The River Cottage

Sea Fishing Handbook

The River Cottage Sea Fishing Handbook

by Nick Fisher

introduced by
Hugh Fearnley-Whittingstall

www.rivercottage.net

BLOOMSBURY
LONDON · BERLIN · NEW YORK

To my own Fisher-family crew, Helen, Rory, Rex,
Patrick, Kitty and our dog Spike, without whom there
would be no point to my fishing or cooking

First published in Great Britain 2010

Text © 2010 by Nick Fisher
Photography © 2010 by Paul Quagliana
Recipe photography © 2010 by Gavin Kingcome
except the following: p.35, p.91, p.105 (bottom), p.108 (top and middle) © Mike Thrussell;
p.92 © Chris Caines; p.98 © Dr Richard Roberts; p.106 (bottom) © Richard 'Tiny' Daw;
p.118 © Matthew Toms; p.147 © John Wright. Cover image © Ed Pavelin/Alamy
Illustrations © 2010 by Toby Atkins

The moral right of the author has been asserted

Bloomsbury Publishing Plc, 36 Soho Square, London W1D 3QY
Bloomsbury Publishing, London, New York and Berlin

A CIP catalogue record for this book is available from the British Library

ISBN 978 1 4088 0183 3
10 9 8 7 6 5 4 3 2 1

Project editor: Janet Illsley
Designer: willwebb.co.uk

Printed and bound in Italy by Graphicom

Mixed Sources
Product group from well-managed
forests, controlled sources and
recycled wood or fibre
www.fsc.org   Cert no. CQ-COC-000015
©1996 Forest Stewardship Council

www.bloomsbury.com/rivercottage

Contents

I've been bewitched by the sea for as long as I can remember. Some of my earliest memories are of paddling around in rock pools, bottom in the air and eyes fixed firmly on the salty puddle in front of my nose, marvelling at blood-red sea anemones and pulling up tiny crabs or shrimp in my neon-yellow nylon net. Forty years on, and I'm at it again, ostensibly tutoring my own brood in the fine art of rock-pool fishing, but in reality just as thrilled and beguiled as I was then, and they are now.

Catching my first fish is a moment firmly etched on my memory too, though my pride is tinged with mild embarrassment. I was five. My dad, taking pity on my lack of success, covertly placed a very dead mackerel on the end of my hook. I was fifteen before the scam was revealed. I should have realised long before then that Richmond Park is not one of the world's great sea-fishing destinations. My first 'real' catch was a 2½lb perch I landed on Lough Corrib in Ireland. Mum cooked it. I ate it. It was delicious. From that point on I was as firmly hooked as that perch.

Since then, what was a passion has become a near obsession. I seize every chance to go out fishing on my little boat, *Louisa*. Even when that's not possible, fishing is never far from my mind. I sort my tackle on winter evenings in front of the fire, browse fishing catalogues and even, when I can get away with it, watch fishing programmes on the telly. That's how I first found out about the author of this book. Stuck on dry land, I discovered Channel 4's *Screaming Reels*, presented by one Nick Fisher. Fishy name, fishy guy. And, I was delighted to find, presenter of the best fishing programme ever made.

Nick's approach was about as far away from a damp day on a river bank as you can get. He was wild, irreverent, slightly dangerous, funny. I decided to stalk him, to reel him in with a view to collaborating on some fishy telly. We met. We fished together. He caught a small roach and I caught, er, nothing. The telly didn't quite happen. I'd like to say we enjoyed our fishing too much to let work get in the way, but since meeting more than ten years ago, we have at least managed to write *The River Cottage Fish Book* together. It's a sizeable tome, which did require us to spend rather too much time at our desks. But it also allowed us a fair bit of time on the water – earnestly researching our subject, of course.

Nick's first fishing memory is, characteristically, rather more swashbuckling than mine. There he was, at the end of a rock pier in Millport on the Ayrshire coast, dipping his toy rod into the sea, surrounded by fishermen with years of experience, buckets of succulent bait, bags of expensive equipment. A tug on the line. A wrasse on the end of it. As the tiny kid struggled to land it, the adults swarmed around him, offering to help. But Nick was having none of it. He insisted on landing it himself.

We've come a long way from bent-pin hooks and plastic rods these days. As our wives are only too quick to point out, we both have far too much tackle cluttering up the house. And we're never short of an excuse to acquire more. Yet in our heart of hearts we know it's unnecessary. That what really marks us down as fishermen is not the extent of our kit, but the fact that we still get that same sense of anticipation when we get our tackle together, and the same surge of excitement when we feel a fish tugging on the end of the line, as we did with our first-ever fish.

Now that you've picked up this book, we'll soon be counting you as one of us. Even if you've never fished before, don't be anxious about your beginner status or your lack of experience. We often fish with beginners who catch more than us on their very first time out. As Nick emphasises from the outset, you really don't have to spend much on tackle to get great pleasure, and great results, from your sea fishing. One well-chosen rod-and-reel combo will see you through a multitude of shoreline scenarios. And an hour or two with this book will put you in with a shout of a memorable catch on your first-ever outing.

Whether you're a beginner or an old-timer, there's no one better than Nick to take you fishing – even if it is a virtual fishing trip taken from the comfort of your favourite armchair. Nick is the one to communicate the vital philosophy that every fishing day is a good day, whatever the outcome. His enthusiasm, knowledge and passion shine from these pages. And the message, above all, is that fishing is not an exclusive pastime, far from it. It's the most convivial way to spend time with old friends, or indeed make new ones. When pursued solo, it's inspiring and contemplative, the perfect antidote to the mayhem of modern life. It is also one of the most fun family days out you can imagine.

And to cap it all, you will, if you're lucky, get the most fantastic prize at the end of it. A delicious supper. I once said to Nick, as we bobbed about somewhere off the Dorset coast, 'So much better than golf, isn't it?' 'Yeah,' he said, 'you can't eat a hole in one.' How very true, I thought…

To eat a fish that you've pulled from the sea yourself is a culinary pleasure, surpassed only by that of sharing it with the friends or family you've just been fishing with. And to make a just-caught fish taste delicious is hardly a chore. A flash of heat, a slug of oil, a bit of butter, a few herbs, some garlic, perhaps a splash of wine, is often all that's needed. But in the spirit of far-flung seafaring adventure, we both enjoy exploring other ideas too – thyme and parsley might be replaced by chilli and soy, a classic crisp chip-shop batter one day, pure, clean escabeche the next.

But whatever the recipe, one thing holds true. Fresh sustainably caught fish from British waters is some of the finest in the world. And, in a country where you're never more than 70 miles from the sea, it is accessible to all of us. I hope you'll pack your rod and reel (and perhaps a bucket barbecue and a travelling selection of seasonings) and treat yourself to a day's fishing soon. In fact, just writing this has got me longing to check the tides, and rummage in my tackle box…

Hugh Fearnley-Whittingstall, East Devon, March 2010

My Fishing Mission

Fishing is a beautiful thing. It is a rich, satisfying minestrone of emotions and experiences that engage your brain, heart, soul and stomach. By its very nature, a fishing trip involves the Great Outdoors in a gloriously active and interactive way. Unlike other outdoor pursuits, fishing is not simply about observing or photographing, or ticking off lists. Nor is it just about cutting a swathe through the Outdoors, fast or slow, under sail, or hanging from a paraglider, or standing on a surfboard.

Fishing is about getting down to the sea and investigating it. Challenging it. Using your brain – maybe parts of it you don't get to use in everyday life – coupled with some well-chosen equipment, to extract something alive from the water. Not wishing to be too dramatic, fishing is about life and death. It's one of the very few interests you can pursue in modern society that still involves going out to hunt and kill your dinner; where you can still feed your family or friends from the fruits of your hunting adventure.

A fishing trip, at its best, has many parts. First there's the preamble – time spent in anticipation and day-dreaming – a period which can take up anything from a snatched moment during a busy day at work, to a lengthy reverie staring out the window of a packed bus. Part of the preamble includes planning the trip: choosing where to go and when to go; deciding whether to plump for a quick mackerel-bashing boat trip or a two-tide, all-day session on some fabulous Victorian pier. It's a time of maps and charts and tide tables, of mates and books, of internet chat rooms and tea-stained lists. Or maybe, for some more confident anglers, this is also a time for thumbing through recipes and amassing ingredients.

All this planning blossoms into the day of 'actually being there'. A day when, if things go well, you might catch a bucket of mackerel, a jaw-dropping sea bass or a thick-scaled, spiny-finned black bream – great fish on which to practise with your descaler and filleting knife.

If the fish capture and the following fish preparation have been successful, they should neatly segue into the fish cooking part of your expedition. A marvellous time of creativity – hot pans, sharp knives, fresh herbs and great smells – which in turn spills over into the very best of all times: the eating experience.

The joy of fishing is that it delivers on all manner of levels from the spiritual to the nutritional. Fishing has a purpose. A point. An end game. And I have to confess, it's the end game – the cooking and eating of fishing – that interests me just as much as the hooking, playing and netting part. I fish mostly because I love to cook and eat what I catch.

In Britain we are fortunate, because there are still an awful lot of fish in the seas around our coast. A multitude of edible species lurk in our inshore waters, from salmon and sardines to cod and pollack. There are beaches, piers, rocks, breakwaters, estuaries and harbours, peppered all around our islands, which provide easy access to fishing, fish and ultimately great seafood. Even at a time when global fish stocks are in a fairly catastrophic state, in our inshore British waters we are still in reasonably good shape.

In order to catch some of our inshore fish, you could, if you choose, fill a couple of sheds with assorted fishing tackle. You could buy yourself an array of fishing rods and reels and rigs and lures to cover every eventuality. Or, like me, you could be pragmatic, limiting your scope and curbing your budget by focusing on fishing for the species that you are most likely to catch, and the ones that you are most likely to want to eat.

With that in mind I've tried to keep rigs, baits and tackle-faffing to a minimum in this book. You may soon outgrow my basic approach, but if I only manage to help you get out and catch a few of your first fish, I will have achieved my goal. Even better if I can help you to prepare and to cook the fish you catch – either on the beach or at home.

My cooking is like my fishing: it's not always clever or fancy or neat. What makes me happiest is when I use every single scrap of every single fish I've killed, in order to feed the ones I love. For me, wasted food – or wasted fish – can spoil the whole experience. Taking fish from the wild to feed ourselves is a privilege, not a necessity. So apart from doing it with a little style, a lot of passion and gratitude, it's also important that we do it with a clear conscience.

Like Hugh, I've been inordinately fortunate in my fishing 'career', and have fished all around the world. I have hunted some very exotic species in some wildly exotic places. All of which is very nice, but ultimately, it does feel a little irrelevant in the big scheme of things. The irony of all that travelling is that I've come to realise now that the greatest pleasure I derive from fishing today is fishing for British fish, catching them as best as I can, doing as little damage as possible along the way, and cooking them into a simple homespun, homemade feast.

Nick Fisher

Glossary

Fishing, like any hobby or passion, is made all the more intriguing and satisfying by having its own special language. At first, this may seem off-putting and exclusive, but once you get the hang of it, this language will become the much-loved lexicon that separates you, the angler, from the non-angler.

Here are a few much-used terms, which are well worth having in your vocabulary. I've included the definitions, too, so that when you use them you have some idea what they mean:

Artificial lure A lure is an example of any 'terminal tackle' that will 'lure' a fish to bite it. It can be anything from a rubber fish mounted on a hook (made to imitate small bait fish), to a mackerel feather (made to imitate tiny fry fish), to a hook-mounted jelly worm (made to look like a marine worm). Rubber baits are also known sometimes simply as 'artificials'. And 'lures' can also refer to metal, wooden or mechanical baits, such as spinners, plugs or spoons, which are 'retrieved' through the water in such a way that they, too, imitate small fish that are slow or wounded and are therefore easy prey for predator fish.

Bleeding Releasing blood from the circulatory system by cutting the gills of your fish, after you've banged it on the head. Bleeding makes the flesh appear 'cleaner' and slows down the rate at which it will spoil, thus prolonging its shelf life.

Bottom-fishing Also known as 'ledgering', this is a method of fishing when your bait is held firmly on the seabed.

Casting The act of propelling your bait or lure some distance out into the water, using a rod.

Demersal fish Fish that live mostly in the demersal region of the sea, which is right down on the bottom, just above the seabed.

Feathering The act of fishing with a string of feathers.

Float fishing Fishing with your bait suspended under a float.

Ground bait Extra bait that you add to the water around your hook bait, to create a focus and act as an attractant to fish in the vicinity. Also known as 'chum'.

Handlining Fishing with a handline rather than a rod and line. A handline is a thick line that is wound on to a wooden frame.

Hook bait Whatever you put on your hook – something a fish wants to eat, that will bait it to bite.

Ledgering See bottom-fishing.

Ledger rig General term used to describe any static rig that is weighted on the bottom, with the bait presented on or near the seabed.

Marks A 'rock mark' is a specific location, on the rocks of a cliff or beach, where you would expect to catch fish. A 'good beach mark' is a place on a beach known to be productive. Even on a boat, the skipper might lower the anchor or else drift over a certain 'mark' because he knows it has given up fish in the past.

Pelagic fish Species, like mackerel, herring and tuna, which are able to feed up and down the water column from the seabed to the surface. Pelagic means 'wandering' or 'nomadic' and these fish also wander from area to area in search of the best food.

Priest A purpose-made instrument of death. The tool you use to bash a fish over the head with; so called, because it administers the last rites.

Retrieving The action of winding in; the opposite to casting.

Rig The construction of the 'terminal tackle'. The type of rig or construction you use might be referred to by the method of angling you're using, such as a 'float rig', or it might be named after the species of fish you're targeting, such as a 'plaice rig'. It can also relate to the location in which you're fishing, such as a 'pier rig'.

Snood Another name for a short hook length. The piece of line on a rig (especially a paternoster rig) which actually connects to the hook. A snood may be stronger than the reel line if a fish has teeth. Or weaker, if the fish (mullet, for example) are easily spooked by thick line.

Spinning A method of angling using a spinner (or spoon or wedge) as bait.

Striking The action of reacting to a 'bite' – the feeling of something nibbling at your bait – by quickly raising the rod tip to the 11 o'clock position, with the intent of driving your hook into the fish's mouth and effect a 'hook up'.

Tackle Anything you take fishing with you, from a rod and reel to rigs and weights, spinners and feathers. All of these constitute part (or all) of your 'tackle'.

Terminal tackle The business end of your line. 'Terminal' refers to the end of your line that interfaces with the water and, hopefully, the finned things. A hook and a weight is all part of your 'terminal tackle'; a reel isn't.

Trolling The practice of fishing from a slow-moving boat, by dragging a bait, feathers or lure along 30 yards or more behind the boat.

When to Go Fishing

When it comes to outdoor pursuits, we can all so

easily get obsessed with tackle, kit and clothing. It's human nature to assume that success or failure in any sort of outdoor quest boils down to what you choose to take with you. But I know, from bitter fishing experience, that it's not *what* you take that matters most. It's *where* you choose to go and *when* you choose to go there.

Tides, past weather and future weather all have an effect on how fish behave and how they feed. You can never guarantee to catch fish, but you can narrow the margin for failure by learning a few basic rules about seasons, weather, tides and time of day.

Time of year

In fishing 'season' has two meanings. There's the natural season when certain migratory fish that live part of the year in deep offshore waters are present in our inshore waters and accessible to the angler. And there's the imposed legal season, which denotes when you're permitted to try and catch certain species. This restriction is a way of protecting vulnerable fish, namely salmon and sea trout, when they're in the process of migrating out of the sea into rivers in order to spawn. The law is designed to give them a better chance of successful spawning and to stop fishermen targeting these fish when they're preoccupied with sex rather than survival.

Although the legal season applies only to salmon and sea trout, it is worth considering in relation to other species. Any fish in the act of spawning, or that have recently finished spawning, are not good to catch. If you catch fish before they spawn, you're depriving them of the ability to reproduce and potentially destroying millions of fish eggs before they've had a chance to be fertilised. What's more, a fish that has recently spawned is not particularly good to eat, because its energy and nutrition have been devoted to creating healthy eggs to the detriment of the rest of its body, particularly its muscle flesh – the part that you most want to eat.

There are no laws to stop you catching sea fish that are just pre- or post-spawning. And at certain times of year it's impossible to know if you're going to catch one in either condition before you do. But if you catch a fish, either swollen with eggs, or with a telltale slack belly and flabby muscle tone, then try to release it safely back into the sea (see p.176). If you then catch another in the same condition, it makes sense to move to another location or change bait or technique, and try for a different species.

Most sea fish are in their prime in the late summer months and through the autumn, mainly because they have spent the last few months of the year gorging on abundant high-protein food and are therefore fat, fit and full of omega-rich oils and life-enhancing minerals like selenium, taurine and zinc.

The adjacent chart breaks down the year into seasons and indicates the best possible time to take each of the most catchable species from the sea.

Seasonal fishing for sea fish

	SPRING	SUMMER	AUTUMN	WINTER
MACKEREL	🐟🐟	🐟🐟🐟	🐟🐟🐟	🐟
DOGFISH	🐟🐟	🐟🐟🐟	🐟🐟🐟	🐟🐟
POUTING	🐟🐟🐟	🐟🐟🐟	🐟🐟🐟	🐟🐟
POLLACK	🐟🐟	🐟🐟🐟	🐟🐟🐟	🐟🐟
COD		🐟🐟🐟	🐟🐟	🐟🐟🐟
WHITING			🐟🐟🐟	🐟🐟🐟
GARFISH	🐟	🐟🐟🐟	🐟🐟	
RED GURNARD	🐟	🐟🐟	🐟🐟🐟	🐟
BLACK BREAM	🐟	🐟🐟🐟	🐟🐟	
PLAICE	🐟🐟🐟	🐟🐟	🐟🐟	🐟
SEA BASS	🐟	🐟🐟🐟	🐟🐟🐟	
DAB & FLOUNDER	🐟		🐟	🐟🐟🐟
HORSE MACKEREL	🐟🐟	🐟🐟🐟	🐟🐟🐟	🐟
HERRING	🐟	🐟🐟	🐟🐟	
SQUID			🐟🐟🐟	🐟🐟
SLOB TROUT	🐟🐟	🐟🐟🐟	🐟🐟	
GREY MULLET	🐟	🐟🐟🐟	🐟	

🐟🐟🐟 = most likely to catch
🐟🐟 = likely to catch
🐟 = a slim chance

Weather

The perfect weather conditions for sea fishing are a day with light cloud cover and a steady light onshore wind coming from one direction, which gives some movement to the surf and should ideally colour the water just a little by churning up small clouds of sand in the shallows.

Always check the weather 24 hours in advance of your intended trip (see Directory, p.249, for weather forecast websites) and be prepared to cancel if the weather is forecast to turn ugly. Don't get me wrong, fishing in bad weather can sometimes be a lot of fun when you already have some sound angling experience. But if you're still near the start of your learning curve it's only going to make the basics, such as tying knots and casting, that much more difficult.

Rain

Even if you've got top-notch waterproof clothing, persistent rain will still mess up a day's fishing. It makes everything so much more difficult to do, and will create a stack of wet kit to deal with when you get home. In saying that, rain splashing on the water can actually help to cover a multitude of angling sins, like bad casting and noisy wading, and rain hitting the water can sometimes put the fish at their ease.

Sunshine

A day of bright sunlight can be surprisingly unproductive weather for going fishing. Fish generally don't like too much sun as most of them don't have eyelids, so they skulk goth-like in darkened depths. This is a tactical move because bright sunlight illuminates the water and airborne predators, like cormorants and gannets, can spot fish much more easily. In addition, most of our native fish don't like water that is too warm as it makes them sluggish and puts them off their food.

The middle of a very hot summer's day might *seem* like the perfect time to sit next-the-sea, rod-in-hand, but bright sunlight really isn't ideal for fishermen either. Believe me, some of the most excruciating sunburn I've ever experienced (and I'm a freckled ginger Scot!) came courtesy of hot summer fishing. I know it sounds very Nanny State, but if you do choose to go and fish in the middle of a summer's day, take lots of fresh water, a hat and lashings of sun cream. And if you're wearing sandals, don't forget to cream your toes!

During hot weather, it's always best to go fishing at dawn and dusk, because the fish come out to feed when the light levels are low and the water is cool. For the angler with a throbbing vein of romance in his soul, it's also the most special time of the day to be by the water, when most non-angling civilians haven't yet ventured out, or have already gone home. Being able to sit and savour dawn and dusk next to the sea is one of the many unexpected privileges of being an angler.

Wind

High winds (20mph plus) are rarely an advantage in fishing. Some locations are more affected by wind than others, as are some fishing techniques. The direction of the wind is also an issue. Here's a rough rule of thumb summary, to help you understand the impact of wind on your fishing:

In an inshore boat It's the responsibility of the skipper to make a judgement on whether the wind is too strong to allow his anglers to fish comfortably and safely. Generally, anything above a Force 5 is deemed to be too 'lumpy' for fishing.

On the beach The main issue is direction. Wind can be offshore (coming from the land heading out to sea), onshore (coming from sea to land), or it can be blowing across the beach in either direction parallel to the sea. An offshore wind is the most comfortable for fishing, because it's at your back and will help your casting by giving it extra wind propulsion. The exact opposite is true of a strong onshore wind. Having a hard wind in your face all day is uncomfortable and tiring, and it'll make casting more difficult and even potentially dangerous. Light to moderate cross winds aren't so much of an issue, except an easterly wind which is colder and rarely the best for a day's fishing, hence the uncannily true adage: 'When the wind's in the east, the fish bite least'. But strong cross winds are a pain to fish and many anglers will find real trouble keeping their weight and bait where they want it on the seabed, due to the sideways drag of the wind and water pulling on the line, moving it off to one side.

Rock fishing A strong wind in any direction is going to make a potentially dangerous place to fish even more dangerous. Erratic winds cause erratic seas and being stuck on an exposed rock above deep water in a strong wind is too much of a risk. I haven't been washed off a rock, but I've been drenched by big waves I didn't see coming. Dragging soaking gear back to the car, knees knocking with fright, is really no fun.

Tides

Tides give me goosebumps – especially when I try and get my head around the micro and macro mechanics of what happens in the period between high tide and low tide. Tides influence the creation and flow of plankton, as well as the movement and feeding patterns of all fish, molluscs and crustaceans. But before focusing on life under the water, first we need to stand back, look up and try to get some kind of handle on how the life of everything in the sea – from a tiny shrimp to a huge bucket-mouthed conger eel – is connected to, and controlled by, the movement of our moon and the sun in outer space.

Along most parts of our coastline, in any given 24-hour period, the tide will be high twice and low twice. When you check the local newspaper's tide table for the times of high water and low water, you'll often find a symbol that depicts the corresponding phase of the moon. Most of us understand that the moon is somehow responsible for tides – and that its influence has got something to do with the moon's magnetic or gravitational pull. And that's all you really need to know (plus the fact that the times of high water and low water will shift forward by about 40 minutes every day. So, if high water is at noon today, it'll be at around 12.40pm tomorrow.)

But for me, grasping a little more about the cause and effect, about *why* the sea behaves the way it does, helps to increase my pleasure and interaction with it.

The moon

The moon revolves around the earth, and the earth and moon together revolve around the sun. The sun is much bigger than our moon, but the moon is much closer. And so the moon has the greater gravitational effect on the earth.

As the moon passes over and around the face of the earth, it acts like a magnet trying to pull the earth towards it. The earth, in its own orbit of the sun, won't shift under the pull of this massive magnet, but the seas – covering over 70 per cent of the planet – will. The sea on the side of the earth nearest to the magnetic moon will bulge upwards towards the moon, drawn by its gravitational pull. This bulge of water on one side of the earth creates a high tide.

The sun

Although it is not so pronounced, the sun also has a gravitational pull that affects the sea on the surface of the earth. And because the moon rotates around the earth and together they rotate around the sun, there are phases when the moon is in between the earth and the sun. Also, there are phases when the earth is in between the sun and the moon, like piggy in the middle. There are phases, too, when the moon and the sun are at right angles to the centre of the earth. If you imagine the earth as being the centre of a clock, this is when the sun is at 12 and the moon is at 3.

Each of these combinations of moon, earth and sun has a distinct effect upon the magnetic pull exerted on the seas, creating a different-sized bulge that affects the height of tides.

Spring tides and neap tides

Spring tides have nothing to do with the season of spring. 'Spring' relates to the notion of the tide 'springing' up; in other words, being at its most mobile and most fierce.

Neap tides are the opposite. These are the weakest or smallest tides, when the difference in height from low water to high water (the tidal range) is much smaller than the difference during spring tides.

Neap and spring tides alternate every two weeks; halfway through each complete phase of a new moon, or lunar month (28 days).

The spring tides occur when the moon's gravitational pull is at its strongest; when it's furthest away from the sun and the earth is piggy in the middle, then both planets are pulling at the sea in opposite directions, which creates a bulge in the seas on both sides of the earth. Springs also occur when the moon is on the same side as the sun and together, with their combined magnetic force, they're pulling the surface of the seas dramatically in one direction.

Neap tides occur when the sun and moon are at right angles to the earth, in the first and third quarters of the new moon. This is when the sun's magnetic power is directly cancelling out some of the moon's magnetic strength.

But all you absolutely need to remember from this celestial dance of moon, earth and sun is that spring tides are strong and big, and neap tides are weak and small.

How tides affect fisherman Knowing the times of high and low water is essential to fishermen. If you're fishing on a shallow, sandy surf beach in Norfolk or Cornwall, the sea could be an awfully long walk away at low tide. And if you set up an elaborate fish camp way down the beach as the tide is coming in, you'll find yourself having to re-site your camp before you've even had a chance to get your first brew on.

So do check the time of tides as a matter of course. The daily shift forward by 40 minutes each day is caused by the incremental movement of the moon on its 28-day orbit of the earth. This means that if the fish came on the feed at a certain time yesterday, chances are they'll do the same towards an hour later today.

How tides affect fish Developing a mental image of how tides work is hard enough, and even if we do get our heads around the physics, most of us will imagine tides as something constant and gradual.

Unsurprisingly, the sea isn't that straightforward or predictable. Most importantly, tide movement – from low to high – *doesn't* happen at an even and constant speed. When the tide comes in, it starts off slow, gets fast, *very* fast, slows down, stops and slowly starts running again, in the opposite direction. The specific pace that a tide is running during the flood (incoming) tide or ebb (outgoing) tide is something that wreck-fishing charter skippers and yacht skippers need to know intimately. Arguably though, if all we intend to do is chuck a float-fished mackerel strip off the end of the pier in our quest to catch garfish for tea, then all we really need to know is when the tide is going to be low and when it's high.

And yet, just knowing that the state of the tide and formation of local geography – in terms of where there are headlands and bays – make a difference to the direction and pace of the sea will ultimately help us to think a little more like a fish. To keep itself alive, well fed and safe, a fish depends on its knowledge of the tides.

Every aquatic life form in our inshore waters is influenced by tide. Some fish and shellfish can use the tide and even *second-guess* tidal movements, to ambush prey or avoid being ambushed. Other life forms, like plankton, are totally at the mercy of tidal currents, which will carry it hither and yon, sometimes straight into the mouths of plankton predators.

Moving up the chain from plankton are the fish that feed on it. These small fish, also known as 'bait' fish, have some ability to swim against the tides, but only up to a certain point. When the tidal run is too strong they get pushed around, while larger predator fish, who are able to swim against the tide whenever they need to, are able to use the corralling power of the tide to their advantage. Bait fish that are bunched and bullied by tidal currents become easy prey for fish like pollack, bass and cod, who make good use of the all-you-can-eat buffet that a fierce tide creates.

Understanding how the tides influence the food chain in turn helps us second-guess what certain fish might be doing at certain times.

As a general rule of thumb, tidal movement is a good thing for encouraging life to exist in the sea. A run of tide is a physical movement of the water and when it flows around rocks, gullies and structures, it will create bubbles of air in the water, pumping it full of life-enhancing fresh oxygen. At the same time, it transports food such as plankton, worms and crustaceans into the mouths of predators.

And yet, when a tide is too fierce, which it does become in some locations around the coast at certain times of the year, even the big fish will have to stop feeding. This is because holding themselves head-on into the full force of the tide starts to demand too much effort and valuable energy. So instead, they'll find somewhere sheltered in the lee of a structure to hunker down and let the bite of the tide pass.

Tides, crabs, worms and clams High and low tides cover and expose areas of mud, sand and gravel on beaches, estuaries and harbours. This twice-daily movement of sea water back and forth across these areas is vital to the creatures that live there.

At low tide, when the water recedes and exposes swathes of the seabed to the open air, crabs and worms bury themselves under the damp sand for safety. Then later, the fresh run of tide will bring them up out of their hiding holes to feed. Clams are filter feeders; they mostly want to filter the first run of a new tide because they know it will be carrying the maximum amount of sediment and plankton and algae as it sweeps them up across the exposed flats. Fish in turn know what the crabs and clams and worms want to do. Fish like dabs, flounders, plaice and mullet will use the new tide to carry them on to the flats to hunt the worms and crabs as they pop out to savour the new wet.

Conversely, when the tide is out and the mud and sand banks are exposed, it's time for anglers to become fork-wielding predators and to dig in the soft mud for fresh live baits with which to tempt those foraging fish species on the next flush of the tide.

Where to Go Fishing

Very tasty and exciting sea fish can be caught from either the shore or from a boat. Undoubtedly, more fish are caught from boats, simply because they can cover a larger area and deeper water much more quickly and efficiently. However, boat fishing is always going to be more expensive and more complicated to arrange. Shore fishing, on the other hand, is instantly accessible to anyone able to wander on to a beach. Pier fishing and rock fishing have the added advantage of allowing you to drop directly down into deeper water than you would normally be able to reach from the beach.

Boat fishing

Boat fishing is, without a shadow of a doubt, one of the easiest ways to get yourself on the other end of a fishing line from an edible sea fish. However, understandably not everyone wants to be spoon-fed their first fish, or wants to invest in an outing they're not sure they'll enjoy. So, although heading out to sea might logically be the quickest way to get a bend in your rod, staying on dry land might be what you feel you'd rather do. And if that's the case, there's plenty of information in this book designed to help you hook up (see pp.30–41).

If you do decide to go boat fishing first as a way of learning the ropes, then unless you happen to be lucky enough to own a boat or have a friend with a boat, the chances are you'll be reliant on booking yourself on to a charter fishing boat.

Charter boats come in all shapes and sizes, from custom-made high-speed craft that only take half a dozen anglers, through large open-decked day boats that specialise in seaside-resort mackerel trips, to serious deep-water charter boats, which normally carry ten anglers and two crew. And then there's always the odd trawler which might take out 'trippers' on days that it's not going out to sea to drag a net.

For anyone new to sea fishing, I would advise against booking yourself on any boat trip that lasts more than 2 hours, simply as a precaution. Because, if you don't like it, or if you don't feel well, at least you know it's going to be over soon. Serious sea-angling charters are normally a minimum of 4 hours, and some are 8 hours or more. Avoid these until you've got your feet wet with a few shorter trips first.

The most effective way to get your hands on something worth cooking is to sign yourself up for a one-hour mackerel trip. There are lots of these mackerel-trip boats in harbours all around the country that run during the summer and sometimes into the autumn months, when the weather allows.

Often these boats provide tackle and some instruction, too. On some boats you will be equipped with a simple handline, or a basic rod and line, attached to a string of mackerel feathers. On others, the handline is standard supplied kit but a rod and line can be provided for an extra charge. Make sure you ask what the arrangement

Locations for catching sea fish

	MACKEREL BOAT	INSHORE FISHING BOAT	SANDY BEACH	SHINGLE BEACH	ROCKY LEDGE	PIER	ESTUARY	HARBOUR
MACKEREL	best	best	best	best	best	best	lucky	best
DOGFISH		best	lucky	lucky	lucky	best	lucky	lucky
POUTING		best	best	lucky	lucky	best	lucky	lucky
POLLACK		best	lucky	lucky	best	lucky	lucky	lucky
COD		best	lucky	best	best	lucky		
WHITING		best	best	best	best	best		best
GARFISH	best	best	lucky	lucky	best	best		best
RED GURNARD		best	best	best	best	best		best
BLACK BREAM	best	best	lucky	lucky	best	best		best
PLAICE		best	best	best	best	best	lucky	lucky
SEA BASS		lucky	best	best	best	lucky	lucky	lucky
DAB & FLOUNDER		lucky	best	lucky	lucky	best	best	best
HORSE MACKEREL	best	best	lucky	lucky	lucky	best		best
HERRING	best	best			lucky	lucky		lucky
SQUID	lucky	lucky				best		best
SLOB TROUT							best	lucky
GREY MULLET					lucky	best	best	best

best = best   lucky = might get lucky

is before you sign up. Some mackerel boats will encourage you to bring your own rod, others advise against it. The simple reason is that it's harder for a skipper to avoid anglers getting into tangles if they're all using different tackle with different line thicknesses and different weights. If everyone is using the same basic tackle, the lines will all behave in the same way and it's then easier for the skipper to control the dangle of the terminal tackle as he manoeuvres the boat.

There is, however, likely to come a point once you've been on a mackerel-trip boat a few times when it dawns on you that, fun though it is, you're not really controlling the whole process. You're on someone else's boat, using someone else's tackle. The skipper has decided where, and when, and how you will fish. And, suddenly, being shoulder to shoulder with a load of people doing exactly the same thing makes you feel less a master of your own mackerel destiny.

This might well be all you really want from a sea-fishing experience – a chance to bag up with mackerel in the simplest and most efficient tackle-lite manner. But, in my experience, the more you can take control of where and how you fish, the fewer fish you might catch, but the more pleasure you'll derive from catching them. In which case, assuming you don't have your own boat, you'll have to think about beach, pier or shore fishing to get your mackerel.

Often people will start off on mackerel boat trips, then get a bit bored and frustrated, so move on to beach and pier fishing, to get the hang of using tackle, tying knots and learning about techniques and baits. Many then progress *back* to boats again in the form of short charter reef trips (also called 'reef-fishing trips' or 'inshore trips') to enable them to go in search of other species of fish which are easier to catch from a boat. These fishing trips are slightly more technical, last about 2–3 hours, and might involve bringing your own tackle.

Boat fishing equipment

ROD	Boat rod, carp rod or spinning rod (see pp.113–17)
REEL	Multiplier or fixed-spool reel (see pp.119–20)
LINE	15–20lb line (see p.121)
HOOKS	1–4/0 hooks (see pp.122–3)
TERMINAL TACKLE	Weights, swivels, booms, beads, feathers, other lures (see Tackle and Kit, pp.125–9 and pp.132–44)
RIG ASSEMBLY	Paternoster, running ledger, float, spinner, pennel (see pp.163–7)
BAIT	Mackerel, squid, lugworms, ragworms (see Bait, pp.153–5 and p.158)

A note on seasickness

Seasickness seems so unfair. Some people will feel seasick just standing on a boat tied up alongside a harbour, while others can be bounced around like a pea on a kettle-drum and never feel even the slightest bit queasy.

In fact, seasickness doesn't have anything to do with the sea; it's simply motion sickness – the same as you might get travelling on a plane, train, car or bus. The brain just gets confused. The inner ear is your balance centre, and your eyes provide your visual information reference. When the two don't agree, vomiting may soon follow. Inside a cabin or a wheelhouse, it's even more confusing. Your eyes tell your brain you're in a stable environment, but your inner ear knows you're pitching around.

According to experts, fatty foods are best avoided for at least 12 hours before a sea trip. And it's always better to travel on deck, rather than inside the wheelhouse or cabin. The best position to plant yourself on a boat is right at the back where it's low down and most stable. And the best place to look is at the horizon, but don't fixate on it. Keep your head as level and still as possible, to avoid further confusion. The sickness is caused by your sensory perceptions being out of synch, so don't use binoculars or try to read – focusing your eyes on close subjects or artificially magnified ones will only exacerbate the symptoms.

Seasickness sufferers – skippers, too – often say that if you feel sick, it's best to be sick: let it happen, rather than try to hold on to your breakfast. Out is better than in, ideally from the back of the boat into the sea or a bucket with the wind behind you.

Shore fishing

As an island, we are surrounded by a stunning range of shore-fishing venues, including sandy beaches, pebble beaches, rocky cliffs, piers, estuaries and harbours.

Choosing where to go on your first few exploratory shore-fishing trips should really be dictated by what's easily accessible to you. Whether you're on holiday and there's water in the vicinity, or you're heading out from home and planning a trip to some nearby stretch of sea, the three most useful tools you can use are a map, a telephone directory and an angling website.

A detailed OS map of your planned destination will show where the water meets the land, the nearest parking spots and passable footpaths to the shore. If it is an estuary, a map will help you identify where and how the river flows into the sea. And if you're intent on trying your luck at a beach, you can study what's on either side of the spot you fancy. Features like rocky headlands, open bays and tight coves all affect the tidal flow and even the weather, especially the wind. If you know the forecast wind direction you can make an informed choice as to which side of a headland or a bay to fish, making sure the wind is on your back, rather than hard in your face.

A phone directory will list fishing tackle shops in the area. And a good tackle shop is a fount of useful knowledge. A quick conversation with a local tackle dealer can save you a lot of time. You might not feel qualified to conduct an in-depth conversation, but never be afraid to admit you're a novice and need all the help you can get. You'll be amazed how helpful anglers and tackle dealers can be if you give them the opportunity. Fishermen love their fishing and love to be able to show how knowledgeable they are. Obviously, it's much easier to have this sort of conversation face to face. And any canny tackle purveyor will realise that you're much more likely to part with cash if you're actually standing in front of his till.

Angling websites are just as important when you're exploring new locations. Anglers are a proactive bunch, who love to expound their wisdom. I've listed the best websites in the Directory (see pp.249–50), but there are many more local ones, and personal blogs that you can track down with a little cybersleuthing. There's so much angling information available that a trawl of the internet is very worthwhile before heading out in the hope of getting your own net wet.

Sandy beaches

Most people love to spend a day hanging out on a warm sandy beach. To be able to swim and paddle, to play with your children, dog or inflatable swim-toys one minute and catch a fish from the self-same sun-kissed sea the next would be a perfect scenario. In reality, it's unlikely to happen. Swimmers and anglers don't make for naturally sympathetic and symbiotic bedfellows. Apart from the obvious hook-in-flesh danger aspect, there's also the problem that humans splashing around in the water are likely to scare away any fish. The best time to try fishing in this type of location is just after dawn and just before dusk, when the light levels are low and there is no glare from the sun on the water. This is when the fish will feel safe to venture into shallow water. And conversely, the best time for beach fun is when the sun is high.

Best tides The most effective stage of the tide for sandy beach fishing is when it's going out or coming in. Not when it's at its lowest or its highest. Tide movement is significant on sandy and pebbly beaches because the motion of the sea on to sand or through pebbles might dislodge any resident fish or aquatic life.

Sand fleas, shrimps, tiny crabs, sand eels and other small sea creatures live in wet sand and among tiny gravel-like pebbles. These creatures also like to be covered by a layer of sea water, as this allows them to move around easily and seek out food and mating partners. All these life forms are acutely aware when the tide is going out or coming in, either because of the change in its direction or the change in pressure as it ebbs and flows. So they know when their covering of sea water is about to disappear. And when this is imminent, they have two choices: either dig into the wet sand and hunker down for the duration, until the water layer returns with the next incoming tide; or else move with the outgoing tide, slipping further and further down the sloping beach, until the tide stops ebbing and starts to come back in again.

Fish such as dogfish, plaice, bass, gurnard and, to some extent, mackerel feed on these beach-dwelling aquatic critters and they know that as the outgoing tide slides down a beach, it is going to be washing a selection of these critters in their path.

Fish also know that when the tide is flowing in over the sun-warmed sand or pebbles, all manner of edible critters who have hunkered down for the duration will pop out of their hiding holes to take advantage of new oxygen and better mobility.

Sandy beach fishing equipment

ROD	Spinning rod (see pp.113–14) or carp rod (see p.116–17)
REEL	Fixed-spool reel (see p.119)
LINE	10–15lb line and shock leader (see pp.121 and 131)
HOOKS	1–4/0 hooks (see pp.122–3)
TERMINAL TACKLE	Floats, weights, swivels, beads, feathers, other lures (see Tackle and Kit, pp.123–9 and pp.132–44)
RIG ASSEMBLY	Running ledger (see p.164)
BAIT	Mackerel, squid, lugworms, ragworms, peeler crab (see Bait, pp.153–5 and pp.158–9)

Shingle beaches

Steep shingle beaches like Chesil in Dorset are also known as 'storm' beaches, because their 45° slope of shingle or gravel leading down to a plateau of sand is the result of fierce wave action. The joy of fishing this sort of beach is that you never need to cast out very far. Most fish feeding takes place along the line where the shingle meets the sand. The onshore waves will erode the sand under the shingle slope, displacing food and attracting various fish, from bass to plaice, to gurnard and small pollack.

Chesil Beach stretches for 17 miles, from Portland to West Bay, so it can be very hard to decide exactly where to stop and cast your bait. One way is to examine the high water line along the upper part of the beach, looking for concentrations of flotsam and seaweed. These indicate that there's an unseen feature, or a convergence of currents just off the beach or further out to sea, propelling floating and submerged matter up the beach at a particular point. This is a good place to start, because the sea in this spot is obviously carrying a lot of matter: sea rubbish and weed that will contain all sorts of small aquatic life, which in turn will attract feeding fish.

Any protruding bumps of shingle breaking the even sweep of the shoreline suggest there is something happening in the deeper water that keeps the build-up of shingle at this position. Any hint of a feature or a tidal anomaly is worth investigating. And it always helps the angler to see what a beach looks like at low water. Any hollows, rocks or ridges represent features. Fish love features. Mark the position of any you spot by taking a visual bearing in relation to the cliffs or background. This way you can aim your bait in that direction once the tide has started to flood.

The tackle is the same as you'd use on a sandy beach. The steep-angled shingle will give you deep water close in on high tide, so mackerel feathers and spinners are easier to use for more of the tide than on a shallow sandy beach. A short lob cast on a shingle beach at high tide will easily put you in water deep enough to hold fish.

Shingle beach fishing equipment

ROD	Spinning or carp rod (see pp.113–14 and pp.116–17)
REEL	Fixed-spool reel (see p.119)
LINE	10–15lb line and shock leader (see pp.121 and 131)
HOOKS	1–4/0 hooks (see pp.122–3)
TERMINAL TACKLE	Floats, weights, swivels, beads, feathers, other lures (see Tackle and Kit, pp.123–9 and pp.132–44)
RIG ASSEMBLY	Running ledger (see p.164), float rig (see p.165)
BAIT	Mackerel, squid, lugworms, ragworms, peeler crab (see Bait, pp.153–5 and pp.158–9)

Rough ground or rocky beaches

Some beaches are just not suitable for enjoyable fishing, especially for the beginner. Beaches that contain a large amount of big boulders and craggy rock are dangerous and tackle-hungry. Fishing on very rocky, rough ground requires specialist tackle and a solid knowledge of local tides and weather. What's more, the species these beaches attract, like conger eel, bull huss and smoothhound, are complicated to hook and land, and not species that I would encourage you to eat.

There is nothing more soul-destroying than getting all excited about going on a fishing trip, only to end up somewhere scary, where you snag against rock at every cast, leaving you confused, bruised and tackle-less.

Pier fishing

Most fish like structure in their lives. Literally. Much of the seabed is a desert – miles of flat nothingness that is constantly scoured by a continually shifting, incessant Sirocco-like 'wind' in the form of tidal currents. Water is pushed and pulled four times a day across this landscape, which, if there's no structure growing out of it, makes it a very inhospitable environment for fish and shellfish, except those that can burrow into the sand to seek sanctuary.

A pier is a sanctuary – a glorious multi-layered, multi-faceted sanctuary – which provides all manner of seductive nooks and crannies for things to lodge and grow, or else hide and dine. Classic Victorian piers have iron legs and stone feet. They stick out at 90° to the coastline, causing all sorts of confusion to the natural flow of the tide, which normally travels parallel to the shore.

So a pier acts as a spit, jutting across the tide, creating eddies and swirls, lees and races – all the things that fish, shellfish and worms favour, rather than the constant exposed stream of tides that exist on a barren, featureless seabed.

The legs and feet of a pier obstruct the sideways movement of the tide, acting as barriers to the flow. This creates a shadow or lee in one direction of the tide, while the side of the pier foot facing the advancing tide will be eroded, creating a series of pockets which, in time, join up to form a trench. The base of a pier becomes a moonscape of craters and hollows, pockets and trenches, all of which impede the flow of worms, crabs and other fish-edible species that drop into the hollows as the tide pushes them in one direction or another.

The pier structure provides footing for seaweeds, algae, mussels, limpets and winkles, while the pier 'floor' is carpeted with compartments to hold various washed-along foodstuffs. All of this food attracts fish. Congers, codling, coalfish, dogfish and pouting get their snouts down in the troughs, while mackerel and mullet and garfish will sit higher in the water, using the vortexes of tide to deliver food. A pier is like a massive seafood buffet that caters for every species of bait fish and predator at some stage of the tide.

End of the pier syndrome Most anglers' natural instinct is to cast to the far side – of anything. If I turn up on one bank of a river, I inevitably try to cast my bait to the opposite bank. If I fish a lake, I try to cast my bait at least into the middle. And the same is also true when I go pier fishing. My natural instinct is to walk to the furthest end of the pier, jostle for position with other anglers and cast as far as I can. In all of us there lurks some competitive desire to cast our bait the furthest, in the erroneous belief that by so doing we'll catch more fish. But, given that the troughs and hollows on the underside of the pier are an advantage for fishing, obviously the best place to fish is actually around the middle of the pier.

Gear and the pier When you arrive at a pier, check which way the tide is running. If it's flowing from right to left, you might feel it's better to fish on the left side, as your tackle and bait will be dragged away from the structure, down the tide, so you'll be able to see your line and more easily recognise any bites. Otherwise, if you drop your bait on the right-hand side, your tackle is going to be dragged *under* the structure by the tide, right into the tackle-snagging, barnacle-encrusted legs of the pier.

The fish, however, are most likely to be tight *under* the pier, feeding in the gullies and holes. And they'll probably be pointing head-on into the tide, watching for food being pushed their way. So, any angler dropping their bait on the down-tide side is actually dropping their bait *behind* the feeding fish, with the scent being washed even further away down tide.

If you drop the bait on the up-tide side of the pier, the scent will be wafted towards the underside, where the fish will notice it quickly and hopefully move to grab it. Fishing the up-tide business-side of the pier is much more snaggy, but you can learn to tune your rigs to make it possible, by fishing with heavier weights and a 'rotten-bottom' or sacrificial link. This is simply a length of weaker line that you attach to your weight when you're fishing over rocky and snaggy ground. The idea is that this weak length with a lower breaking strain will break before the main line does. This way you sacrifice only the lead when it gets stuck, because the weak link will snap, and you won't lose your entire rig. Another way of creating a weak link is to tie a paper clip to the bottom of your line and hook the weight on to it. When the lead gets stuck, the paper clip will bend straight under strain as you pull hard, letting your weight fall off but freeing the snag and saving your rig.

Pier fishing equipment

ROD	Spinning rod (see pp.113–14) or carp rod (see p.116–17)
REEL	Fixed-spool reel (see p.119)
LINE	10–15lb line and shock leader (see pp.121 and 131)
HOOKS	1–4/0 hooks (see pp.122–3)
TERMINAL TACKLE	Floats, weights, swivels, beads, feathers, other lures (see Tackle and Kit, pp.123–9 and pp.132–44)
RIG ASSEMBLY	Paternoster or running ledger rig (see pp.163–4)
BAIT	Mackerel, squid, lugworms, ragworms, peeler crab (see Bait, pp.153–5 and pp.158–9)

Estuary fishing

Not all harbours have a river running through them, but all estuaries do. The estuary is where the river widens out from a clear channel cut through the land to an open plain, where it meets the sea. The estuary is the point where fresh water meets sea water and it mixes together to make 'brackish' water.

For some fish, such as sea trout and salmon, this brackish water zone acts as a kind of no man's land, where they stop to make the difficult transition from sea fish to river fish for the purposes of breeding.

For other fish, like slob trout (see pp.97–9), the brackish water and intertidal zone is like a bizarre purgatory – a place where they stay because they can't make up their minds whether to remain in the river and be brown trout, or else bite the bullet and take to the ocean, to become pukka sea trout.

For yet others, like immature juvenile bass, the estuary is a safer option than the outside sea. Less likely to contain 'A list' predators, the estuary acts as a nursery area, providing somewhere for the young fish to feed and grow in relative safety.

Mullet cruise around estuaries for much of their lives as they like warm shallow water and the weed, maggots and algae it offers. Flounders and dabs love estuaries, too, because the soft silty mud provides camouflage and is normally home to their favourite food: shrimps, crabs and worms. Flounder fishing is an ideal way to fish an estuary. While targeting flounder with ragworm, you might also accidentally catch sea trout, slob trout, bass, pollack, dab or plaice, so it's a practical catch-all approach.

The best way to start is at low tide and follow the incoming tide upwards from the estuary mouth towards the source of the river. Travel light, with just one rod, a couple of spare rigs and a pair of wellies or waders to navigate the muddy spots. In fact, be very careful of muddy spots, don't venture away from the rocky shoreline by too far. If the mud is exposed then wait for the tide to cover it. Don't try to cross it.

As you move up, look for gullies and hollows which are exposed but soon to be filled by the incoming tide. These are good spots to fish, and are places where dabs or flounders will hole up, waiting and feeding while the incoming tide covers the ground ahead, forging the way. Dabs like to hunt in small packs too. So, if you do hook a fish, send your next cast back to the very same spot; there may well be a bunch of his hunting buddies waiting to chomp your bait.

There's nothing to stop you float-fishing up an estuary too, with a worm suspended just a couple of feet below an easy-to-cast but not-too-bulky float.

Estuary fishing is best when you're mobile and covering a lot of water. You're unlikely to catch a monster, but you'll be surrounded by wading birds, wild mussels, cockles, winkles and maybe even the occasional wild oyster, seal or otter. All of which go to make the estuary experience in the world of brackish water really quite special.

Estuary fishing equipment

ROD	Spinning rod (see p.113–14)
REEL	Fixed-spool reel (see p.119)
LINE	10–15lb line and shock leader (see pp.121 and 131)
HOOKS	1–2/0 hooks (see pp.122–3)
TERMINAL TACKLE	Floats, weights, swivels, beads, feathers, other lures (see Tackle and Kit, pp.123–9 and pp.132–44)
RIG ASSEMBLY	Float rig (see p.165)
BAIT	Mackerel, squid, lugworms, ragworms, peeler crab (see Bait, pp.153–5 and pp.158–9)

Rocky cliffs and ledges

Fishing off rocks works well because, unlike gently sloping beaches, the water around rocky outcrops is often instantly deep. Rocks also attract algae, which attract larger life forms, which in turn attract fish. Rocks provide cracks and crevices for seaweed to root and this provides food and shelter for all manner of aquatic life, including fish and larger crustaceans such as crabs, shrimps, prawns and lobsters. A rock face that is always partially submerged by sea water is like a mini reef, providing a permanent habitat which can support a whole food chain of sea life.

Fishing off rocks that always have sea around them is easier in some ways than a beach, because there's always water, whatever the state of the tide. And a simple drop of a bait from the rocks gives you instant access to this reef-like habitat.

However, the disadvantages of rock fishing are numerous. It's a naturally snaggy environment, which will rob you of tackle. And it adds an extra dimension of difficulty when landing a fish. Trying to drag a fish up a snaggy rock face so often turns a moment of triumph to one of tears and regret. To overcome this, use a drop net (see pp.146–7) or a long-handled landing net.

The most worrying aspect of rock fishing is that it's potentially very dangerous. I've known experienced anglers who have broken ankles climbing to rock marks. One of the most common accidents befalling rock fishermen is tripping on a rabbit

hole, while lugging fishing tackle across cliffs. And these accidents are ones which happen *before* they've even got to the really dangerous spot. The bit where the rocks meet the sea.

Every year a number of anglers are swept off rocks by crashing waves. And even more have to be rescued by lifeboat crews, because they get stranded by rising tides and frighten themselves rigid by climbing down to places which they then discover they can't climb back out of. Make no mistake, rock fishing is fraught with danger. If you're determined to try it, then:

• Make sure you go somewhere that is recommended by an experienced angler or tackle shop.
• Before you go, listen to a relevant local weather forecast and check the tide table so you know what the tide is doing and when (see Directory, p.249). Don't go in bad weather.
• Take a mobile phone and put the coastguard number on speed dial. In some rock-fishing locations, mobile phone signals are poor or non-existent, so as an added precaution, let someone at home know exactly where you're going and what time you intend to return. That way, if you don't pitch up, they can contact the coastguard and let him know exactly where you went.
• Pack a torch – just in case of emergency.
• Wear good boots with ankle support and a decent grip.
• Travel light.
• Don't take young children with you.

Rocky cliff fishing equipment

ROD	Spinning rod (see pp.113–14) or carp rod (see p.116–17)
REEL	Fixed-spool reel (see p.119)
LINE	10–15lb line and shock leader (see pp.121 and 131)
HOOKS	1–4/0 hooks (see pp.122–3)
TERMINAL TACKLE	Floats, weights, swivels, beads, feathers, other lures, drop net or landing net (see Tackle and Kit, pp.123–9, pp.132–44 and pp.146–7)
RIG ASSEMBLY	Float rig (see p.165)
BAIT	Mackerel, squid, lugworms, ragworms, peeler crab (see Bait, pp.153–5 and pp.158–9)

Harbours

Harbours are built to provide a safe haven for boats, giving them somewhere to moor protected from the direct force of the prevailing wind and weather. And what works for boats works for fish too. A harbour is like an office foyer with fish passing in and out through the doors, some just to drop off or pick up, others to hang around and wait, and a few more going straight through to the elevators and on up to higher levels.

In the event of storms, some fish will take refuge inside harbours, especially small fish like sprats, which don't have the strength to fight against stormy seas and strong currents. Where there are sprats or other bait fish, then sure enough bigger fish will follow. Bass and big mackerel are opportunistic feeders and will cruise into any harbour that's providing a temporary home to some nervy sprats. And so, just before and just after stormy weather, the temporary population of harbours might explode with refugees and refugee predators.

In the late summer and autumn, when the sea temperature is at its warmest, prawns are attracted to the weed and algae that grow on the submerged harbour pilings. And, where there are prawns, there are always cruising fish, trying their hardest to eat them.

Cold weather can have an effect on the aquatic population of a harbour too, by offering a shivery siren call to certain species. The first frosts of winter attract squid as they migrate in from deeper water. Like any of the finned predators, these violent cephalopods are on the hunt. They target small fry – fish born earlier in the year – who are taking cover in the shadow of the harbour walls. Squid also have huge eyes, which gives them a night-hunting advantage.

Winter fish like whiting will gravitate towards harbour mouths, especially at night when, like squid, they feel less conspicuous.

As most harbours also have a river running into them from their landward side, there's a continual flow of fresh water which flushes food along the river bed and into the harbour itself. Sea fish will hang out where the fresh water spills into the harbour in order to intercept this conveyor-belt of food. The more rain that's falling inland and the more swollen by flood the river is, the more potential food it will carry. (That said, there is a limit to how much fresh water the average sea fish will stand.)

Certain fish 'smell' fresh water and get excited by it, for reasons other than food. Salmon, sea trout and eels all require fresh river water for their breeding cycle. Mature salmon and sea trout return from feeding at sea and seek to enter specific rivers, in order to run upstream to search out tiny gravel-bedded tributaries where they can lay their precious eggs in cool, well-oxygenated fresh water.

One fish which is synonymous with harbour cruising is the grey mullet. These fish are the 'homies' of the harbour neighbourhood, who cruise around the calm water, simply seeing and being seen. Grey mullet are understandably often mistaken for bass by novice harbour groupies who see a big silver fish (often in excess of 5lb) cruising in the sunlight as if he owns the place. Many assume it must be a high-ranking predator like a bass, rather than a vegetarian algae-sucking pacifist mullet.

The truth is that bass are much more wary and inconspicuous than mullet, who are conspicuous in their disregard for prying eyes. You'd be forgiven for thinking that a fish that makes himself so easy to spot would also be easy to catch. Nothing could be further from the truth (see grey mullet, pp.100–103).

Harbour fishing and the law Many harbours will have local restrictions about where you're allowed to fish. A quick chat, or a phone call to the harbourmaster, or even a look at the website, will clarify what you're allowed to do, when and where.

As a rule, boat owners are unhappy about people fishing around their craft. I've seen mooring ropes snagged, tackle left snapped and hanging from fenders, and gel-coat yacht surfaces chipped and scratched by carelessly cast terminal tackle. As a boat owner myself, I've experienced all manner of madness in the harbour mouth during summer, and believe me, getting someone's terminal tackle wrapped around your propeller is extremely annoying, potentially dangerous and expensive.

It's these accidents and discourtesies that create bad feeling between anglers and boaters in harbours and, because it's boaters who pay the mooring fees (and, thus, the harbourmaster's wages), boaters will always have the greatest leverage. Antagonising boaters will only ever restrict your fishing.

Harbour fishing equipment

ROD	Spinning rod (see p.113–4)
REEL	Fixed-spool reel (see p.119)
LINE	10–15lb line and shock leader (see pp.121 and 131)
HOOKS	1–4/0 hooks (see pp.122–3)
TERMINAL TACKLE	Floats (waggler and bubble), weights, beads, swivels, feathers, other lures, drop net or landing net (see Tackle and Kit, pp.123–9, pp.132–44 and pp.146–7)
RIG ASSEMBLY	Running ledger (see p.164), float rig (see p.165)
BAIT	Squid, mackerel, ragworm, bread (see Bait, pp.153, 155, 158 and 159)

Fish You Might Catch

'If you caught something every time, it would be called "catching" not "fishing", wouldn't it?' This is the sort of philosophy that gets bandied about amongst sea anglers to make you feel better about going home with an empty cool box. These words alone might be enough to heal your disappointment, but I doubt it. However, you should be aware that even anglers like me and Hugh, who have spent decades in the pursuit of fish, often come home fishless – even on the most promising of days in the most ripe and fertile fish locations.

Most of the fish that you can catch around our shores are not only edible but delicious, and the species in this chapter are arranged roughly in order of the ones most likely to put a bend in your rod, to those least likely to put in an appearance.

Some species don't taste as good, or take too much effort to prepare, or are too small to bother with; I've identified these (on pp.104–6). And there are some fish that taste good, but are in serious danger of being overfished and should be released, as they're much better for the marine environment alive than dead (see pp.107–9).

Unlike wild mushrooms or berries, there aren't any fish that will poison you if you eat them, although there is one British fish – the weaver fish (see p.106) – that *will* poison you if you accidentally stand on it with bare feet, or prick yourself with its three stiletto-sharp fin spines. But if you pan-fry it and eat it on toast with butter and horseradish sauce it will do you no harm.

One myth that I feel should be exploded at this point is that learning to sea-fish is a means to access cheap fish. It isn't. If cheap fish is what you want from sea fishing, then stop now. Don't fool yourself that learning to fish will save you money, it won't. The ratio of spend – in terms of money, time and effort – to fish on plate doesn't make any personal economic sense whatsoever. And yet, what fishing does give you, if you catch the bug and really take to it, is ultimately priceless. The joy and satisfaction of learning new skills and being able to convert a day out at the seaside into a smashing feast of bitingly fresh fish is a gift for life.

The location (see pp.27) and season (see pp.17) affect what you might catch. Where fish dwell in the water column is also a factor (see adjacent diagram).

Key:

1 Garfish (top, middle)
2 Grey Mullet (top, middle)
3 Herring (top, middle)
4 Horse Mackerel (top, middle, bottom)
5 Mackerel (top, middle, bottom)
6 Black Bream (middle, bottom)
7 Sea Bass (top, middle, bottom)
8 Squid (middle, bottom)

9 Pollack (middle, bottom)
10 Cod (bottom)
11 Red Gurnard (middle, bottom)
12 Dogfish (bottom)
13 Whiting (bottom)
14 Pouting (bottom)
15 Dab (bottom)
16 Flounder (bottom)
17 Plaice (bottom)

Where sea fish dwell

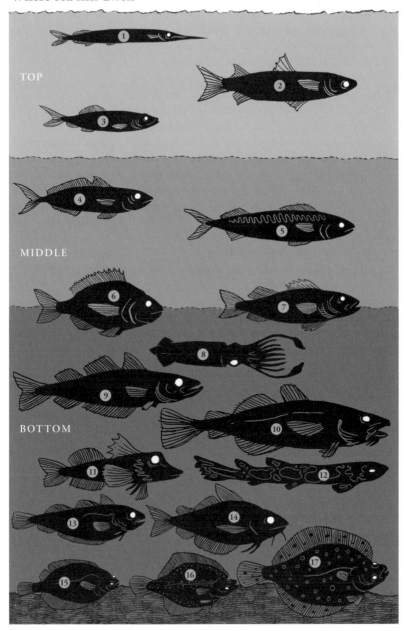

TOP

MIDDLE

BOTTOM

Mackerel *Scomber scombrus*

SEASON	All year in the Southwest. Generally April–October in the rest of the UK
LOCATION	Beach, pier, rocks, boat
METHOD	Spinning, feathering, float-fishing with small strips of bait (mackerel or squid)
CONSERVATION STATUS	Healthy

So many love affairs with sea fishing have started with a mackerel bite. Without a shadow of a doubt, these are our finest sea fish. Not only are they plentiful, they are co-operative, they taste good and they're chock full of life-enhancing omega-rich oils and other nutrients.

Always excitable and hungry, mackerel are like perennial puppies. The reason why they are so ravenous and therefore happy to attack practically any sort of bait – from a bare shiny hook to a fancy thrumming spinner – is because they are 'pelagic' or wandering fish. These are fish that are continually on the move, both in terms of migration, as well as moving up and down the water column, hunting food at various depths, from the surface to the seabed. Mackerel are in effect the British equivalent of tuna or marlin, which criss-cross entire oceans in the pursuit of top-class feed.

Mackerel behave in the same way as these big-scale pelagic fish, only they do it over a smaller range. They might not cross oceans, but mackerel will migrate up and down the English Channel, or along hundreds of miles of our coastline, in their quest for top nourishment. And their pelagic nature, this continual searching and swimming, necessitates that their flesh be oily. Mackerel require a continual ready source of energy on tap, as 'fuel' for their hard-working muscles. Conversely, white fish, such as cod and pollack, have a much less active lifestyle and so can carry their oil energy supplies in the reservoir of their liver.

Finding them

Mackerel are eternally obliging fish, which can be caught from a range of locations (see chart, p.27), using various methods, from small baits float-fished, to cast spinners, feathers or plugs.

During the spring, mackerel migrate to inshore shallow waters as the sea first begins to warm. In winter, the deeper water offshore maintains a higher temperature than the shallower inshore water, so mackerel move offshore to follow the food and more consistent water temperatures. When spring returns, they move back inshore as the food supplies migrate and the sea temperature rises.

Most of the time you won't actually catch sight of mackerel, even though they may be feeding near the surface. Occasionally during the late summer and autumn you may detect evidence of their presence in two ways: showers of tiny fry fish hopping out of the sea and seagulls diving into it. The fry leap out of the water in an attempt to escape mackerel, which are hunting the shoal from below. And the sea birds dive in to take advantage of the mackerel's endeavours, picking off bait fish that have been wounded or disoriented by the mass mackerel attack.

Catching them

If you're fishing from a boat, the easiest way to catch mackerel is with a string of mackerel feathers (see pp.134–5). You just have to lower them over the side and jig them up and down at various depths, or let them hang out the back, 20 or 30 yards behind, as the boat putters slowly along. This latter method is known as 'trolling' (see p.13).

Using mackerel feathers is trickier if you're casting from a shallow sandy beach, where they'll sink and possibly get caught up on the seabed. But it's still likely to be the most productive method. I often cut a string of six feathers down to three, which still gives three chances to attract a mackerel but reduces the weight of your string and the possibility of accidentally hooking the seabed. Choosing the right weight – just enough for a decent cast but not too much to take it down to the seabed too quickly – is another way of fine-tuning your beach feathering approach.

Because of their high oil content, mackerel spoil much more quickly than white fish like whiting, cod or pollack. So, they need to be killed, bled and chilled soon after they're caught (see pp.177–9); there's a particular method for killing mackerel which bleeds them at the same time (see p.178). And to enjoy them at their best, you really need to eat mackerel as soon as possible – ideally on the day you catch them, or at least within the next couple of days.

Eating them

Mackerel are laughably easy to cook; their natural oils make them conveniently self-basting and hard to spoil, either on the grill or in the oven. I love mackerel made into sashimi (see pp.206–8), pickled (see pp.210–11) and in escabeche (see p.213 and pp.216–17).

It is also delicious barbecued with bay leaves (see p.230), baked with potato chunks and lemon wedges (see p.233) or fry-poached and then generously drizzled with lemon juice or crab apple juice (see pp.242–3). And a great way of cooking mackerel on the beach is to poach it in a bucket of sea water (see p.228).

Dogfish *Scyliorhinus canicula*

SEASON	All year
LOCATION	Beach, pier, boat
METHOD	Fish a bait (worms, squid or mackerel) on a bottom-fishing rig
CONSERVATION STATUS	Healthy

Most fish are hard to catch and easy to eat. Dogfish are the opposite: sometimes catching them is too easy. Their rabid hunger and terrible table manners makes them suckers for swallowing hook bait. If you happen to alight upon a whole pack of doggies, then you might find *all* you catch is one dogfish after another. A rowdy pack can scare every other self-respecting species away and then squabble amongst themselves over the pickings left on the feeding ground.

Dogfish are tricky to eat, but it's not because they don't taste good, far from it; a bite-sized nugget of deep-fried beer-battered dogfish is about as delicious a fish-eating experience as any sane angler could wish. No, it's the *packaging* that dogfish goujons come in that is the problem.

The Lesser Spotted Dogfish (aka the LSD), our most common dogfish, and our most prolific member of the shark brotherhood, is covered in a thick, gritty sandpaper-like skin, which is so tightly fitted that it requires a real knack to get it off without shedding your own blood, or tears, in the process. So tricky is the art of dogfish skin removal that I've devoted a whole section to the techniques (see pp.194–7).

But please don't be put off. Think of a dogfish as the marine equivalent of a pomegranate – there's some serious fiddling to be done to get to the good stuff. However, when you succeed, the hidden fruit is sweet and succulent, easy to cook, and well worth the effort.

Finding them

Dogfish don't go anywhere. Even in the depths of winter, when most other species have sought out warmer and deeper climes, the dogfish, bless him, can still be found snouting around all his usual haunts searching for food. Sometimes the cold weather or a change in feeding patterns causes them to hunt in packs, which means there may be a thinner spread of dogfish over a large area, but a large concentration at specific marks.

Most of the year, dogfish like to feed over sandy, gravelly or muddy ground, but they'll occasionally hunt over rocky ground too. They can be found in deep as well as very shallow water.

Catching them

Catching dogfish isn't too difficult. They'll eat more or less anything, so baits don't have to be fancy, or fresh – sometimes stinkier is better. Dogfish are used to hunting out baits in dark murky depths, so they've developed a highly tuned sense of smell, and use their snout more than their dark, beady satanic eyes to find food. Baits don't need to be carefully presented on the hook either: a doggie will bite chunks out of a whole dead dolphin if it needs to. So a lump of old mackerel, rancid from defrosting and refreezing, ragworms, fish guts, tails, heads, limpets, whelks or hermit crabs will all work. Dogfish are very partial to a cocktail, so don't be scared to be inventive and mix squid and worm or fish and crab on the hook. But remember, like all true scavengers, dogfish are members of the bottom-feeding fraternity, so whatever bait you do use, it needs to be well weighted, so it's in contact with the seabed.

I generally prefer to use fine wire hooks when I'm fishing for any of the species I've covered in this book. However, dogfish do have thick cartilage in their jaws, covered by that incredibly tough sandpaper skin, which can make hook removal quite tricky. Thin wire hooks are inclined to bend very easily in a dogfish's jaw as you try to remove them, and then they become useless. (It always helps to have a pair of long-nosed pliers in your box to help remove hooks.) If you're in the middle of a dog pack, and are catching more dogfish than you intend to keep, it makes sense to swap to using thick wire hooks (a 2/0 or 3/0), which bend less easily, and then also use the

How to hold a dogfish

pliers to squeeze the barb down flat. That way you'll be able to unhook the dogfish easily and return the ones you don't want to eat totally unharmed.

Unhooking a dogfish can be a painful business for the angler, because a dog's flapping and curling tail can easily wind itself around your wrist as you fumble at the hook, inflicting a very nasty graze with its highly abrasive skin – one which will take a long time to heal.

To get around this, some anglers take a rag with them to wrap around the fish while they perform hook removal surgery. Another technique I often use is simply to fold the fish sideways so that the tip of its tail is level with its chest, and hold the tail fin firmly against its body with the thumb and fingers of one hand (as shown above), while you deal with the hook with your other hand. The friction of its skin against skin makes it easy to hold it still.

Because they're such primeval thick-skinned sharks, dogfish don't die easily. To despatch one properly, it's necessary to club it hard, two or three times across the centre of the head, with a well-weighted 'priest' (see p.146). And remember there are special techniques for skinning dogfish (see pp.194–7).

Eating them

Dogfish is easy to cook. It doesn't flake or fall apart like white fish or oily fish, so it makes fantastic stew (see p.224). And because it's a cartilaginous fish, which doesn't have skeletal bones, it is a popular choice with even the fussiest fish eaters. Simple dogfish goujons, deep-fried in breadcrumbs (see pp.238–9) and dipped in homemade tartare sauce (see p.205), are about as eminently edible as any fish can be.

Pouting *Trisopterus luscus*

SEASON	All year
LOCATION	Boat fishing is best. Also try the beach, rocky cliffs and harbours for small pouting
METHOD	Bottom-fishing with mackerel strip for bait, or ragworm, lugworm or squid strip bait
CONSERVATION STATUS	Healthy

Pouting are members of the cod family, so they're related to whiting and pollack, yet they don't get treated with anything like the respect that their cod cousins receive. For as long as I've been sea fishing, I've known pouting to be sneered at by serious sea anglers, mostly because they're regarded as an unwanted accidental catch landed during the more serious business of targeting fish like cod, bass or black bream. Pouting are not even considered worth keeping for crab-pot bait or for hook bait, and because they rarely survive being released back into the water, they are often left to drift away at the torturous mercy of eye-plucking seagulls.

The reason why pouting don't survive when they're released is because they're very sensitive to pressure change. Being brought up from a depth of even as little

as 30 feet can cause their swim bladder to 'blow' and the membrane over their eyes to inflate (as a consequence, they've been given the uncharitable moniker 'bug eyes'). In this inflated state, they're unable to swim back to the seabed, and so float helplessly on the surface.

If you catch a pout, especially from a boat, then the chances are it's going to die. This may be a tragedy for the pout and his family, but it is good reason for the fish-loving angler to celebrate because pouting, despite their ill-deserved reputation, are very good to eat.

Finding them

Pouting can be caught nearly all year round, the spring, summer and autumn months being the most pout productive. The bigger ones tend to stay in water over 40 feet deep, so the best method for catching them is from a boat, but occasionally big ones will be caught from beach marks too, especially in the evening and at night. Rocky cliffs and harbours usually hold a resident population of small pout.

Catching them

As pouting are bottom-feeding fish, you need to use a bottom-fishing rig baited with a mackerel strip/chunk, worm or squid. They also respond well to mackerel feathers with a chunk of bait attached to the bottom couple of hooks. Pouting have big mouths and greedy bellies, so hook size and even bait size is unimportant. They'll wrap their gums around anything vaguely edible.

If you catch a pouting, bleed it, gut it and chill it as soon as you can. Removing guts swiftly is the key to pouting success. Many pouting detractors claim they smell bad, and it's true their guts do have a distinct smell, which is more 'composty' than other fish. This is simply because they eat more weed in their diet and have a different digestive system. But if you gut them and chill them within an hour or two of catching, they smell and taste as fine as any white fish in our seas.

Eating them

The proof of the pouting is in the eating. In countries where they worship freshly caught fish of all species, like Spain, Portugal and France, you'll see pouting or *faneca* fillets in every local fish market. And in my house, they're a firm favourite too. Usually I serve them as fried breadcrumbed fillets (see pp.238–9) or battered fillets (see p.240), sometimes popped into a crusty roll with a dab of homemade tartare sauce (see p.205), garlic mayonnaise (see p.204) or tomato ketchup.

Pollack *Pollachius pollachius*

SEASON	Inshore during summer and autumn
LOCATION	Over rocky ground, weed beds and near inshore reefs and structures
METHOD	Ragworm bait, spinner, rubber worms, rubber fish. Caught on paternoster rigs, trolled lures and float-fished ragworm
CONSERVATION STATUS	Healthy, but more vulnerable now they're commercially fished as a replacement for cod

In the last few years, pollack has gone from zero to hero. A fish once considered fit only for cat food now regularly sells for the same, if not more than, cod. Chefs rave about pollack now, when not so long ago cod and haddock were the only white fish deemed worthy of note. And anything you might do with cod, you can do with pollack, in the knowledge that it's a faster-growing, more plentiful fish, which doesn't carry anything like the same conservation issues that cod does.

Unlike herring and mackerel, which are pelagic oily-skinned fish, pollack and cod are white demersal fish. They inhabit the demersal zone of the sea, close to the seabed, where currents are less strong and life is less frenetic. Unlike pelagic fish, they don't swim around all day long, and instead hide around features out of the force of the current where they can ambush their prey.

As pollack don't need a constant ready supply of fuel oil, they store it in their liver, where it can be slowly tapped when needed. Pollack liver oil shares the precious health-giving properties that have made cod liver oil so famous. (In Iceland, I've stayed in hotels where at the end of the breakfast buffet line stands a decanter full of chilled cod liver oil and a stack of shot glasses, for diners to dose themselves for the day ahead.) It's mad not to do something with the livers of any pollack you catch; personally I would highly recommend keeping the liver for popping into the pot whilst making fish stock, to add extra flavour and nutritious oils.

Finding them

Really big pollack of 15lb plus are a deep-water fish, so they are rarely caught from the shore or from inshore boats. However, when the water is warm during the summer and autumn months, small pollack (around 2lb) are often found in shallow water around rocky outcrops or kelp seaweed beds. Pollack love a feature, such as a small reef or ledge, a sunken wreck, or ancient concrete pilings – somewhere to lie in ambush for small fish and crabs that are washed along by the tide.

Catching them

Being voracious predators and sometimes opportunistic bottom-feeders, pollack can be caught on all sorts of baits and rigs, from feathers and baited feathers to ragworm and peeler crab. From a boat they can be caught trolling, drifting or even while sitting at anchor. My favourite way to catch pollack from a small boat is to drift while fishing a lightly weighted paternoster rig on a spinning rod, or light boat rod, with 15lb line and a fat trailing ragworm as bait. Of course you can use rubber worms and artificial baits instead, which are a lot cheaper and will work well in most conditions. But there's just something very satisfying and exciting about fishing with what you know in your heart is a pollack's favourite meal. The bites are rapacious. A pollack will chase a big ragworm with all the enthusiasm of a hungry lurcher.

An important thing to note, though, is that even fishing into no more than 20 feet of water, pollack, like pouting, don't fare well after being brought out of the sea. Catch and release doesn't really work with pollack, so if you do happen upon a good pollack spot, stop as soon as you've caught your feed. Don't be tempted to go on fishing for 'sport' afterwards; it will only cause more pollack demise.

I recommend gutting your catch at sea or on the shore, because it's less messy than doing it in the kitchen, and more importantly, it gives you a chance to put ice directly into the belly cavity.

Eating them

Small pollack make very good eating. Because of their delicate white flesh, they're not really suitable for barbecue cooking, unless you cook them in a protective foil parcel. But they're a very good fish to practise your filleting skills on.

I always save the heads and skeletons of my pollack (along with the liver), because they make such excellent fish stock (see pp.218–20). Like a cod's head, a pollack's head is full of cartilage. When boiled and then allowed to cool, this creates the most magnificent fishy jelly, which is wonderful as a base for fishy risottos and soups. If you make stock from pollack, you don't have to use it straight away. More often than not, I pour the cooled stock into a double layer of freezer bags and pop it in the freezer for another day.

To cook pollack fillets, I lightly salt them first, distributing 1 tbsp salt over both sides of each fillet and leaving them to stand for around 15 minutes, before giving them a good rinse in cold water and a pat dry with a tea towel.

I then coat the fillets in a tempura-style batter or breadcrumbs and deep-fry (see pp.238–9), draining them well on kitchen paper before serving. Or I shallow-fry the fillets in olive oil, with some capers and lemon juice.

Otherwise fillets of pollack can be steamed and served with a soy, chilli and garlic sauce (see pp.236–7) or baked with green beans and stock, and topped with a pesto crust (see p.234).

Cod *Gadus morhua*

SEASON	Winter (October–February). In recent years, early-summer runs appear in the Channel
LOCATION	Shore fishing over rough, rocky ground or shingle beaches. Early-summer inshore boat fishermen concentrate their efforts over beds of brittle starfish
METHOD	From shore, use big baits (peeler crab, lugworm, mussel and black lug) ledgered on pennel rigs. Over starfish beds, boat anglers use rubber fish, wedges and baited feathers
CONSERVATION STATUS	Not too healthy; use discretion

Cod is not a smart fish. In fact, I'd go as far as to say that it's really quite a stupid fish. When cod are present in any number, they're easy to catch. They're greedy, lazy big-mouthed slobs, who'll eat just about any bait you put in front of them, and swallow it whole – from a single ragworm on a size 1 hook, to a pennel rig-mounted cocktail of baits the size of your foot.

A few years ago, I was evangelical in my cod preservation stance and put more than a few noses out of joint when I insisted every cod caught while drift fishing from our boat off the Portland Race, outside Weymouth, was returned. They often get caught in amongst the bass and bream shoals feeding in the fast current. Since then, I've become more easy-going and have even kept one or two cod myself as I've seen their numbers inshore increase. But that's one or two fish over the same number of years. Even if we know there's good cod fishing to be had, we have to be abstemious and careful. Make no mistake, if the cod species is abused, it will disappear.

In saying all that, anyone who has the opportunity to catch a couple of cod, now and again, would be mad not to make the effort and, if successful, to take the odd fish home. Yet, here is where we need to have a healthy fish conscience. In my opinion, one fish from a trip is acceptable, two is an absolute maximum, and if you keep catching cod, for whatever reason – because the planets are aligned and you find yourself 'in the zone' – then you need to have the discipline to stop.

Finding them

The trick of cod fishing is almost entirely down to location: being in the right place at the right time, either on a rocky beach mark when a bunch of feeding fish are passing during the winter months; or in early summer on a boat drifting over a bed

of brittle starfish, which have caught the attention of a feeding shoal. Sometimes beach fishing at night works best as the cod will come closer to the shore under the cover of darkness. When I was living in Norfolk, in my very early teens, night fishing was considered the only way to catch cod from the beach. Along with my dad, I would crunch over miles of pebbles carrying a ghostly glowing Tilley lamp and just occasionally we'd get lucky and tease a couple of codling from the wind-chilled North Sea.

Catching them

I take my hat off to anyone who catches a cod from the beach. It takes dedication and perseverance to track down cod; it might even require cold, blustery night sessions, many blank trips and much investment in bait. So, if you're someone who likes a challenge and is prepared to put in the hours and the effort, then you definitely deserve your cod. Use big baits – peeler crab, lugworm, mussel and black lug – on a pennel rig (see p.167).

Boat fishing for cod is slightly less noble and deserving, in terms of the ratio of effort to reward. Unless you're skippering your own boat, chances are you're going to be taken out by a skipper who knows where the cod are, and can put you above a co-operative feeding shoal (of which, let's face it, there aren't statistically that many). There you'll be able to pretty much fill your boots fairly easily. Usually a few drifts over a feeding shoal with rubber fish Storm lures (see pp.143–4) or baited feathers (see pp.134–6) will result in multiple hook-ups. In this situation, it's not unusual with feathers to even hook two or three cod at a time.

This is when recreational cod fishing is dubious, in my opinion. Any cod caught and killed should be justly earned. Cod is not a fish we can afford to get greedy or complacent about, nor is it one that we recreational anglers can over-target or abuse from boats, while commercial fishermen are governed by strict quota restrictions.

If you do catch a cod – well done. And if you do kill it, just make sure you treat it with total respect from the killing, chilling, preparing cooking and eating perspectives, so that you leave not a single morsel unloved.

Eating them

Cod bones, skin, head and fins all make fabulous fish stock (see pp.218–20). The cod head alone, if it's big enough, can be roasted (stick a couple of rashers of thick streaky smoked bacon on top and a bunch of rosemary inside) with fennel root to make a finger-licking, bone-picking, eye socket-sucking feast.

Fillets of cod can be steamed (see p.235) or baked with green beans and stock, and topped with a pesto crust (see p.234). And there is no finer fish to wrap in an eggy batter and deep-fry (see pp.238–41), then drain and serve with tartare sauce (see p.205) or a sweet chilli or soy and garlic dipping sauce (see p.205).

Whiting *Merlangius merlangus*

SEASON	Autumn and winter
LOCATION	Inshore boats over sandy, muddy or shingle ground. Occasionally from the shore too, especially at night, when fishing on to a sandy seabed
METHOD	From a boat, mackerel feathers baited with chunks of fish work, as will any paternoster rig baited with worm and fish baits. From the shore, use a bottom-fishing paternoster rig with small fish baits such as mackerel, sprat, herring and even strips of fresh whiting
CONSERVATION STATUS	Healthy

My most clearly etched memory of whiting lingers from my childhood in Scotland, where these fish were used in a perverse form of culinary torture executed upon sick people. Whiting poached in milk is the Protestant equivalent of Jewish chicken soup: a cure-all for the bilious and nauseous. In my granny's kitchen, the pressure cooker was the most prized instrument of torture. Sadly, poaching whiting until it's the consistency of zoo plankton really does its flaky muscular flesh a terrible disservice.

Since moving to Dorset, I've learned to let go of my lowland Scots Presbyterian roots and recognise fresh whiting for the fabulous Arctic white-fleshed fish that it really is. Not only delicious to eat, but satisfying and challenging to catch at times too. I now love cooking and eating whiting. And I can say, with unabashed pride, that I've managed to turn the whiting legacy around, and now my whiting fish fingers or tempura fillets in a sweet chilli dipping sauce are firm crunchy favourites with my own four children.

In so many ways, it is hard to find a more boring fish than whiting. They are the masters of beige. Beige in flavour, beige by nature, and beige in their behaviour, preferring to inhabit the most middle-of-the-road patches of seabed – not too deep, not too shallow, not too rocky. They like a nice sandy patch where they can ferret around *en masse* for crabs and worms.

Whiting don't appear to have any very interesting friends either. Winter shoals are often mono species. It's as though no self-respecting species wants to be associated with whiting. This is probably a result of their timing though, arriving inshore when most of the other more interesting fish have departed offshore to deeper, warmer, more constant and less storm-affected seas.

Finding them

Like a winter version of the mackerel, whiting arrive in our inshore waters around September, usually travelling in large shoals. The peak period for catching them around Britain is probably between late October and late November, but certainly on the south coast, they can often hang around right through until February and even into March. After Christmas is when the big ones (up to 2lb in weight) are normally caught. These tend to be more the lone wolves with big teeth and big appetites, unlike the smaller shoal fish that busy themselves along as members of a pack in the autumn.

The trick with catching whiting is location. They love clean sandy ground, but also have a penchant for a bit of flat muddy ground too if there's plenty of food to be found. Along shingle and surf beaches they'll cruise any gutters or troughs that have been scoured out behind the breaking surf. At night they'll venture into very shallow water, less than a couple of feet in depth, if they're finding good food.

The big spring tides of the late autumn are the ones that bring whiting right in to the beach. Then, in sporadic shoals, they hug the coastline in the same way that mackerel do in summer. Whiting will move along the shore against the flow of the tide. They're hunting for crabs and small fish being pushed along by the current and by heading into the flow they're able to use their keen hunter's sense of smell to its best advantage.

Catching them

Once you've found a shoal, the hard work is over; whiting are normally very easy to catch. Oddly, for such a cautious fish, they are actually not too fussy about what they'll pop in their mouths. Place just about any bait in their face and they'll hang themselves on your hook like floppy wet lemmings, limply pursuing mass suicide.

Unlike mackerel, whiting are demersal or bottom-feeding fish, closely related to cod. So they'll always be caught on, or very near, the bottom, usually using ledgered baits of mackerel or squid, or ragworm or lugworm. They are suckers for baited feathers too. Mackerel feathers, baited with chunks of mackerel flesh or squid, fished in the usual jigging manner, but down deep, bouncing off the seabed, is one very productive method to haul a few in, once you've found your shoal.

And for all their beigeness of character, whiting are, rather surprisingly, not averse to a bit of bling. Many committed and serious whiting anglers (which may seem like a cruel contradiction in terms) will fix silver flashing and rattling beads (known as Booby beads) to their feathers or paternoster rigs in order to attract the fishes' attention.

For all their lack of pizzazz, a whiting's mouth does conceal an impressive array of small pointy teeth. These teeth can eventually rasp right through fishing line, especially if you're banging out a bucket in a session. So use a 20–25lb hook length.

Normally, however, whiting weigh less than 1lb, although there are shoals of larger ones, known as Channel whiting, which can regularly be found weighing 2–4lb. These are the real bad boys of the otherwise bland whiting world. Not surprisingly they put up much more of a fight than the beige 1lb clones and, if you're lucky, might well put an unexpected curve in your carbon.

As with their close but sadly misunderstood cousins, the pouting (also known as the pout whiting), they should be cracked on the head, bled and chilled quickly. Warm whiting will deteriorate fast because their muscle flakes are very small and tightly packed, and the flesh will turn soft if it's not kept well chilled.

Eating them

A bunch of whiting, big or small, will always give terrific fillets – as well as some cod-like heads and frames that provide the basis of a truly classic fish stock (see pp.218–20). Most of the whiting I catch I'll fillet and fry in breadcrumbs or tempura batter (see pp.238–9), or possibly grill with bacon lardons or chorizo (see p.245).

I also like to fry-poach whiting fillets with olive oil, garlic and lemon and serve them over a bowl of brown rice (see pp.242–3).

Sometimes I'll just coat them lightly in a mix of cornflour, salt and black pepper and fry them quickly in very hot corn oil (see p.239).

Alternatively, neatly trimmed slices are perfect candidates for a quick ceviche marinade (see pp.214–15), especially with thinly sliced peppery-hot red chilli.

Garfish *Belone belone*

SEASON	Spring, summer and early autumn
LOCATION	Around piers, rocky headlands and from inshore boats
METHOD	Mini mackerel feathers, baited feathers and float-fishing with small mackerel, sand eel or even garfish strips for bait
CONSERVATION STATUS	Healthy

Garfish are extraordinary-looking creatures – rather like a cross between a swimming dinosaur, a baddie from *Thunderbirds* and an early blueprint for the Trident missile. They have a long pointed beak and a sleek, hydrodynamic body, with a sharply forked tail to provide them with forward thrust. But these are not their only distinguishing features. Garfish have luminescent green scales and a remarkable turquoise skeleton. You can always recognise anglers who have had a successful garfish catching experience, because their hands, bag and clothing possess an unmistakable green glow from all the dislodged scales.

I've often heard even experienced anglers say that garfish can't possibly be eaten because the green colouring is poisonous. This is totally untrue. The green of their scales and the deep green pigment of their bones is caused by a harmless mineral called vivianite, which is commonly found in rock formations around the English Channel. If you can get over the radioactive sheen of their scales and bones, you'll find that garfish are truly delicious to eat. Their lovely white flesh has the consistency of very firm mackerel and, because they are an oily pelagic fish, they're packed with beneficial nutrients.

Finding them

Summer is the best time to catch garfish. They're known in some areas as 'the mackerel guide' because they'll appear just in front of the spring shoals of migrating mackerel. And generally they'll hang around the same places as mackerel for the rest of the summer. This means that piers, seaward harbour walls and rocky headlands are classic garfish haunts.

Being oily pelagic fish, garfish tend to favour warmer water, and they'll happily swim in the very top layer of the sea during the summer. In fact, they're one of the few British sea fish that you might actually witness leaping out of the water. Their slender acrobatic design makes it possible for them to leap over rocks and navigate into very shallow water close to cliffs and rocks, in their predatory hunt for small fish, and to avoid less agile predators.

Catching them

Because they hunt small bait fish, garfish are occasionally caught on micro feathers or small baited feathers. Some adventurous anglers even pursue them with a fly rod, using small white or silver lures, although, in my experience, these flies work much better if they're tipped with a tiny strip of fish flesh or fish skin.

However, the most enjoyable and successful way to catch garfish is from a rock jetty or pier, using a light spinning rod and a sea float or bubble float rig, with a small hook size 1 suspended a few feet beneath it, weighed under by a drilled bullet lead. The hook should then be baited with a tiny sliver of mackerel flesh, sand eel fillet, or whole small sand eel. If you get lucky, try using a sliver of garfish flesh instead. (Like so many other sea predators, they are enthusiastically cannibalistic.)

Garfish are immense fun to catch. They'll put a serious bend in your rod and will often leap out of the sea during the ensuing fight, like a mini marlin or super-streamlined rainbow trout. The rows of sharp teeth inside their bony beak of a mouth does make them a little tricky to unhook. It helps to keep a wet tea towel and pair of pliers handy. Hold the garfish in the wet towel, use the pliers to turn the hook bend back on itself, and pull it from its mouth. If you've already caught enough for a meal, or feel a bit unsure about eating the fish and so intend to let them go, the wet towel minimises abrasion of scales, which might otherwise damage a garfish's chances of survival. Indeed, if you're not intending to keep many or any, you can squeeze the barb flat on your hook before you start fishing and the garfish will probably release themselves during the battle unharmed.

To kill a garfish, I would normally grab it in a rag or towel and give it a sharp crack over the back of the head; you don't need to wield the priest (see p.146) with a heavy hand. There's very good flesh in the neck and 'shoulders' so keep your killer blow accurate. You can hold them by the beak too, if you find this an easier way to keep the head perfectly still while you aim.

Eating them

My first garfish eating experience was in Guernsey, the Mecca of garfish fishing and eating. I had two cooked for me by a delightful septuagenarian who ran a local B&B. She grilled them briskly and served them with mushy peas, horseradish sauce and toast. It was a meal I'll never forget and I've cooked garfish in various ways since. My favourite is probably baking them in an open dish with wedges of par-boiled potatoes and lemon (see p.233). Horseradish sauce (see p.205) is a fine accompaniment.

Escabeche (see p.213 and pp.216–17) is another great option for garfish fillets. The oiliness of the flesh lends itself perfectly to being flour-dusted, quick fried and then doused with a tangy, vinegary marinade. Or you can simply grill chunky batons of garfish with a handful of chorizo slices and let the paprika-coloured oil baste the green-tinged garfish for a quick dish that is as colourful as it is delicious.

Red gurnard *Aspitrigla cuculus*

SEASON	Summer and autumn
LOCATION	Most easily caught from an inshore boat. They favour sandy, muddy or gravelly ground. Gurnard can be caught from beaches and piers too, though usually smaller fish
METHOD	Bottom-fishing with running ledger or paternoster rigs, using bait of worm, squid or mackerel, works well. Occasionally caught on mackerel feathers or baited mackerel feathers
CONSERVATION STATUS	Healthy

Catching a red gurnard always feels like winning the lottery. They are a gift of a fish; a ruby-red jewel that comes rising out of a grey sea in an explosion of colour, so bright you practically have to shade your eyes from the glare. My heart always skips a beat when I catch a gurnard, not least because I can practically taste the fish feast that lies ahead.

To look at, a gurnard has the face and forehead of a Glaswegian pub-brawler, and skin the colour of a Moroccan sunset. The Dutch call gurnard the 'Englese soldaat', in reference to the scarlet red coats of the traditional English battledress.

In centuries past, soused gurnard was considered a delicacy, which in truth it is. But then the tide of gourmet taste changed and they were relegated to the bottom rung of the dinner ladder. Until recently, red gurnard were rarely ever eaten or sold by fishmongers in Britain, and they were most commonly used as crab-pot bait.

Gurnard were favoured by potters because they had tough skins and lots of firm flesh, which meant they lasted for a couple of days or more in a crab pot. They do, it's true, make for great pot bait because of their handy size and because their delicious flesh is held together very tightly in a thick wrapping of skin. This means that crabs and lobster are forced to pick away at them for ages, trying to get all the flesh off and attracting even more crabs and lobster into the pot in the process. Using them as pot bait is such a terrible waste of great food though.

Thankfully gurnard is now being appreciated for the fabulous fish it is and has cruised on to menus around the country. The best gurnard I've ever eaten was served up in a small hotel restaurant in Penzance. The fish was coated in a spicy flour and fried whole, head and all, in very hot oil. Done this way, all the fins and skin became golden and crispy. Served with a green salad, new potatoes and huge chunks of fresh lemon, it was a finger-licking, flesh-picking, fin-crunching joy.

Finding them

Spring through to autumn is when most gurnard are caught. The best time, as for so many of our inshore species, is towards the end of summer and beginning of autumn when the sea is at its warmest and the fish are all well fed.

With their low-slung mouths and large fin feet, gurnard are ostensibly bottom-feeders. They feel their way across sandy and muddy flats, as well as rock-strewn portions of seabed, using their hook-like fin 'toes' to grip on to the seabed, and their feeler feet to poke around in the sand and unearth small crabs and tasty molluscs. They aren't glued to the seabed though; gurnard will move up in the water column to chase prey fish if there's nothing available on the floor. Most gurnard are caught from boats although smaller fish can be caught from sandy and pebble beaches too.

Catching them

If the weather is right and the tides are not too strong, it's not actually that difficult to catch gurnard, because they're not a fussy fish. Most are caught by accident, either when feathering from a boat for mackerel (they especially favour baited feathers), or when bumping a bait across sandy ground in search of flat fish like plaice or sole. When trying to catch bream on paternoster rigs bottom-fished with squid and ragworm baits, it's very common to pick up gurnard too. They're not faddy feeders – if they see bait, they'll usually eat it.

Although they look a bit prehistoric and slow, don't be fooled. Gurnard will often snatch a bait (such as squid, mackerel or worm) immediately after it's been cast into the surf. Their extra big eyes give them great quality of vision, even in murky conditions. And they're lightning quick to move in on anything that flashes silver or kicks up dirt. If you feel a bite on your line before your bait's even properly touched the bottom, it's likely to be a gurnard.

If you catch a gurnard that's under 8 inches, it should be released if it appears well enough to swim away. If you're catching a lot of small fish, then squeeze down the barb on your hook to make it easier to unhook and release them.

And when you handle your gurnard, don't be surprised if it starts making bizarre croaking noises. The Scottish colloquial name for gurnard is 'crooner', a name which refers to their habit of singing or snoring when caught.

This fish has a monstrously hard head and a square-topped bar-fighting forehead. So when you want to kill a gurnard for the pot, it'll need to be walloped extra hard. And I always snip through the gills with my fishing scissors in order to bleed them.

Eating them

Gurnard are without doubt one of the best eating fish in British waters, like a cross between sea bass and monkfish. There's a lot of bony head on a gurnard too, which makes fabulous fish stock (see pp.218–20). I like to dust the fish in spicy flour and fry them in very hot vegetable oil to crisp up their skins (see p.239), then finish them for a few minutes in the oven.

Gurnard also makes very impressive sashimi (see pp.206–8), sushi (see p.209), and is a shoe-in for a great fish soup (see pp.222–3). It is also one of the all-time best fish stew ingredients, because of its robust nature and its righteous refusal to flake up and break up in a pan (see pp.224–5).

Black bream *Spondyliosoma cantharus*

SEASON	Late spring, summer and autumn
LOCATION	Boats over inshore reefs and rocky ground. Occasionally beaches and cliffs
METHOD	Bottom-fishing with running ledger or paternoster rigs, using small mackerel and squid strip baits
CONSERVATION STATUS	Commercial targeting is on the increase but is still relatively light

I have to confess I couldn't help myself from jumping around like an over-excited schoolgirl the first time I hooked one of these off my own boat in Dorset. I've always had a soft spot for black bream. They fight hard and they taste better than practically any other fish from our local waters. In fact, I'd swap a bass for a black bream any day of the week.

Bream fishing is such an exciting, pleasing affair. Bream bites are so positive and their fight so tenacious, teasing and rod-rattling. Then the sight of a black bream as it appears at the surface, nearing the landing net, is inspiring. And unforgettable, as bream flare their great long spiny dorsal fin and the male fish also gleams with steel-blue and black mating colours. Then, tragic as it is to kill them, this is offset by the promise of great eating. Raw, marinated, grilled or fried, few other fish can equal them. If ever there was a prince among fish, the black bream is he.

Finding them

Black bream fishing on the south coast is a summer and autumn affair. They're migratory fish that come to our shores in the warmer months from warmer seas. Some early fish may be caught close to the foot of cliffs or around deep inshore rocky marks in springtime, when the fish are spawning. But the main bream-catching season is during the summer, when they're hanging around reefs and wrecks, hunting for protein to recondition themselves after the rigours of reproduction.

Whilst a few black bream get caught from beaches and cliffs or rocks, most are caught from inshore boats. So check with local charter boats that do half-day inshore reef trips and ask about the potential for black bream. Huge numbers of bream are caught along the south coast every season, within just 2 or 3 miles of land.

When you hit upon a good black bream mark, they can be a surprisingly co-operative fish. They are not overly fussed about tide and will happily feed through the slack periods, unlike bass and many of the other Channel fish.

FISH YOU MIGHT CATCH   73

Catching them

The way most good skippers catch black bream from a boat is to anchor over a reef, ledge or wreck in a position where the baits will sit just up tide of the structure. The scent of the baits is then dragged into the wreckage by the movement of the water, which in theory teases fish out of the protective structure to investigate.

Bream tackle couldn't be simpler. You need a spinning rod or carp rod or light boat rod. Use a simple one- or two-hook paternoster rig with size 1 or 2 Aberdeen hooks. Black bream average around 1–3lb in weight, with the occasional big one coming in around 4–5lb. But even at this size they still have very small mouths, so hooks need to be small and strong. Their limpet-crunching teeth can easily bend or break hooks that are too wiry and weedy.

The baits you use should be small, too. Strips of squid, about the width of a pencil and half as long, work best. Just hook them once through the tip of the widest end and they'll flutter enticingly in the current. Black bream also respond well to tiny chunks of fresh mackerel (about half the size of a first-class stamp), single small lugworms, ragworms or scallop frills. And a bream will even take frozen worms or frozen prawns. Don't fill a hook with loads of bait hoping to make your offering seem too irresistible to ignore, as the bream will just nibble away at it, leaving you with no bait and no dinner. (Or else, you'll simply attract the bigger-mouthed pouting to your bait.)

A black bream will never just grab a bait and gobble it down; they're more inclined to worry a bait, pecking away like a demented bantam cock. Sometimes after a series of half-hearted bites, if you reel in, you'll see teeth marks all along the length of the bait, where black bream have nibbled but never fully committed to necking your offering.

You do need to strike a bream bite. 'Striking' is simply the action of sharply lifting the rod tip upwards in response to the pecking, hoping to drive the small hook home into the cartilage around the bream's toothy mouth. The timing of a bream bite strike is worthy of a thesis all of its own. Strike too early and you pull the un-mouthed bait away from the fish, probably spooking it off in the process. Strike too late and the bream will have fleeced your hook, leaving you bare-hooked and unlikely to catch anything.

What happens so often is that you'll strike a bite and miss, and then you're left wondering if there's any bait still on your hook or not. Then an internal debate starts: *should I reel in and check?* Which, of course, would be the sensible thing to do. But, if you do still have bait on your hook, you'll be wasting precious fishing time. The world of bream fishing can be fraught with frustration and insecurity.

Hooking a black bream on light tackle in a steady tide makes for a really decent bit of rod-bending action. As the fish come up in the water they'll turn and get their heads down, taking line in fast jerky pulls. Their fighting technique is very distinctive

– they use fast movements and jaggy head-shaking lunges. You'll know you've got a black bream on immediately it's hooked.

Once you've reeled in your catch, be very careful of the skin-puncturing spines along their fins and around their gills. They also have thick scales, which make them great for cooking on a barbecue, as the scales help to protect the flesh from the heat.

If you're taking the fish home, then consider descaling them on the beach or harbour first, as it can be a messy business at home. If, however, you do descale them in the kitchen, hold the fish underwater, either in a bucket or in the sink, to stop the scales flying around.

Eating them

Black bream are ideal for baking (see pp.231–3) or grilling (see p.245). Their laterally flat shape makes them perfect for scoring across the flank – squeeze butter mashed with garlic and rock salt into the slashes and it will ooze delectably into the flesh as the fish cook, giving a crispy garlicky coating to the skin. Baby new potatoes and carrots from the garden are all you'll need for a fantastic meal.

I particularly like to fry-poach black bream fillets with garlic, lemon and fresh herbs (see p.244). They also make great sashimi (see pp.206–8), sushi (see p.209) and a classic ceviche (see pp.212–13 and 214–15).

Plaice *Pleuronectes platessa*

SEASON	Spring, summer and autumn
LOCATION	Shore fishing from sandy beaches and shingle beaches, or an inshore boat fishing over a sandy seabed or mussel beds
METHOD	Use long baits made up of lugworm and squid, fished on the bottom, either ledgered from the beach or slowly dragged along the bottom from a drifting boat with a plaice rig or a plaice spoon
CONSERVATION STATUS	Healthy

The Florida-orange splodges on a plaice's top side make it an instantly recognisable fish. And it's one of the few common inshore fish that has always been regarded as a 'proper' fish. Like cod and haddock, which have – rather unfortunately for their own sustainable safety – become the staple fodder of the great British fish and chip eater, plaice is one of those fish that commands respect. Trotting home with a couple of pouting and a dab might not make you a hero, but walk through the door carrying a plaice and respect is guaranteed. Because of its heroic nature, plaice is one of those fish that serious anglers can get rather obsessed and compulsive about.

Finding them

Plaice are usually caught fishing from the shore over sandy ground, or drift fishing or anchor fishing from a boat over a sandy bottom or mussel beds. Fishing around the south coast can be at its best in the late spring and early summer, when adult fish are ending their mating and spawning period and starting to feed voraciously in order to put some real girth back on their shrinking love handles.

Catching them

All tackle shops sell 'plaice rigs' if you don't fancy tying your own. And there are even special devices you can buy or make, known as plaice 'spoons'. These were originally made by serious plaice specimen hunters from teaspoons. The handle is sawn off to leave just the bowl of the spoon, into which a hole is drilled in one end, and a ring looped through for attaching to a swivel.

The plaice spoon is attached a few inches above the bait and it is designed to attract a big flattie's attention by kicking up puffs of sand, as the bait is dragged along the sandy ground from a slowly drifting boat. These mini sand clouds suggest that something crustacean-like is feeding on the bottom, and the plaice, in theory, will then venture over to investigate and happen upon a tasty-looking bait.

According to purists, a perfect plaice bait is made of lugworm and squid, woven together in a tantalising cocktail, and big – up to 6 inches long. Trouble is, a bait that good will also attract practically every other fish feeding on or near the bottom, from a dab to a dogfish, so it's hard to be too selective.

Even if you're fishing in the spring/summer post-spawning period, when plaice are in desperate need of a post-coital blow-out, they can still be very hard to catch. This is because they become totally focused on one particular food source and won't even look at a mouthful of anything else. They particularly love eating mussels at this time of year and get their love-weary heads down to gorge themselves silly on the small cherry-sized seed mussels that lie in beds often close to rocky shorelines.

When plaice are grazing on bite-sized mussels, which an angler cannot duplicate for bait, experienced plaice hunters may resort to cheap sensationalism – flashing glittering baubles and beads to solicit intrigue. Plaice rigs at this time of year may include rattling Booby beads, spinning vanes and sequins; anything flashy enough to distract a plaice who has his nose hard-pressed to the mussel trough. But often the feeding plaice are unmoved and remain uncatchable to rod and line anglers.

Plaice baits might be huge, but plaice bites aren't. Even very large plaice will often only have a pathetic nibble bite like a two-day-old sparrow chick. And because they use their wing-like fins to stir up the sand as they feed, they often simply disturb a bait with their fins rather than truly mouth it. This can be a crucial moment, because if you strike a nervy bite too early, you'll scare any serious-sized plaice away. They don't grow big and fat from being stupid. So patience definitely pays dividends when pursuing the picky plaice.

Sometimes big flat fish, which already have what looks like a very squashed head, appear hard to kill with a priest or bosher (see p.146). Being flat to begin with means there's not much skull to fracture. A couple of proper hard cracks to the head will usually suffice, but with some fish you might also want to puncture the brain cavity with a screwdriver or blunt knife.

Eating them

If handled well, plaice make for epic eating, although I personally wouldn't choose to cook mine on the beach. They need, and deserve, a little more special treatment and controlled heat, either on the hob in a large non-stick pan, or under the grill (see pp.246–7), or else baked whole in the oven, head and flesh still on the bone (see pp.232–3). I've recently taken to slashing the top side of my baked plaice as they go into the oven and adding a few small strips of smoked streaky bacon across the slashes. Then, when I take it out of the heat after a short fierce baking, I'll squeeze lemon juice or even half an orange into the gaping gashes.

Sea bass *Dicentrarchus labrax*

SEASON	Summer and autumn
LOCATION	Rocky outcrops and storm beaches, inshore boats over rocky ground and reefs
METHOD	Use ragworm or sand eels for bait. Use spinners, plugs or rubber fish as lures
CONSERVATION STATUS	Healthy. MLS of 40cm

Sea bass are the Holy Grail of sea anglers. Both shore and boat anglers talk of sea bass in hushed tones, because they're considered so special. The reasons for this are manifold. With their gleaming silver flanks and hydrodynamic torpedo shape, bass look magnificent. They also have a reputation for being hard-fighting, rod-bending apex predators, and to top it all, their culinary repute is second to none.

Then of course there's the monetary value. Just a portion of pan-fried sea bass in a modest seaside restaurant could cost you north of twenty quid. And a whole 5–6lb sea bass, bought over the counter in a fishmonger's shop, would cost you a fortune.

In short, bass look great, fight well and are among the top three most sought-after and expensive of British fish – so, why *wouldn't* any angler want to catch one?

It's worth noting, before we start plotting how to get a portion of rod-caught heaven on your plate, that sea bass are one of the few British sea fish to have a minimum legal landing size limit. Measured from tip of the nose to fork of the tail, this is currently set at 40cm or 16 inches (though some regions have variations; these should be posted in the harbourmaster's office.) This regulation applies to *everyone*, from the recreational angler to the commercial fisherman. Even if you're only idly flicking a spinner from the beach – and not trolling or netting from a commercially registered fishing vessel – it doesn't exempt you from this important byelaw.

The MLS for bass exists primarily because they are slow-maturing fish, which only become sexually mature when they're at least 5 years old. So in order to protect our inshore breeding populations, the size restriction is instigated to allow all sea bass around our coastline a chance to spawn and reproduce. Mostly bass spawn in estuaries and shallow protected bays, which is why you'll find many estuaries have restrictions on bass fishing, to prevent juvenile fish from being disturbed or killed.

Finding them

Bass can be found in pockets around most of our shoreline. In the South and Southwest they're predominantly a summer and autumn fish. They'll sometimes hold in small areas right through into the depths of winter too, depending on what

food is available to them. Bass like to hunt small fish and crabs, so wherever these are in abundance – over reefs, in rocky patches of seabed, around pier pilings or close up to rocky cliffs – you might just get lucky and catch one.

Catching them

For all their kudos, small bass are not hard to catch. They're young, stupid, hungry and fearless. And they'll wrap their gums around anything that looks even potentially edible. Catching bigger bass does get more difficult, not least because the biggest fish have lived the longest, seen the most, and developed the greatest sense of suspicion and self-preservation.

The two most likely ways that you'll actually catch a bass yourself from the shore are spinning with a plug, spoon or wedge, or else fishing a big whole squid bait, ledgered just behind the surf line.

Spinning for bass

Spinning for bass is really no different from spinning for mackerel or pollack from the beach. The same spinner or lure that will catch a pollack will catch a bass. However, some big bass will more happily take a bigger-sized spinner, spoon or plug than a similar-sized mackerel or pollack. This is simply because bass have huge mouths and are more aggressive and predatory than mackerel or pollack, so they will attack much bigger prey.

There are two schools of thought concerning summer spinning for bass. One is the careful and exacting approach, the other is the chuck-it-and-suck-it approach. The careful, thoughtful bass angler will go to the beach at break of dawn, when all is calm, the shore is as yet undisturbed by humankind, and the sun hasn't started to shine its glaring spotlight on the haunts of the wary bass. But I've also heard tales, told in tackle shops up and down the coast, of 'grockle' anglers who buy their first-ever rod, reel and Toby spoon, walk down to a known mark and catch a 3lb bass on their first cast. Nothing about angling is predictable.

So it's definitely worth having a bash for bass. Stick on a big plug or spoon and go for a wander along the beach or fish off some rocks. Fish with an open mind and a hungry belly – who knows what might tug your string. And the joy is, if your plug or spoon isn't too large, you might be compensated for your effort and lack of bass with a big pollack or jumbo-sized mackerel instead. Both of which are every bit as good as bass to eat.

Surf ledgering for bass

Ledgering with one whole or even two whole squid on a pennel rig (see p.167) is a tactic that only really works after a storm. The water needs to be rough from the earlier storm winds, but beginning to calm down, and the sea needs to be cloudy.

The theory behind this technique is that the bigger bass will come close inshore (as close as 10–15 yards) to feed on crabs and other shellfish that have been dislodged by the crashing waves and scouring action of the storm surf. The cloudy, stirred-up, sediment-filled water affords them a feeling of security, where they would otherwise be nervous and flighty if the sea was sun-illuminated and clear.

Bass feel safe surrounded by murk, and with their armour-plated heads and steel-like gill rakers, they're properly equipped to feed nose down into the whirlpool of sand and gravel. They also have a highly tuned sense of smell, so in this murk they can still home in on a free meal.

The noise of the surf and constant churning up of the sand and gravel helps the angler too. The sea noise will mask the vibrations of your movements on the beach, which in calm circumstances would easily spook a bass. You need to use big fresh succulent squid baits and to refresh them regularly, so they emanate maximum scent. The more attractive a bait smells, the easier it is for a big bass to find it.

If you try this method, by all means do use a tripod rod rest, but make sure you stand close to it at all times; a big bass will easily pull a rod off a rest and out to sea. It's happened to a surprising number of experienced anglers. You'll also need to use a minimum of 15lb reel line and a 40lb shock leader too if you're fishing near snags or sharp rocks. It's not easy to hook one of these surf-hunting bad boys, but if you do, it's usually even harder landing him. Don't even attempt to do it on light line. Tears and regret will be the only possible outcome.

Bass are every sea angler's dream fish. If you should be so lucky as to catch one above the MLS of 40cm, by all means kill it, bleed it and chill it. Then descale it, cook it, and make stock with every morsel you don't eat. But should you catch two, then I'd urge you to think hard about letting the second one go. A 3lb bass is the thing of anglers' dreams, but it's also a very important marine resource, capable of one day spawning and producing many more sea bass. One bass is more than enough to keep on any day's fishing. Two is starting to take them for granted.

Eating them

One of the most impressive things about bass is how easy it is to cook. You can't really go wrong, unless you desperately overcook it. And even then, a good bass can be quite forgiving. From sashimi (see pp.206–8) and ceviche (see pp.212–13 and pp.214–15) to fry-poached fillets (see pp.242–4), to baked whole in the oven (see pp.231–3), even to barbecued, scales on (see pp.226–8), bass will taste fantastic. Lemon juice, olive oil, salt and black pepper are all the flavourings you'll ever need to add to this great natural-tasting fish. If you get lucky and have a lot of bass to eat, try it cold (or rather at room temperature, not chilled) maybe with a tiny smidgen of horseradish sauce (see p.205) just to eke the flavours out, or mixed with warm lentils and a splash of sweet vinegar like balsamic or rice vinegar.

Dab *Limanda limanda*
Flounder *Platichthys flesus*

SEASON	Late summer, autumn and winter
LOCATION	Estuaries, creeks and off sandy beaches
METHOD	Bottom-fishing with worm or shellfish baits
CONSERVATION STATUS	Healthy. Rarely sold commercially

Most anglers and fishmongers tend to group dab and flounder together. They certainly look very similar and both are poor cousins of the mighty plaice. In fact, the flounder is often mistaken for a plaice, because it can sometimes have a smattering of orange spots across its back – though flounder spots rarely have the same eye-watering Florida-orange intensity of the plaice's big abstract blotches.

The best way to tell the difference between a plaice and a flounder is by examining its bumps. A plaice has a smooth even skin, sloping all the way over its back, gently continuing right down to the tips of its dorsal and anal fins. A flounder, on the other hand, has a row of weird sharp bumps called tubercules which lie in a line separating its body from the base of both of its major fins. It also has a line of the same tubercules running along and behind its head.

You can easily distinguish between a dab and a flounder by touch. The skin of the dab is much rougher, spinier and more abrasive than the smooth skin of the flounder. (The Latin name for dab, *Limanda limanda*, is derived from *lima*, meaning a file or rasp.) Another obvious difference between the two fish is that flounders can grow a bit larger than dabs (12 inches on average as opposed to 10 inches), but otherwise they're fairly similar in terms of their diet, seasons, and indeed the methods you might adopt to try and catch them.

Finding them

To catch these fish in tip-top condition it is better to fish in the autumn, when they're well past spawning and have fed hard through the summer. Neither dab nor flounder worry too much about tides; they'll feed on both the biggest 'springs' and the smallest 'neaps' (see pp.20 and 22). And what they like best of all is feeding close to the shore just after a storm, while the sea is settling down. They come close in to hoover up crabs or shellfish that have been dislodged by the storm's wave action. Although both dabs and flounders can be caught during the day, even in bright sunlight, the most productive time to fish for them is after the sun has gone down. They feed voraciously at dusk and during the night too.

Flounder

Both flounders and dabs like to feed over sandy or muddy ground, either off a beach or particularly in, or adjacent to, a river estuary. Although both are committed sea fish, they also have a love affair with fresh water. The flounder is the most passionate about river water and will migrate so far up rivers that it will pass beyond the furthest reach of the sea, where it no longer experiences any aquatic salinity. Because of this love of fresh water, flounders are often found in lochs, and in the Netherlands they have even been farmed entirely in freshwater ponds.

Dabs don't do fresh water with quite such abandon. They will venture up estuaries, feeding in small packs through the hollows and depressions in mud and sand, but they'll always return to the sea proper with the outgoing tide.

Neither dabs nor flounders are freaked by shallow water or too much sunlight. Their camouflage abilities, which involve burrowing into or covering themselves over with sand and silt, make them abnormally brave in the shallows.

Catching them

The flounder's habit of moving into shallow muddy creeks has given rise to one bizarre method of fishing for them, known as tramping. Every year in Palnackie in Scotland, there is the World Flounder Tramping Championships, which involves contestants stepping through thigh-high water in bare feet, in the hope of treading on a flounder hidden under the mud. The fish is then pinned down by the tramper's foot, and either stuck with a barbed spear, or else grabbed by the head and slipped into a wet sack tied around the waist of the tramper.

Dabs are not subject to tramping, but they were once fished in the shallow creeks around Blakeney on the North Norfolk coast by spearing with long bamboo poles.

The more conventional way to fish for dab and flounder is by bottom-fishing with baits such as ragworm or lugworm or any form of shellfish that you can get to stay on a hook, from mussels to razor clams; flounder in particular won't turn their pug-like nose up at a strip of fresh fish or squid. Use small size 1 and 2 Aberdeen hooks, casting on to sandy or muddy ground from beaches, piers and harbours.

Dab and flounder bites often take the form of three or four swift 'knocks', which happen with such machine-gun-like rapidity it's hard to react to them. So don't. Just wait. And if another series of taps occurs, simply pick up the rod and start to reel in. You don't need to 'strike' (see p.174) on a dab or flounder bite, they'll normally hook themselves, simply from pulling against the weight of the lead.

Eating them

Both flounder and dab are delicious grilled with a well-massaged smear of butter (see pp.246–7), pan-fried (see pp.242–3), or baked with a splash of cider or wine (see pp.231–3). And they're great eaten in a crusty bap with garlic mayonnaise (see p.204) or tartare sauce (see p.205) and a smattering of salad leaves or chopped chives.

Horse mackerel *Trachurus trachurus*

SEASON	Spring, summer and autumn
LOCATION	Inshore boats and mackerel-trip boats, or from piers, rocks and outer harbour walls
METHOD	Feathering, or float-fishing with mackerel or squid strips
CONSERVATION STATUS	Healthy

Horse mackerel is also known as 'scad' or 'scad mackerel' or even occasionally 'Jack mackerel'. Although it shares a name with our Atlantic mackerel, it isn't actually related to it in any way. Scad are part of the global Jack family (along with fish like blue runner, Jack Crevalle and amberjack), a very tasty and much-loved variety of fish that appears all the way down the eastern American seaboard and across the Atlantic to South Africa. The name 'horse' mackerel is said to have been given to these silver-sided, fork-tailed fish because legend has it that other species would ride upon their backs to cross the wide Atlantic.

Like so many of our 'forgotten' species, scad has got something of an undeservedly bad reputation. Just the other day, I was told by an experienced charter boat skipper that horse mackerel are impossible to eat because they're full of bones. This sort of prejudice against certain fish is rife amongst British anglers and skippers, and cooks too. People say things about eating – or rather not eating – fish like scad, pout and garfish as though they're giving you established facts, yet often they're simply repeating what they've heard, without ever trying them. I've eaten scad mackerel hundreds of times and I can honestly say that it's firm fleshed and delicious. So please don't pay any attention to anti-scad propaganda.

Scad mackerel is not only delicious, its flesh is full of omega-rich oils and has high levels of taurine, an organic acid often added to energy drinks. Taurine is thought to be essential for skeletal muscle development, useful in reducing high blood pressure, helpful in avoiding congestive heart failure, and even thought to promote better neurotransmission in the brain. In other words, the scad mackerel is not just edible, it's a super fish super-food.

And if you really want to hear how totally brilliant scad are, listen to the Japanese, who religiously hunt a very close relative of the scad called aji. This is a fish so revered by Japanese sushi and sashimi chefs it's even honoured with its own special celebration day know as Aji Himono Day. If you're ever lucky enough to get your hook into one, be grateful, be gracious and treat it with respect, because this is a crowned prince amongst fishes.

Finding them

Just like mackerel, scad mackerel are most prevalent in summer and autumn. And like mackerel, they will follow and hunt any shoals of small fry or sprats around the coastline, so they're often found feeding very close in to shore, especially as it starts to get dark. It's difficult to set your sights on catching scad alone, because they rarely seem to occur in mono-species shoals, but are instead mixed into mackerel shoals.

Generally speaking, scad are normally found nearer the seabed than mackerel, except in the darkness of twilight or night where, in calm water, they may head up to feed nearer the surface.

Catching them

Strings of feathers, especially the smaller-sized or even micro feathers, are, in my experience, probably the most reliable scad seducers. Next in line I would plump for using small strips of squid on a paternoster rig (see p.163) just as you might for targeting black bream. Float-fishing 1-inch to 3-inch squid strips is another reliable method. It helps to give the float rig a tweak from time to time to make the float splash and the squid strip move up then flutter down in the water. Scad are used to hunting for sprats, so any small splashes at or near the surface are likely to attract their attention.

If you do catch yourself a scad or two, kill them swiftly, bleed them and keep them cool. They're an oily fish, not quite as oily as mackerel or herring, but they'll go off quickly if they get warm.

Eating them

When you prepare scad for cooking, you need a slightly different approach from mackerel. Scad have scales that need to be removed (see p.183) and the distinctive bony ridge along either side of its mini tuna-like tail needs to be sliced off with a sharp knife, or trimmed off with your sharpest kitchen scissors.

Contrary to the myth, scad meat is less bony and easier to fillet than mackerel because the fish has more of an oval profile, like a black bream. The flesh is firmer than mackerel flesh and perfect for light pickling (see pp.210–11) or escabeche (see p.213 and pp.216–17), or plain grilling or frying. The Japanese use scad for sushi (see p.209) and sashimi (see pp.206–8).

Another favourite Japanese way is to coat scad fillets in wheat flour, then lightly fry them, let them cool and then marinate in vinegar and soy sauce with slices of sweet red pepper.

Being an oily fish makes scad perfect for grilling (see p.245) or barbecuing (see pp.226–8), as they self-baste and don't spoil too quickly under the heat of the grill or over hot charcoal.

Herring *Clupea harengus*

SEASON	In the Southwest herring turn up in summer swimming with mackerel shoals. North of the Bristol Channel and the Thames Estuary they tend to be around more during late autumn and spring
LOCATION	Mackerel boat, or from the beach, piers and harbour breakwaters
METHOD	Mostly caught using mackerel feathers or micro mackerel feathers
CONSERVATION STATUS	Healthy

Victorian naturalists referred to herring as a 'gregarious' fish. This always makes me think of herring as a happy-go-lucky party animal, forever in search of the right crowd to hang out with. In truth, I think it simply refers to their habit of travelling around in large shoals.

In Dorset, we very rarely come across any large shoals of herring; instead, the few we do catch are normally mixed in among mackerel shoals. I don't really know if this is because these herring get lost and just hook up with any old shoal that appears to know where it's going, or because they're suffering from some deep-seated identity crisis. Whatever the cause, all the recent ones I've caught have been on mackerel feathers and plucked from the centre of a mackerel shoal.

Along the east and northeast coast, herring shoals are more plentiful, but they are nothing compared to the biblical shoals that existed before the 1950s trawler-fishing boom. At that time, herring shoals typically measured several miles wide and tens of yards deep, containing trillions of fish. These once provided massive seasonal employment all the way down Britain's east coast – from Wick to Great Yarmouth.

Sadly, the diesel-powered trawler revolution and the use of massive purse seine nets was devastating for our national herring stocks. The overfishing had such a damaging effect that a ban was imposed on commercial herring fishing in the 1970s. There has been some recovery in certain areas since then, and there's now even a certified sustainable herring fishery in the Thames Estuary. Herring do crop up, here and there, all around the coast, caught from angling boats, often when least expected, and normally sandwiched in amongst shoals of other species.

Although herring stocks have been decimated by industrial-scale commercial fishing fleets, the recreational angler doesn't have to fear inflicting damage by catching a few for tea. In my experience, fishing on the south coast in particular, there might be a run of herring for a week or so, in tightly packed shoals, easily as big as mackerel shoals and often mixed among them, but they won't stay like the mackerel do; they move on, only to leave us all wanting more.

Finding them

Herring are a pelagic fish, like mackerel, so they wander around the coast, but also up and down the water column. They are plankton feeders, so they move up to the surface at dusk, as the clouds of zooplankton rise upwards with the cooling water. (Zooplankton is the collection of minute animals that in turn feed on phytoplankton, the near-microscopic plant plankton.)

Most herring are caught from mackerel-fishing boats, but like other fish species they are occasionally caught from the shore, especially from piers and deep-water rock marks. There may be some reliable herring spots along the east coast where herring shoals are most prolific (see Directory, p.249, for websites to investigate further), but down on the south coast it's hit and miss.

Catching them

The best way to catch herring is on mini or micro feathers. These are arranged just like normal mackerel feathers but on much smaller hooks, sometimes with glow-in-the-dark luminescent colours.

The smaller your feathers, the more chance there is that a herring or two will mistake them for the tiny sea creatures they voraciously hunt. Should you ever be lucky enough to hook into a couple of strings of herrings, then you are destined for a tremendous feast. Pound for pound, herring are the most nutritious fish in our waters. They contain even more omega-rich oils, essential minerals and life-giving fatty acids than mackerel, which takes some doing.

Just like mackerel, their high oil content means herring spoil very quickly once they're dead, as the oils in their flesh will oxidise and attract bacteria – a process that you can slow down by getting them on ice as quickly as possible.

Eating them

In medieval times, a suitable portion of herrings was defined in law, by the monks of Westminster Abbey. The religious fervour of the day imposed a staggering 215 fasting days each year, during which the eating of meat was forbidden. Fish was the preferred food on fast days and, according to the monks, a suitable portion for a devout brother was firmly set at four or five herrings, depending on size (of the herring that is, not the monk). Personally, I would wholly concur that about four or five herrings apiece is a very good portion. Any less is sacrilege.

Because herring were so plentiful, but also very perishable, many different methods of preserving them were devised during their heyday, ranging from salting

to pickling, to curing in wine and mustard, to smoking – either hot or cold – as red herrings, kippers, bloaters or buckling. Pickled and smoked herrings are certainly delicious, but fresh herrings offer great potential, too.

If you do manage to catch a few and the weather's amenable, you'll find that fresh herrings barbecue beautifully, with a taste and texture somewhere in between a mackerel and a sardine (see pp.226–8). And because herring come ready infused with their own self-basting oil, they're also perfect for grilling (see p.245).

I love herring cooked escabeche-style (see p.213 and pp.216–17) too, because the fillets crisp up well on the outside, remaining soft inside, and their oiliness contrasts perfectly with a vinegary marinade and slightly crunchy shallots.

But I have to say that my mum's traditional Scottish recipe of coating filleted, splayed herring in coarse oatmeal and frying them in butter or beef dripping, then serving them with a dollop of stewed rhubarb or gooseberries, takes a lot of beating.

Squid *Loligo forbesi*

SEASON	Winter
LOCATION	Harbours, piers and breakwaters
METHOD	Using squid jigs or slow-retrieving a small dead fish bait, mounted on a treble hook
CONSERVATION STATUS	Healthy

Most people know squid as 'calamari', which they generally encounter only on menus, in pickled seafood salads, or occasionally on the fishmonger's slab. I often find people are shocked to learn squid not only inhabit our inshore waters, but that they can actually be caught relatively easily. The biggest bother about catching squid, in fact, is that it's only really possible in the cold winter months, from November onwards, and that the best time to fish for squid is when night is falling.

A cold winter's evening is, understandably, not everyone's favourite time to sit for hours on a pier, breakwater, harbour wall or inshore boat. But, if you do brave the elements and the gloom, you could be in for one of the most extraordinary experiences you'll ever have with a rod in your hand and a bucket at your feet.

Finding them

Squid migrate to shallow inshore water from their normal haunts of deep offshore waters in the winter months to breed and to hunt. Although they appear to be passive almost jellyfish-like creatures, squid are in fact active and aggressive predators, who will bite big chunks out of any small fish, alive or dead, with their sharp, horny parrot-like beak, situated in the centre of their web-like cluster of tentacles.

The fish squid like to hunt best are small juvenile whiting and poor cod. These vulnerable fish know there are a lot of hungry predators in the big sea eager to swallow them whole, and so they make an effort to protect themselves by moving into shallow safe havens in the evening – places where big fish are loath to tread. Small whiting and poor cod seek sanctuary alongside harbour walls, deep breakwaters and piers at dusk, where they'll also find some bonus sustenance in the form of shrimps and snails, who too are hiding amongst the weed and algae growing from the shadowy underwater structures.

Squid are blessed with enormous eyes, which give them enhanced night vision. This means they're very well equipped to slope into the shadows, in search of the nervy small fry, and are able to pick them off with sniper accuracy using their sucker-encrusted tentacles. The place to find squid, then, is close against these structures, at nightfall.

Catching them

The best way to catch squid is to use either a small dead fish as bait, or a factory-manufactured squid jig.

Using squid jigs

There are two types of squid jig available in tackle shops. One is made of glow-in-the-dark luminescent material. It has a skirt of upward-pointing hooks encircling its base and a body which glows green in the dark. The other type looks like a prawn, wearing a tight velour tiger-striped jacket (which comes in a variety of colours), with a spiked dorsal fin and a couple of layers of hook-bristling skirts around its tail.

Both of these lures are supposed to attract the squid's attention: the dumpy one because it glows with mesmeric luminosity and the fat prawn one because, well, it looks like a fat prawn. On sight of a jig, the squid should shoot out its sucking tentacles, wrap them around the lure and attempt to drag it towards its beak.

Meanwhile, the angler, in theory, made aware of some action occurring underwater through the vibrations at his rod tip, will start to reel in – pulling the jig in the opposite direction to the squid. This should entangle the tentacles in those needle-sharp hooks, which means with a constant reeling pace the squid should stay attached, until he's lifted from the sea, destined to become lightly battered tempura squid rings. Oh, if only it were that simple!

In my experience, the glow-in-the-dark dumpy lures don't work so well around our stretch of coastline. I don't know why. In Weymouth harbour, I've found it's the prawn variety that works best.

Using a small fish as bait

Using a small dead fish as bait to attract the tentacle attentions of a squid is often more successful than a jig. I suppose that when the water is slightly cloudy, squid can detect the dead fish bait through smell, as well as using their amazing sight. If the water is clear, jigs can attract them from a long distance but jigs rely totally on the fish being able to see. The scent of the dead fish provides a whole other sensory attraction. A poor cod is, after all, a real example of what they're hunting, rather than an optical imitation.

Normally, I'd suspend a 4-inch freshly killed poor cod a couple of feet above a lead weight of 3 or 4oz. The best rig to use is a two-hook rig, with one hook to hold the poor cod on the end of the line and the other hook, preferably a small treble, just nicked into the skin of its flank, with two of the three treble hooks facing out, ready to snag into the squid's inquisitive tentacle. The two hooks of the treble facing out will never work as well as the multi-hook skirts on the prawn-shaped jigs do. And so, the technique of fishing the small dead fish rig is slightly different from the jig. Because it doesn't have the same grappling skirt of hooks, it won't snare the squid so

Prawn-style squid jig

Glow-in-the-dark-style squid jig

easily, so you need to reel in much more slowly and evenly. While the squid is busy nibbling at the bait, you're trying to coax him up to the surface, without him becoming aware of what's occurring.

Using this technique, once you get your squid to the surface, you'll need to get a net under him quickly. Often the squid isn't actually hooked at all, he's simply holding on, munching at your bait, quite unaware that you're slowly reeling him in. So unless he's actually entangled and snagged by one of the small treble hooks, he can just let go at any time and disappear back down to the deeps. It's a tense and tricky moment.

Once you've got him in the net, the best thing you can do is to leave him inside it, holding the net out over the water to see what he does next. Often, but not always, squid will squirt their load of ink at this moment, when they feel themselves trapped by the netting. This ink is better unloaded into the sea than all over the deck of your boat, or all over your clothes. Getting fresh squid ink out of clothing is not an easy task. Whether he does or doesn't squirt at this point, it's still best to put him into a bucket of water next, because if there is more ink to come, containing it in the bucket makes for less washing. Do not underestimate the indelible blackness of a fresh squid squirt. It's so unbelievably black and sticky I have a couple of squidding shirts that have been boil-washed umpteen times and yet still bear the black residue of a November night's fun.

To kill a squid, you can either just leave it in a bucket of water, which is a slow way to go, or you can put it on ice, which will kill it quicker. Or you can clamp it hard, on either side of the head, with a pair of long-nosed pliers. If I have ice I'll use it, but as we normally fish for squid in the depths of winter I rely on the bucket of sea water technique. Keeping them alive for a while in the bucket also allows them to purge more of their ink.

Eating them

Preparing squid (see pp.198–9) is almost as satisfying as catching them. Seeing such an alien-like creature turned into pure snow-white slabs of sweet calamari flesh is indescribably gratifying. And squid rings or squid strips dipped in spicy flour and fried in hot oil (see pp.238–9), then served with lemon wedges and a homemade sweet chilli dipping sauce (see p.205), are just about the most wonderful hot tangy squid experience you can have.

It's also possible to fry squid pieces in a very hot pan with just a smidgen of oil and then squeeze over lemon and lime juice (see fry-poaching, pp.242–3). They take only a couple of minutes and once cooked you can toss them in a dressing of oil and rice vinegar spiked with a little chilli.

Squid rings and pieces are perfect for adding to a risotto (see p.221), or to a light tangy fish soup (see pp.222–3) too.

Slob trout *Salmo trutta*

SEASON	Spring, summer and autumn
LOCATION	River estuaries
METHOD	Earthworms trundled along the river mouth with a light weight
CONSERVATION STATUS	Healthy

The trout family, aka the salmonids, are an awe-inspiring tribe. Brown trout inhabit water from the clear mountain streams of the Himalayas to the shopping-trolley-strewn creeks of central London. And one shocking, otherworldly thing that brown trout do – or at least *some* brown trout do – is suddenly decide, during their infancy, to stop being a freshwater fish and, instead, convert to become a sea fish. And so, over a period of a couple of years, a spotty, fragile river-dwelling trout, no longer than your middle finger, will transform to become a huge silver-sided gleaming beast of a trout, weighing up to 6lb. Big enough and tough enough to eat at least five finger-sized brownies for breakfast.

The point of this bizarre transformation is to venture out to sea, to become big and strong and exceedingly fertile, and then to return to the river, packed full with millions of eggs, in order to multiply and thus enhance the evolution of the species. The fuel that powers this survivalist evolution is high-protein seafood, such as shrimps and crabs, which are much more nutritious to trout than any food to be found back home in the babbling brook of their birth. The place for a brown trout to put on serious weight, then, is in the all-you-can-eat seafood buffet that lurks beyond the mouth of the river estuary.

Making the passage from lean-pickings fresh water to fat-boy sea buffet sounds easy. Geographically it's only a couple of miles, or less, but physiologically the leap is enormous. The difference between living as a fish surrounded by fresh water, and living as a fish surrounded by sea water, is akin to you or me deciding we're going to live on the moon. Then, over the space of a couple of months, actually growing the physical equipment to help us survive in an alien environment.

The brown trout who undergo this unbelievably fundamental and dynamic metamorphosis and go to live and feed in the sea, then come back to rivers to spawn, are called sea trout. Sea trout, in other words, are simply brown trout who have chosen to go and live some of their lives at sea.

There's a huge amount we don't know about sea trout, including how far a sea trout will migrate out to sea in order to find good food. We know salmon swim all the way to Greenland, but sea trout are generally believed to stay within a 5-mile

radius of the shoreline. They might migrate along the coast a greater distance, but they don't feel the need to go far out.

Slob trout, on the other hand, are lacking in motivation. A slob trout is a brown trout that *thinks* it wants to become a sea trout, but lacks the bottle to go the whole hog. Instead of leaving the river, traversing the estuary, and forging ahead to pastures new and menus large, a slob trout starts the journey – then wimps out. It gets as far as the estuary and goes no further, deciding instead to live an in-between life, moving up and down the estuary from the edge of the scary sea to the mouth of the safe river, with every ebb and flow of the tide. Probably saying to itself, 'That's it. I'm going. I am. I'm off. Er... No I'm not. I'm staying. No. I'm going. I'm *definitely* going. Nope. I'm staying...' and so on, for tide after tide, year after year.

I've always liked to believe that slob trout are so called because they live a slob-like existence, committing to neither one thing nor another. I may be wrong, there may well be another totally different explanation. But if there is, I don't want to know it. To me, they will always be estuarine couch potatoes, who like to pretend they've left home, but keep coming back every weekend, bringing their washing with them.

Finding them

Slob trout move up and down the muddy and gravelly terrain where the flow of the river cuts across the wide open estuary. They will lie head towards the flow, usually on either side of the fast-moving water rather than in the middle of it, watching for any food washed along towards them. At this point they're becoming opportunistic feeders and may take from the bottom or the top of the water, especially if it's shallow. Slob trout are always easiest to catch in the summer and autumn months. In theory they're still stuck in their intertidal purgatory during the winter but they may seek places to lie low and sulk rather than feed when the water's too cold.

Catching them

The best bait I've come across to catch slob trout is worms. In the west coast of Ireland where I've caught plenty of slobs, the preferred bait is actually garden lobworm. It seems to work very well. The tackle and rig I always use for estuary slobs is a spinning rod with 10lb line, a drilled bullet weight, with a 6lb hook length to a thin-wire size 1 or 2 Aberdeen-style hook, which has a perfect long shank to thread on a worm halfway with plenty of tail left hanging off.

I normally wear waders and walk to a point where I can cast near the centre of the river flow as it cuts across the estuary, although the near edge of the flow is perfectly good enough, especially if the flow is strong.

The start of the ebb tide is my favourite, as the flow of the river begins to beat back the push of the tide. All you need to do is cast out, let your weight hit the bottom and then keep a gently taut line and a well raised-up rod tip, so you're able to feel the weight bump along the bottom. When fishing using this method you always want to keep your lead weight gently on the move, which is why it helps to use the marble-sized drilled bullet leads. If your weight is too heavy it will sit firm and not trundle. And if it does get caught up on something, just raise the rod tip to lift it out of its snag, and then bump on.

It takes a bit of practice, but it's a fabulous way to fish. It keeps you in touch with your bait, and you can keep walking or wading upstream with the tide or downstream with the flow, depending on which is stronger, so you're always covering new ground. What you should picture in your underwater mind is the slob trout facing into the oncoming current, nose down, looking for food being washed out by the flow.

You'll often pick up dabs, flounders, the odd small pollack, a miracle mullet or possibly a bass with this technique. If you find a suitable estuary site to fish it's really worth a try. I think it's a wonderful engaging and exciting method to fish.

Once you've made your catch, a sharp crack with a priest (see p.146) and a scissor cut across the gills to bleed slob trout is all that's required. Then you only have to gut them and they can be cooked whole.

Eating them

Grilled trout (see p.245) is my favourite, with a knob of butter, salt, pepper and chives. But cold trout is also a treat with lemon mayonnaise and chopped herbs. Another great way to cook trout is whole in the oven (see pp.231–3), or on the barbecue, or in wet newspaper parcels over an open fire (see pp.226–8).

Grey mullet *Chelon labrosus*

SEASON	Spring, summer and autumn
LOCATION	Harbours, estuaries and sometimes several miles up river
METHOD	Float-fished bread flake on tiny hooks, float-fished maggot, ledgered bread flake on a single running ledger rig, or Mepps spinner tipped with ragworm
CONSERVATION STATUS	Healthy

Of all our native sea fish, grey mullet are without a shadow of a doubt the greatest rod tease. They are by far the most conspicuous sea fish, so often seen cruising around harbours or nudging their way up shallow estuaries, unafraid of the sunlight, basking in the glare of a hundred frustrated anglers' eyes, yet there is no easy way to catch them on rod and line.

Grey mullet are more or less vegan in their approach to life. They live by a Buddhist philosophy of doing no evil to other swimming finned things and exist on a diet of algae, weed and the very occasional worm or maggot. They are also the world's pickiest nibblers, and show no passion or real appetite for food. Like harbour-dwelling supermodels, they seem to exist on nothing but sunlight and sips of chilled water. When it comes to bait, they have only one weakness, and you'll need an awful lot of skill and patience to catch one out…

Finding them

Summer is the mullet's favourite season. Unlike most fish, they like to see and be seen, unless cormorants are flying overhead. Mostly you'll see them close to shore. They're found most easily in harbours where they cruise round at any stage of the tide, and sometimes they appear in shoals edging their way around rocky headlands.

Rarely have I ever been aware of them out at sea, mainly because they're not attracted to normal boat-fishing methods. However, netsmen who set gill nets across the direction of the tide runs will often pick them up miles out to sea. So they are there, they just don't make themselves obvious to anglers.

Catching them

There are many ways you can try and catch mullet by rod and line, but the four most successful methods are float-fished bread flake, ledgered bread flake, spinner and worm or float-fished maggot. None of them are easy. But the heady satisfaction of hooking and landing a big mullet, because it is so difficult to do, is unsurpassed.

Float-fished bread flake method

A grey mullet's only Achilles heel, in his vegan-esque diet, is bread. The cheapest, whitest, nastiest, cotton-woolliest white bread, broken into minuscule granules, is just about the only thing that can tempt a grey mullet to part its luscious Angelina Jolie-esque lips.

To employ the float-fishing technique, use a bread 'flake': a torn first-class stamp-sized portion of the fleshiest, most crust-free section of the slice. This is then dipped in sea water and pinched between thumb and forefinger to expel excess moisture. And finally it's mounted on a tiny size 14, or smaller, freshwater coarse-fishing hook. The wetting and squeezing is done to help the flake to stay on the hook longer, because bread is a very fragile, easily unseated bait. For this reason, cast it with care.

If this sounds fiddly and faffy to you, believe me, it is. Seriously so. And it gets worse. Really dedicated mullet anglers don't use sea-fishing gear at all, they only use coarse-fishing tackle, designed for catching small things like a ½lb roach. Mullet maestros use 12- or 13-foot coarse float rods, a small fixed-spool reel, fitted with 6lb main line, tapering to 2lb tip section. This rig is then fished under a skinny, delicate waggler float. Their approach is all about achieving perfect presentation of a tiny bread bait, with zero visible evidence of the angler. Basically, if your teeny-tiny hook isn't completely and neatly covered by your minuscule morsel of hand-wrung bread flake, and a glint of steel should shine through, then you might as well be fishing with a crane hoist and a sack of spuds, because no self-respecting mullet is ever going to give it the time of day.

To increase your chances, you can try hanging an onion sack of dried, stale mushed-up bread just upstream of where you intend to fish. I've seen this done on the river Medway estuary in Kent, the home of the Mullet Club, with pretty impressive results. Done on an outgoing tide, tiny fragments of bread are taken downstream with the flow, siren-calling mullet to follow the stream of morsels towards the source. The waggler rig is then fished close to the bread chumming sack, so that a feeding mullet might suck in the hook bait instead of a free chum offering.

If you're faffily inclined, it's worth a try. The fight of a grey mullet on a float rod with light line is as sensational a battle as you'll ever experience from any British fish.

Ledgered bread flake method

In Guernsey, I once fished with a mullet fanatic who used a totally different technique, fishing on the harbour basin floor. He would wade out across the exposed mud at very low tide and lay a bed of broken-up white bread in a sofa-sized patch. Then he'd wait on the harbour wall and watch as the tide came in and covered his bread. He would cast a pinch of bread flake on a tiny hook, weighed down with a ½oz lead, and so the bait was 'ledgered' on the bottom close to the bread patch. He'd then wait as the tide filled the harbour and the mullet nudged their way along the bottom, entering with the fresh flood of tide. They'd happen upon his tempting patch of bread and eventually suck up his sneakily positioned hook bait.

Spinner and worm method

This is probably my favourite mullet technique, because it's active and immediate and doesn't involve too much fiddling.

Basically this is a way of spinning for mullet using a conventional spinning rod with a small size 5 Mepps spinner, which is slightly modified to increase your chances. The modification is simple: remove the treble hook from the spinner and replace it with a 1½-inch length of 6lb monofilament line with a size 14 carp hook tied on the end. Now, take an inch of fresh ragworm and very lightly snag it on to your hook.

In my experience this method works best in cloudy tidal water. I've fished this way off the back of my boat when it's been tied up to a harbour buoy and caught several passing mullet. If you see signs or splashes of cruising fish, just cast near them and retrieve the spinner at a quickish pace. Slow down and speed up until you find the pace that the fish best respond to. For a peace-loving species, it's hard to explain what it is about half a ragworm and a French-designed spinner that suddenly gets them all excited (which it does *some* of the time). There are times, of course, when this method has zero effect. And then there are other times when the spinner will keep being bumped and plucked by mullet without any proper hook-ups.

The last method involves maggots…

Float-fished maggot method
This will work in two locations, either from the beach fished over rotting seaweed in the summer, or over a sewage outflow pipe where the mullet are used to seeing maggots as an opportunistic source of food.

Fishing near sewage pipes Mullet like nothing better than hanging around sewage outflow pipes and snacking on assorted effluent solids. I know, for a fish that acts like a committed vegan Buddhist most of the time, this behaviour seems outrageous. The truth is, most fish and shellfish love an outflow pipe pumping effluent. Thankfully these pipes are much rarer around our coastline than they used to be.

One of the consequences of outflow pipes is the preponderance of maggots. Grey mullet, in the right mood, love a maggot. I've fished a heavy-bodied waggler float straight into the brown river of an outflow (ironically on one of the prettiest stretches of the country's coastline) with a double maggot on a size 16 hook, and had stunning rod-bending success. But telling you to 'First find a sewage pipe' really doesn't feel like a healthy way to set you on course for a tempting mullet supper.

Fishing amongst rotting seaweed The other maggot technique is a lot less nausea-inducing, but it does require an awful lot of complicated cosmological things to happen, in just the right order. First you need a storm. A storm that washes a large amount of kelp and seaweed far up a beach. Then you need a period of hot weather, to make the now rotting seaweed warm enough to encourage flies to lay their eggs in the stinking bacteria-ridden weed mounds. Then, as the eggs hatch into maggots, you need a super-big spring tide to wash up to and through the line of rotting weed and flush out the adult maggots.

In a calm but high sea, these maggots will get carried out into the water, acting like a dinner gong to any grey mullet in the vicinity. Sea fly-anglers like to fish a maggot-imitating fly pattern at these incoming mullet. You could also fish a tiny clear waggler float with a small hook and single maggot on the outgoing current.

If you've been successful with your mullet-fishing quest, firstly, you have my sincerest respect, and secondly, remember that mullet need to be killed, bled, chilled and gutted swiftly after landing. A solid crack across the back of the head with a priest (see p.146) will suffice.

Eating them
Big mullet can be cut into cutlets and cooked in foil parcels or baked (see pp.231–3). Smaller mullet are great baked whole, stuffed with herbs and lemon slices. Recently I ate one stuffed with feta cheese and chutney, which tasted delicious. Nothing wrong with filleted and grilled either. Mullet does benefit from a tasty sauce (see pp.224–5), as it has a good meaty, flaky texture but not a huge amount of flavour of its own.

Fish you might catch... but can't eat

One of the most exciting things about sea fishing is that you really don't know what you might catch. Even within just a few miles of my local harbour, I've seen sun fish, normally found in the Caribbean, and caught trigger fish, which hail from the eastern seaboard of America. There are resident colonies of reef-dwelling sea horses, and local anglers who have caught such oddities, and exciting hook-ups with mako sharks and thresher sharks are reported practically every summer. The sea is full of rather astonishing surprises. But that also means that you're fairly likely to hook into a few inedible species, which I'd really recommend you release (see pp.176–7 for details on how to release fish).

The reasons for not attempting to add these particular species to your menu are twofold: either it's simply a waste of time and a waste of fish trying to eat them, because no matter what you do to them, they're never going to taste good; or else, it's because they're too small to warrant your culinary attentions and would be much better returned to remain part of the indigenous food chain.

The fish you're most likely to catch but can't eat include three types of wrasse – ballan, cuckoo and corkwing. Then there are the rocklings (they sound like a delightful boy band, don't they?), which include the three-bearded rockling and the five-bearded rockling. There's the blenny brothers (a Country and Western duo), which include the tompot blenny and the common blenny or 'shanny'. Finally there's the weaver fish. The weaver is occasionally caught on rod and line, but it's mostly encountered by shrimpers, pushing their hand-held shrimp nets through shallow sandy-bottomed tidal lagoons. Weaver fish are very easy to recognise and are worth being aware of, because they have three sharp spines protruding from their backs which can give you a ferociously painful sting. The weaver is about the only fish in British waters (apart from jellyfish) that is likely to cause you any sort of harm.

Ballan wrasse
Labrus bergylta

Usually caught over rocky ground, either from beach, boat or cliff marks. They will eat practically any bait and can be used to make fish stock, if they've been badly hooked or have 'blown' (see p.176). Otherwise, always release them, gently.

Cuckoo wrasse
Labrus mixtus

Mostly caught from boats when fishing over rocky ground or kelp beds. They are impossible to confuse with any other British fish. Always release them when you can. If you have to kill them, because they've 'blown' (see p.176), use them for stock or give to crab potters to use as bait.

Corkwing wrasse
Crenilabrus melops

Usually caught over rocky ground and kelp beds. They are a little more colourful than a ballan, but not nearly as exotic as the cuckoo (above).

Poor cod
Trisopterus minutus

Poor cod can be caught from the shore or a boat, usually over rocky ground or reefs. They can be used as an effective bait for bass or squid, but otherwise always release them. If you do catch one that accidentally dies, you can eat it; they're just very small and much better for the marine environment left alive.

Tompot blenny
Parablennius gattorugine
Shanny/Common blenny
Lipophrys polis

Both types of blenny are caught in shallow water from the beach, or around man-made structures such as piers and breakwaters. They're extraordinary-looking fish, which have no food value and are just too pretty and too unusual to use for bait.

Weaver fish
Echiichthys vipera

Weaver fish tend to be caught from sandy beaches. Be careful how you release a weaver – you need to avoid getting stuck by the obvious spines. If you're fishing at night or twilight check any small fish on your line with a torch first before you grab hold of it, just in case it's a weaver.

Fish you might catch… but shouldn't eat

If you're going to be an angler and start taking home your catch to cook, then I think it's important to understand, right from the start, that there are some species in our UK waters which we have all to agree not to kill.

These species, which take in all of the rays and also the shark relatives, including the smoothhound, starry smoothhound, bull huss and tope, should be off-limits to all anglers because the stocks of these species are in danger of being overfished to a potentially disastrous level.

The reason why this cluster of shark relatives is so at risk is because they don't breed in the same way as other species. Unlike pollack, cod or pouting, which can produce several million eggs a year, rays and huss and hounds produce a small number of eggs, which are fertilised inside the mother's body, greatly reducing their overall number of young. Rays and hounds will lay large purse-like eggs, which already have partially developed young inside them. This means the ratio of eggs laid to young produced is high, but the number of overall eggs is only a fraction of the number laid by fish who fertilise their eggs externally.

As a consequence, when stocks get low, it can take a great many successful years of breeding to slowly boost them back up again to sustainable proportions. Hounds and rays do not repopulate their numbers anywhere near as efficiently as other egg-laying fish, but they do survive well after being caught and released.

Cartilaginous fish (sharks and rays) don't have swim bladders like demersal fish, which are very sensitive to pressure change caused by being reeled to the surface from a depth. In contrast, dogfish, hounds, huss, sharks and rays are all seemingly unaffected by being reeled in and can return to the depths again quickly. For this reason, it's safe and ecologically sensible to let them go (see pp.176–7 for details on how to release fish). A ray or a huss will return to the depths and get on with its life, unharmed, if you release it carefully. So there is every reason to release them and no reason, other than greed, to keep them.

Tope
Galeorhinus galeus

Tope are mostly caught from boats, but can sometimes be caught from the shore too, especially during the summer. Tope is our largest inshore shark (record weight of 82lb). It is often caught while bream fishing over rocky ground with small squid baits. This is now a protected species and must be released.

Bull huss
Scyliorhinus stellaris

Mostly caught from boats, though sometimes from the shore. Bull huss tend to be caught over rocky ground, and are fond of crab bait. They often turn up in crab pots, having been attracted by the bait. Also known as the greater spotted dogfish, the bull huss is much bigger than the dogfish and has larger spots.

Smoothhound and Starry smoothhound
Mustelus mustelus and *Mustelus asterias*

These are shallow-dwelling sharks, often found in the mouths of estuaries because they like a muddy bottom to hunt for crabs, worms and small fish. A female will only have 10 pups maximum every 2 years, so they are very sensitive to overfishing.

Undulate ray

Skates and rays
Rajidae family

Most rays are caught from boats but
they can be caught from the shore too.
They like clean open sandy ground
or muddy flats where they can pounce
on crabs, small fish and sand eels. The
thornback ray (*Raja clavata*) is our most
common ray species. (A useful skate
and ray identification chart is available
from www.sharktrust.org.)

Conger eel
Conger conger

Mostly caught over very rocky broken
ground or near wrecks or reefs. Also
may be caught at night-time from the
shore, as they're nocturnal feeders and
like to feed in shallow water. There
are many conger recipes, but I've yet
to find one I like. Exciting to catch,
this is one fish that truly deserves to
be released.

Tackle and Kit

One of the most exciting aspects of taking up any new hobby is buying kit. It's a form of identifying and engaging with your sport. *I have a fishing rod – therefore I am an angler.*

In my 40-odd years of fishing, I have coveted all sorts of tackle, from all over the world. Through an over-exposure to tackle fanaticism I've now achieved an almost Zen-like state where I've satisfied all my wants. I've accumulated so much kit over the years that recently I've turned into a kind of tackle-vegan, and now enjoy going fishing virtually kit-less.

Where I might enjoy the sensation of being almost naked (in a tackle sense) while heading out fishing, a lot of anglers will experience a lack of tackle as a rabid insecurity. Many anglers' greatest fear is that they'll go fishing somewhere and discover once they get there that they haven't brought along the right gear. As a result, most anglers hideously overcompensate when they pack their kit and take far too much tackle.

Having gone through my own tackle addiction and come out the other side – one day at a time – I do feel uniquely qualified to reduce the weight of your tackle box, by detailing only the essentials.

Main tackle: rods, reel and line

The rod, reel and line can be thought of as the 'hardware' of your fishing tackle, and are the first essentials when you're getting your kit together. It's worth spending money on a good-quality reel and line because these are the constants of your fishing trips. The reel and line in particular have a lot demanded of them every time you cast and retrieve, they receive the most wear and tear, so they're the pieces to invest in. Without a working reel and reliable line, your fishing trip will soon end in tears.

Rods

To catch the fish you most want to eat, you'll probably need a rod too. You can catch fish with a handline (see p.118) but I think it's safe to assume that most anglers will need at least one rod. The rod has two main functions. It acts as a springy whip-like device with which to cast out your bait from the shore, and it's used as a lever to help you lift your weight and hopefully your fish out of the sea.

Rods get named after functions, such as spinning rods, or after locations, such as beach rods and boat rods, or after species, such as carp rods or bass rods.

Spinning rod A spinning rod has been given its name because it is designed for use with a spinning reel (otherwise known as a 'fixed-spool reel') and for casting an artificial lure called a 'spinner' (see pp.138–40). So it's designed for 'spinning' as a technique, which you might use to catch mackerel, pike, salmon, pollack, bass or grey mullet. But most rods are capable of performing a lot more functions than their name implies.

For instance, you might think a carp rod is only good for catching carp, but in fact it's great for a whole range of species. Really these are only manufacturers' names, given to certain designs of rod to afford the purchaser confidence that one particular rod will perfectly suit the species he's setting his sights on. In reality, it's a bit of a ruse to make anglers buy a different rod for every species. This is by no means necessary.

An 8–9-foot spinning rod is capable of catching and landing all of the fish mentioned in this book. It is the most versatile rod you will ever buy.

Spinning rods normally come in two sections: butt section and tip section. You can also buy four-piece or six-piece 'travel' spinning rods, or 'telescopic' spinning rods, which concertina down into their own handle section. These rods will fit in a suitcase, so they are great if you're travelling on a plane and want to avoid having to check-in your rods separately to the oversized baggage section.

If you're tempted to buy a travel or telescopic spinning rod, be warned, you get what you pay for. Because they require complex engineering to fit all the pieces together, very cheap telescopic and multi-piece rods do tend to break more easily. Unless they've been carefully engineered (which costs money), the sections often don't slot together very well and fishing with the resulting rod feels like using a giant stick of wholewheat spaghetti that's been chopped into sections and then 'Araldited' back together again.

The most reliable and most effective spinning rod is a two-piece rod, rated to cast a weight of up to 20–50g (about ¾–2oz); this rating is normally printed on the shaft, just above the handle.

You can buy rods with either cork or rubber handles. My personal preference is cork. I like the way it looks and feels. However weather-resistant rubber handles are practical, last longer and require zero maintenance.

The most important part of any rod is the 'blank' it's made from. The blank is the body or spine of the rod; the carbon-fibre stick on to which the rings, handle and reel fixtures are all attached. The definition of a good blank is one that is light but strong, and which bends in the right place for the job you want it to do. Tackle dealers and manufacturers talk in terms of 'fast tapered blanks', and 'powerful upper sections flowing into a stiff butt', etc. Getting your head around rod technology and design when you're new to angling is unnecessary, unless it's something that grabs your curiosity. You certainly don't need to know how rods are designed and made; so long as you're buying from a reputable dealer, buying a reputable brand, and it's a rod that feels comfy to hold, then you can't go far wrong.

Just as with men's fashion or designer sports cars, there is an elite top-end of manufacture, which is crazily expensive. There are spinning rods that will cost you upwards of £600 which, frankly, is just silly. When you're starting out, don't pay more than £50 for a spinning rod. Buy a reputable make. By all means buy online – there are usually stacks of customer reviews on websites where you can compare makes – but I confess I'm a sucker for buying a rod in a tackle shop, because I like to buy a rod from a man or woman who knows what they're talking about. And you just can't beat *feeling* a rod – giving it a good waggle and just seeing if you like it. Even if you don't really know what you like, you'll get a much better idea if you're holding it in your hands rather than reading about it on a website or in a catalogue.

There are other considerations to rods, like rings, reel-seat fixtures and 'action' (the way a rod bends when it's under strain from a fish), but my advice is to assume all that stuff is okay. If you like the colour, the grip, the price and the way it waggles, go ahead and buy it.

Boat rods I'm not going to cover deep-sea, wreck and reef fishing in this book. It's not really appropriate to anyone who is starting out, because the commitment required, in terms of both tackle and time (the average deep-sea trip is 6–8 hours), is too much. If you've never been sea fishing before, then a deep-sea trip is not the place to start. I want to stick to inshore, shallow-water fishing, where there are lots of great fish to be caught without having to use complicated or heavy gear.

Boat rod-bending action

So, the long and the short of it is; you don't really *need* a boat rod. Even if you go out on a summer mackerel trip, the chances are you'll use tackle provided by the skipper, which might be rod and line or else handlines (see p.118). (If you're booking a trip, don't forget to ask about tackle.) Or, with the skipper's permission, you could even use your own spinning rod, set up with a 3 or 4oz weight and a line of mackerel feathers (see pp.134–7). But it can get tricky for mackerel-trip skippers if anglers are using a mixture of rods and handlines. They all sink at different rates and have differing degrees of water resistance and drag, which can soon turn a mackerel trip into a tackle-knitting session. So be sure to check with the skipper before booking that he's happy for you to have your own rod on board.

At 9 feet, a spinning rod takes up a lot of room on a boat. Most boat rods are around 7 feet, which makes them easier to use on a confined deck space. Apart from being shorter, boat rods are stronger than spinning rods. They need to be able to lift ½lb of lead off the seabed, occasionally attached to a fish of 10–15lb, which also has tidal current to help it fight.

In saying this, the mistake most people make when buying a boat rod is to buy one that is too thick and too strong. It's hard to resist, I know. We're only human, and by nature we assume that the beefier the rod we buy, the beefier the fish we'll catch. This is absolutely not the case. Some of the biggest fish I've caught – fish well over 100lb – have been landed on spinning rods or carp rods. I've seen enormous conger eels brought to the boat on light bream rods and a 15lb line. It's not the breaking strain that matters so much as the technique you use to land it.

If you do want to buy your own boat rod for mackerel trips and inshore reef-fishing trips, all you need is a one-piece or two-piece rod. Boat rods don't have casting weight printed above the handle like spinning rods, they are sold by line class. So they'll say something like 20–30lb, or 50–60lb. I personally haven't used a boat rod in this country in excess of 20lb class in years. There's no need. Don't spend more than £50–100. And be aware that you'll need a boat reel, otherwise known as a 'multiplier' reel (see pp.119–20) to go with it too. Boat rods are not designed to be used with ordinary spinning reels.

Carp rods Even if you never intend to fish for carp, a carp rod is a good weapon to have in your carbon-fibre armoury. Carp rods aren't that different from spinning rods, they're just stronger, less bendy at the tip and capable of casting a heavier weight. They are very versatile and are becoming increasingly affordable.

A new carp rod shouldn't cost you more than £50–100, and there are loads of great secondhand bargains to be had, because the truly committed carp angler is a tackle fiend who will change and upgrade his rods about as often as normal people change their socks. And a carpist's castoff casting stick is certainly good enough for sea fishing. So check out local classified ads and auction sites.

Look for a carp rod with a 'test curve' of 1½–2lb. I often use carp rods to fish from the beach and one with a 2lb test curve will cast a 4oz weight and a bait with ease. Of course, a carp rod isn't going to chuck a lead 200 yards out to sea, like a proper beachcaster rod (see below) would. But at most of the beach marks suitable for a relative novice, a carp rod will cast far enough to catch fish and they're so much easier to use and to store than beachcasters.

Fly rod You'll only need a fly rod if you want to go fly fishing. Fly fishing requires a very different set of tackle, skill and knowledge from the other styles of fishing I cover in this book, and revolves around a different command of mechanics.

All other forms of fishing involve casting something weighted, whether it's a bait, a float, a spinner or a set of feathers with a lead weight attached. And so the rod acts as a simple flexible lever, with a weight at one end. Get the weight moving through the air, using the whip action of the rod, and the moving weight will pull the line off the reel as it goes.

Throwing an imitation fly, weighing a fraction of a gram, more than a couple of feet is impossible because it has no weight or inertia, and it will be held back by even the slightest breeze. You can't add a weight to the fly, because then it'll just sink in the water, and flies are meant to float on the surface. So the only way to propel a weightless fly with a rod is if the line that carries it is heavy, yet buoyant. This can be achieved, but it requires a completely different style of casting and another set of specialised tackle. So if you want to learn how to fly-cast, I'd recommend taking one or two casting lessons from a qualified instructor (see Directory, p.250).

If you want to buy a fly rod that will work for catching trout, sea trout, mackerel, garfish, grey mullet, sea bass and even pike, buy a two-piece 8 weight (this refers to the weight of the fly line), in either a 9-foot or 9-foot-6-inch rod. Again, don't spend more than £100. And don't buy a fancy fly reel, the cheapest one will do perfectly well to begin with. But do spend money on getting a medium-to-good quality weight-forward floating or slow-sinking fly line. 'Weight forward' describes the design of the fly line itself. This means the line is designed and profiled so that the inherent weight of the line is distributed towards the forward end. This is done specifically to make it easier to cast.

Beachcaster rod This is a huge and powerful rod designed to cast large weights over long distances from the shore. Beachcasters can range from 12–14 feet long and cast huge lumps of lead up to 6–8oz.

In my opinion they are not easy things to use and not much fun – either to cast or to land fish. If you progress at beach fishing you may want to buy a beachcaster and try for long-distance casts. But I'd prefer to leave the mechanics and techniques of beachcasting to more technically advanced books than I intend this to be.

Handlines These are simply thick lines used without a fishing rod or reel. They're normally stored on a wooden frame and can be unwound, weighted, hooked and baited, and then dropped over the side of a boat or from a pier. They can be fished with baits or with mackerel feathers.

Handlines are great pieces of kit, especially when used from a boat. They're hard to find in tackle shops, except for the ubiquitous orange nylon stranded crab line, which does the job for mackerel and small pollack, but is a pretty horrible thing to use. My preference is for a very thick monofilament line (see p.121) or thick braided nylon line (illustrated below), with something in the region of 150–200lb breaking strain. Old-fashioned handlines wound on wooden frames are particularly good – look out for secondhand ones in car boot sales and household auctions.

Handlines are the opposite to rod and reel lines: rod anglers strive to fish with a light rod and a thin line to increase sensation through the rod; however, with handlines, thicker is better. The beefier the handline, the more movement and information will be transmitted from the hook to the hand. With thin handlines there is less 'communication' travelling down the line, and if you do hook a fish thin lines bite into your flesh more.

The true joy of handlining is about having direct contact with the fish. Being able to feel every nibble and bite with your fingers on the line, as well as every lunge of the ensuing fight, is so much more exciting than having the sensations filtered through line, reel, rod and padded handle before they reach your fingertips.

Reels

A good reel is more important than a good rod, because it's working much harder and there are many more parts that can go wrong. Unless you want to go fly fishing, the only two types of reel you'll need to cope with are spinning reels (also known as 'fixed-spool reels') and multiplier reels (also known as 'boat reels'). Most usually, spinning reels are used from the shore and multipliers from a boat. Both types of reel are illustrated on the following page.

Spinning or fixed-spool reel A spinning or fixed-spool reel is a vital and versatile piece of kit. Technically speaking, the very same reel can be used in sea water and fresh water, but some fixed spools are made specifically for sea use. These tend to be bigger, because they're used for casting more weight and thicker line. They also have more protection against the corrosive effect of salt water.

Even fixed-spool reels that are designed for sea fishing will grind to a halt after a few outings if they're not maintained. The simplest and most basic precaution to prolong their life requires that you rinse your fixed-spool reel in fresh water after use at sea, then roughly dry it with a rag and spray with WD40.

In a perfect world, you would have two spinning reels: one for sea, one for fresh water. Apart from anything else, you can get away with a smaller-sized reel in fresh water. The most versatile-sized reel you can buy is a 5000 or 050.

In terms of its internal engineering, a spinning reel works hard. If you're casting and retrieving all day long, chucking out a couple of ounces of lead with each cast, then the stresses and strains on such a compact mechanism are considerable.

For this reason alone, very cheap reels don't last. The gear wheels in cheap reels are made of plastic or soft metal and really won't survive much abuse. And, be warned, if your reel does die in the middle of a day out fishing, there's not much you can do to improvise. It's an essential and fundamental part of the fishing process. Sadly, a broken reel equals an early bath.

So, for a reel you intend to use in sea water, be prepared to invest around £40 plus. Most reels come with a free spare spool, which can prove very useful. Buy or beg a third spool too, because then you can fill each spool with different thicknesses (or types) of line to cover a range of eventualities. Having an extra spool of line is like having an extra reel without having to carry the extra weight.

Multiplier or boat reel The difference between a spinning/fixed-spool reel and a multiplier/boat reel is like the difference between a two-wheel-drive car and a 4x4. The multiplier is mechanically a much more efficient piece of machinery. It is mounted on the rod just like a proper winch, at 90° to the line. It has a handle at one end, which cranks a bobbin, creating a simple and direct drive, rather than the complicated system a fixed-spool reel uses.

Spinning (fixed-spool) reel

Multiplier reel

A multiplier can handle more weight and it can reel a line in quicker, which means it's most suited to fishing from a boat, particularly in deep water where you might be using a heavy lead and reeling in is hard work. The multiplication of revolutions of the spool, created by the clever engineering of the reel's internal gears, means the reel gears take some of the strain out of reeling up from a depth. The downside of the multiplier reel is that it's a very tricky thing to cast. However, when you're simply using a multiplier from a boat, you don't need to be able to cast. You just lower your gear over the side, by taking the reel out of gear and letting it drop.

For shallow-water boat fishing, multiplier reels don't need to be expensive. If you're never fishing in more than 100 feet of water then a reel is not being asked to do too much grunt work. But they still need to be resilient to the gear-clogging salt water. Very cheap multipliers do tend to rot and jam quickly, sometimes within half a dozen outings. The lower end of mid-range reels will do the job. You shouldn't have to spend more than £30–50.

Multipliers don't come with spare spools. Unlike spinning reels, spools are not easy to remove and change. So, when you choose the line for your multiplier, make sure it's the line you want, because changing it again later is a very finicky job.

Fly reel You'll only need a fly reel if you're using a fly rod. Fly reels are the most simple and basic design of any reel. Normally fly anglers don't even use the reel for retrieving a fish, it's only used as a line holder and the fish is played by holding the line in the hand, feeding it through the fingers. For this reason alone, fly reels aren't worthy of much consideration. Any old thing will do.

Line

There are two types of fishing line that you're likely to encounter: monofilament and braid. Monofilament is the most common. It's what most people think of as fishing line: clear or translucent single-core nylon polymer line, which is extruded by machine and ranges in strength from ½lb breaking strain to 1000lb. The most useful range for you to have is between 10 and 15lb. It is also helpful to have a spool of 30–40lb to use to make up rigs and to tie to the reel line as a shock leader if you're casting hard from the beach.

If you've got a spare spool or two for your spinning reel, you might want to consider loading them with braid of about 20–25lb breaking strain. Braid is a fairly recent invention. It is composed of interwoven strands of Kevlar-like man-made fibres which create a very strong, very thin line.

The key characteristic that makes braid interesting to anglers is that, unlike monofilament line, it doesn't stretch. Monofilament line is inherently elastic: the more line you have out in the water, the greater the amount of stretch and recoil it will have. The downside of this elasticity or stretch is that it 'muffles' sensation over distance.

At 50 yards, you'll feel a bite on the braid line much more clearly than you will on monofilament line. Braid also cuts through the water more efficiently than monofilament, because pound for pound it has a much slimmer profile and so it creates less resistance to the water current.

The disadvantages of braid are that it can be very tangly and it's trickier to tie efficient knots with. Braid's inelasticity can sometimes prove problematic too. A little amount of stretch is useful at the hook end of the line. Without it, braid can be too unforgiving and will rip a hook right out of a fish's mouth, or else straighten out the bend in your hook, making it useless.

Using braid is a subjective issue and you probably won't have a view on it until you've had a few years' experience of different types of sea angling. In very deep seas (which probably you won't be fishing, at least for some time) it's more common as it causes less water drag and gives better 'communication' at depth. In shallow-water fishing you don't need to use braid, but you might at some point like to experiment.

If you do use braid, you'll need to join it to a short length (8 feet) of monofilament line in order to tie on your hook. Braid should never be used all the way through to the hook; it isn't translucent like monofilament, so it can spook fish and prevent them taking your bait.

Terminal tackle

This is the 'software' that you add to the 'hardware' of your rod, line and reel to transform them into something that can catch fish. The term 'terminal tackle' describes everything that interfaces with the sea (and hopefully with the fish), including hooks, floats, weights, swivels and lures. These pieces of terminal tackle can be assembled into various types of 'rig'. Different types of rig, such as running ledger (see p.164) or paternoster (see p.163), are used either for specific locations, to catch specific types of fish, or to present baits on or just above the seabed.

Hooks

Hook technology is mind-boggling. There are so many sizes, shapes and metallic compositions of hook to choose from, I could easily fill this whole book with amazing hook facts and still barely scratch the surface. There is a hook designed for every fish, every bait and every technique of angling known to man. My personal approach though, is Forrest Gump-like in its simplicity.

In the early days of your fishing adventures, a lot of terminal tackle that you might use (such as spinners, plugs, feathers, Storm lures and pre-made terminal rigs, such as 'pier rigs') will already come with hooks fitted. Experienced and purist anglers may well baulk at the quality of some of these hooks, but when you're learning the ropes, I think it makes perfect sense to be thankful that one part of the puzzle is already in place. If it comes with a hook already tied on it, then use it. You may lose

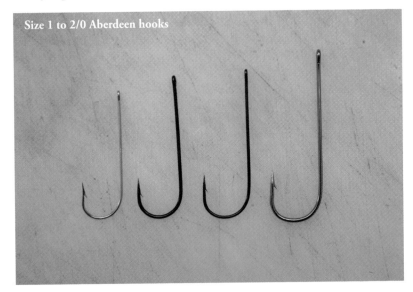

Size 1 to 2/0 Aberdeen hooks

a fish or snap a hook because they're not up to spec, but I think it's better to get to the point of losing a fish rather than never even getting your tackle wet because you haven't quite mastered the knots.

This is my must-have hook shopping list, from the smallest to the biggest. With this selection in your tackle box, you'll be covered for all the species you're likely to catch or want to catch. (One thing to remember is that small hooks catch big fish but big hooks rarely catch small fish.)

- Size 14 freshwater hooks are a specialist size used for catching finicky mullet, when bites are hard to come by. Otherwise most mullet anglers would normally use a size 10 freshwater hook.
- Size 1 and 2 Aberdeen are perfect all-round hooks for catching any of the species mentioned in this book, particularly black bream, pouting, whiting, mackerel, dogfish and garfish. The 'Aberdeen' part of this name refers to the shape of the hook and the length of the shank (the straight bit of the hook before the bend). You might find, if you're catching a lot of dogfish, that the 1 and 2 hooks bend rather too easily when you're trying to remove them from a dogfish's tough mouth. In which case, move to a bigger size (below) and squeeze the barb flat with a pair of pliers to make it easier to remove.
- Size 3/0 is a better hook to use for catching pollack, bass and gurnard. The smaller ones will also work, they just might straighten during the fight if the fish are a decent size.
- Size 4 treble hooks are ideal for squid rigs and for replacing broken spinner hooks.

Floats

A float is simply a flotation device, fixed to a specific point on your line, from which your chosen bait is suspended (see diagram on p.165). A float keeps your bait at a fixed depth in the water. Depending on the location and the species you're trying to catch, you might suspend your bait just under the surface (for example, using bread flake for mullet in a harbour), or in mid water (targeting mackerel with squid strip). Or you might want to suspend the bait (sand eel or ragworm for bass) deep down, just above the seabed, especially if it's weedy or snaggy with sharp rocks, which you want to avoid.

Floats are very sexy. They're shiny, colourful, and come in a range of figures from the anorexic supermodel profile to the chubby big-bottomed bung. The shape of the float and its overall size relates to the type of sea that you are going to use it in.

If the sea is dead calm you can get away with a small float, which is a good thing because a big float might, if the bait is suspended close to it, spook any nervy fish. A big float makes a big splash and casts a big shadow on the water. The smaller the float the sneakier you can be. And small slim waggler floats are best for finicky fish like mullet, because they're easy to pull under. So if a fussy mullet pulls on a suspended

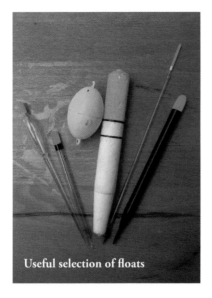

Useful selection of floats

Split shot

bait, he'll feel minimal resistance and might commit to bite. But a fat float will create too much pull against the bait and the wise old mullet will smell a rat.

Over the years, I have owned thousands of floats. Having said that, out of all those that have seduced me into buying them, pitifully few ever venture out of the tackle box on to my line. By all means, indulge any natural predilections, but being pragmatic, these are the floats you'll actually use:

Thin bodied, self-cocking waggler This is used for grey mullet, perch in rivers and grayling. The important feature of this float is that the body has a built-in weight, which makes it easy to cast and forces it to stand upright in the water, without having to hang extra weight beneath it.

Sea float A simple polystyrene wide-bodied float, which comes in a range of sizes. Perfect for mackerel, garfish, bass and pollack, it also works in fresh water for pike.

Bubble float These come in bright orange for long-distance sea fishing, and clear plastic for more sneaky stuff in fresh water, harbours and estuaries. Bubble floats are an old but brilliant invention. Some even have two plugs which allow you to add water to the float to give it weight, but won't make it sink. The bubble float is fabulous for casting, but its spherical profile means it is not a very sensitive instrument. It's heavy and suspicious to fish. It can, however, be used successfully for mackerel, garfish, pollack, grey mullet or perch.

Bullets and bombs

Weights

A weight exists to make things sink. Baits and lures and feathers are shackled to a lead weight in order to get them down deep enough in the water to where the target fish are feeding. In poorer countries around the world I've fished with fishermen who use pebbles, rusty bolts or old spark plugs attached to the line to provide sinkability. Needless to say, in this country you can buy weights in a dizzying selection of shapes, sizes and materials. Carp anglers have a penchant for lead weights that are carefully manufactured and disguised to look like stones!

Of all the tackle you buy, weights are the thing you're most likely to lose. Every time you get snagged, it's the weight that gets lost first. So don't bother to buy anything but the cheapest. Some anglers even make their own. It's also worth noting that they are by nature heavy, so the fewer you decide to take, the less of a burden your tackle box will be.

This is all you really need to keep in your weight munitions:

- A small selection of bombs, from 1–5oz, used when ledgering or feathering (see pp.135–7).
- A small selection of drilled bullets, from ⅛–2oz, used under big floats and for worming or touch-ledgering (see pp. 102 and 165).
- A box of various lead-free split shot, which are nipped on the line beneath smaller floats to make lightweight baits sink. Never use more weight than you need. The more weight you attach, the bigger the splash and the bigger the lump of lead falling through the water, both of which will spook fish.

Swivels

Swivels are useful for creating joins between two lengths of line of different strength. For example, if you have 20lb line on your reel, but only want to present 10lb line to the fish on your hook line, then a swivel makes the joint easy to tie and it will also minimise the potential for tangles.

Swivels are great for joining rigs to the main line. Because of their mechanical construction, swivels can rotate in the water, with either end of the swivel turning in either direction, which means they stop the line from getting kinked or twisted up. In water with a strong tide, the swivel allows a rig to twist and twirl in the current without winding itself into a hideous tangle.

A swivel also makes a perfect stop for a running ledger rig (see p.164). It stops the weight from sliding all the way down to the hook, as well as providing a tangle-resistant buffer between reel line and hook line.

Clip swivels These are most useful when you tie them to the end of your line as the junction between your line and a weight, or between your line and a type of terminal tackle like a spinner, wedge or plug (see pp.138–42), all of which need to be able to rotate as they pass through the water. Without a clip swivel, they would be constantly twisting and kinking the reel line. The clip swivel allows them to rotate freely – and allows you to change them as often as you want without having to tie any knots.

Swivels, clip swivels and three-way swivels

Clip swivels are used to connect to the weight because they can be easily undone, so you can change the size of your weight quickly to match the tide, current or fishing technique. A larger or smaller weight can be attached without the bother of cutting line and tying new knots. They also provide some protection for your line. If you tie your line directly to the loop in your bomb weight, it'll get damaged and nicked every time the weight hits a rock, eventually fraying and breaking, so you'll lose your lead. Because the clip is metal, it won't be affected.

Clip swivels are perfect for using with spinners because you can chop and change as often as you like without having to tie new knots. In fact, if you're new to fishing, knots might still be a bit of a challenge, in which case you can use clip swivels at *both ends* of your mackerel feather string, from the reel line as well as to the weight. That way, you can swap from feathers (see pp.134–7) to spinner (see pp.138–40) to paternoster rig (see p.163) without having to tie knots.

The most useful-sized swivels to have are:

• rolling swivels size 1 or 2
• clip swivels in size 2/0
• three-way clip swivels

Three-way clip swivels are used to make quick paternoster rigs, with the reel line from the top eye, weight link line from the bottom eye, and hook link (snood) from the middle.

None of the fish in this book are big enough to break any medium-sized swivels. Size isn't too much of an issue, but avoid having a huge swivel or clip swivel that's almost as big as the spinner it's clipped to, and similarly avoid anything that's made of such fine wire that it's hard to fit your line through the swivel eye! Tackle shops stock perfectly serviceable swivels. I've fished for decades and still don't fully understand how swivels are sized. Use common sense. If you can't break a swivel or a clip with your bare hands, chances are a 2lb fish can't break it either.

Booms

The function of a boom, on a one- or two-hook paternoster rig (see p.163), is to provide a stiff right-angled 'branch' to the main vertical 'spine' of your rig. The end of the boom, furthest from the spine, is where you hang your hook, suspended on a 'hook link': a piece of monofilament line no more than 8 inches long.

The function of a boom in these basic rigs is to put some distance between the hook and the main line of the rig, in order to stop them becoming tangled together when you cast out or drop your bait down from a pier or boat. If your hook and bait get tangled around the main line of the rig, it'll make your bait presentation ineffective and obscure the bait from a fish's hungry eyes. A boom holds your bait out on a cantilever, keeping it separate and suspended away from the main line, where it can flutter and float attractively in the water, begging to be eaten.

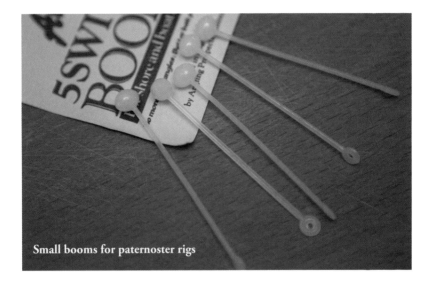

Small booms for paternoster rigs

Most booms can be moved up and down the line, so that you can position them at the preferred distance from the weight. And when you're fishing vertically, either from a boat or from a pier, or off a rocky cliff into deep water, you can determine the depth you want your bait to be presented at by setting the boom height above the weight. By setting the boom 3 feet above the weight you know your bait will be stationed 3 feet off the seabed. This can be useful if you're trying to keep your hook and bait above a bed of seaweed or a bunch of snaggy rocks; the boom holds it in open water, just above the structure where fish will find it easily and where it avoids getting caught up in tackle-thieving snags.

There are various booms on sale. Some are hollow tubes that can be used like zip sliders for making running ledger rigs (see p.164), some are wire. The booms you want for simple paternoster rigs or single-hook rigs are solid plastic, 3–5 inches long, with a hole at one end through which to tie a short hook link. At the other end is a means of attaching the boom to the 'main spine' line of your rig. The method of attaching can vary according to the type of rig; some require knots, most don't.

I'd advise you to buy a basic, cheap boom (because you're bound to lose plenty, we all do), which is easy to attach under adverse conditions. Check out a few shop-bought rigs that include booms. Consult websites like worldseafishing.com and see what patterns they have on offer. And do ask in a local tackle shop which pattern they would advise. Even ask them to show you exactly how to tie one on. There's nothing worse than getting a boom out of your box on the high seas or on a crowded pier and not having the faintest idea how to fit it. All the more reason to keep your tackle purchases simple.

Beads

Beads

Beads are used as a shock absorber between the swivel and the weight's wire loop on a running ledger rig (see p.164). In theory, they prevent the monofilament line from being crunched between the metal of the loop and the metal of the swivel, which will eventually cause it to snap.

I don't always use beads. In fact, if my hands are cold or sticky from bait or fish, I won't even bother to try. They're so annoying to use in bad weather conditions that I think I've lost more beads than I've ever used. However, they are important if the loop on your weight is bigger than the size of your swivel. If the swivel can pass through the loop, then it won't work as a stop. Sticking a big bead between them will prevent the swivel slipping through the weight loop.

Another way of using beads is when you're tying simple rigs for plaice or flounder fishing. Threading eight or ten beads along the line just above the hook will provide something eye-catching and alluring that flat fish respond to and which will, in theory, draw their attention to your bait. Whether you believe this or not, it can't do any harm, and you never know, the extra resistance of the beads in the current may make the bait flap a little more enticingly.

Zip sliders

The zip slider is normally a rigid tube of plastic with a clip attached to one side. The reel line is threaded down the centre of the tube and the weight is attached to the clip. This allows the line to pass freely through the tube, without moving the weight. So, when a fish pulls on a bait, the line slides through the slider without disturbing

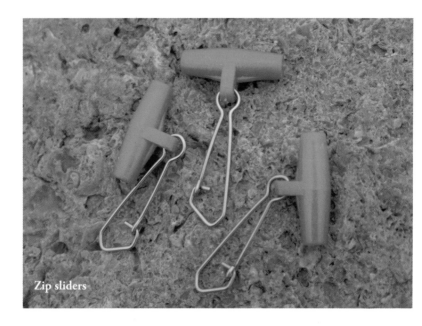
Zip sliders

the bait. This way the fish isn't spooked by feeling any resistance of the weight, and yet, the pulling of the line will still register on the flexible rod tip as a bite. This type of set-up is known as a running ledger rig (see p.164). A zip slider is so called because it acts like the handle on a play-area zip slide, where you can slide down a taut wire, holding on to a handle.

Hook link

The line which is attached to your hook is known as the 'hook link' or 'snood' or even, just to complicate things further, the 'leader' – not to be confused with the shock leader (see opposite). It makes sense for this hook link to be no thicker than absolutely necessary, because some fish are particularly aware and wary of thick line near the bait and will refuse to bite if the mouthful looks strange or acts suspiciously.

Most anglers carry a spare spool of line, which they'll use only for hook links – in other words, the final section of line in your rig that leads to the hook. Some serious anglers will buy a very good-quality line for this short but important section, often a fluorocarbon line, which is specifically designed to appear less visible in water. It's thin and transparent, but strong.

Personally I don't think fancy and expensive fluorocarbon line is necessary, unless you're targeting a really finicky species, like grey mullet. A spare spool of ordinary monofilament is always useful to have, though, as it means you can tie a new hook length without having to cannibalise your reel line.

Shock leader

A shock leader, for general beachcasting, is a length of 40–60lb mono line, which should be about twice the length of your rod. It is designed to absorb the initial shock of heavy lead weights (2oz or more) when you're casting hard from the shore.

The strength of main reel line you'll want to use while casting with a spinning rod or a carp rod (or even a beachcasting rod) is no more than 15lb. Heavy line increases aerodynamic resistance. Anything upward of 15lb is too heavy to be practicable casting over any distance. But just using 15lb line with a 3 or 4oz weight will end in potentially painful disaster, because the force of the cast with that weight is greater than the strength of your reel line. It will snap like straw, unless you use a shock leader to cushion the force of the cast.

A shock leader is a beefed-up extension of your reel line which takes all the initial strain of casting. It is tied to the business end of your reel line and runs to the top of your terminal tackle rig. The important thing is that the shock leader is long enough to wind a few times around your reel spool, up the rod and down to the start of your rig when you're in the casting position. A shock leader should be between 20 and 30 feet long. This will absorb all the shock of the cast, thus protecting the more fragile reel line. Shock leaders also combat abrasion when fishing over rough seabeds.

There's a formula for judging the necessary breaking strain of shock leaders, which equates to 10lb of shock leader for every single ounce of weight cast. Given that you will have a minimum of 10lb line on your reel to begin with, no shock leader is needed for a 1oz weight. If you've got 15lb line on your rod, you will probably get away with casting 2oz, if you're careful. Above 2oz you'll definitely need to add a shock leader, and remember that each extra ounce requires an extra 10lb breaking strain:

- 3oz weight: 30lb shock leader
- 4oz weight: 40lb shock leader... and so on.

If, like me, you prefer to use a spinning rod or carp rod for beach fishing, you'll never cast more than 4oz, so a 40lb shock leader will more than suffice.

I always keep a spool of 30lb or 40lb in my tackle box and tie on a 20-foot length if I'm fishing hard with a string of mackerel feathers and a 3 or 4oz weight. There is a special knot for tying shock leaders on to your reel (see p.170).

Bait elastic

If you want to use peeler crab, mussels, hermit crabs or razor clams as bait, buy a spool of bait elastic from a tackle shop. It is gossamer-fine elastic, which you can just wind and wind around a squidgy bait. Even herring baits, which can quickly turn mushy, benefit from being lashed to a hook with bait elastic. It's very easy to use because it has a sticky, self-gripping surface and doesn't need to be knotted, just wound around itself a dozen times or more.

Artificial lures

An artificial lure is quite simply any piece of terminal tackle that is designed to attract or even annoy a fish, to the extent that the fish then attacks and tries to eat the lure. So, a lure might be designed to look like a tiny fish, or a worm. Or it might simply be made with a reflective surface or from brightly coloured material that creates a flash in the water, interesting enough to make the fish strike.

Artificial lures are used instead of a bait (see pp.150–9). A bait is just a piece of recognisable food hung on a hook to try and attract the hungry attentions of a fish. Lures are used either because a bait isn't available, or because the thing a lure does a good job of imitating, such as a small sprat or a sand eel, is impractical to find and keep alive for use. Baits can be messy and smelly; artificial lures are clean and re-usable. Artificial lures may cost a bit to buy, but they can last for years. Fresh live baits are very hard to buy because not many tackle shops stock them and if they do, they're far from cheap.

Spinners, plugs, jelly worms, rubber fish, mackerel feathers, spoons and wedges are all examples of artificial lures.

The adjacent chart gives you some idea of the best luring or baiting approaches for different types of fish. Thank God there will always be mind-boggling exceptions to every rule and fish, bless them, will always surprise you in their determination to break any rules we devise. But as a rough 'how to get started' guide, this marries up the most likely species with the most likely techniques.

Surface popper plug for bass fishing

Bait and lure techniques for sea fish

	MACKEREL FEATHERS	MINI FEATHER	BAITED FEATHERS	SPINNER OR PLUG	JIG/ STORM LURE	FLOAT-SUSPENDED BAIT	BOTTOM-LEDGERED BAIT
MACKEREL	BEST	BEST	BEST	BEST	BEST	BEST	MIGHT GET LUCKY
DOGFISH			MIGHT GET LUCKY				BEST
POUTING	MIGHT GET LUCKY		BEST				BEST
POLLACK	MIGHT GET LUCKY		MIGHT GET LUCKY	BEST	BEST	MIGHT GET LUCKY	MIGHT GET LUCKY
COD	MIGHT GET LUCKY		BEST		BEST		BEST
WHITING	MIGHT GET LUCKY	MIGHT GET LUCKY	BEST				BEST
GARFISH	MIGHT GET LUCKY	BEST	MIGHT GET LUCKY	MIGHT GET LUCKY		BEST	
RED GURNARD	MIGHT GET LUCKY	MIGHT GET LUCKY	BEST	MIGHT GET LUCKY	MIGHT GET LUCKY		BEST
BLACK BREAM			MIGHT GET LUCKY		MIGHT GET LUCKY	MIGHT GET LUCKY	BEST
PLAICE							BEST
SEA BASS	MIGHT GET LUCKY	MIGHT GET LUCKY	MIGHT GET LUCKY	BEST	BEST	MIGHT GET LUCKY	MIGHT GET LUCKY
DAB & FLOUNDER							BEST
HORSE MACKEREL	BEST	BEST	BEST	BEST		BEST	MIGHT GET LUCKY
HERRING	BEST	BEST	MIGHT GET LUCKY	MIGHT GET LUCKY	MIGHT GET LUCKY	MIGHT GET LUCKY	
SQUID					BEST	MIGHT GET LUCKY	MIGHT GET LUCKY
SLOB TROUT				MIGHT GET LUCKY		MIGHT GET LUCKY	BEST
GREY MULLET				BEST		BEST	MIGHT GET LUCKY

KEY: ✦ = BEST   ✧ = MIGHT GET LUCKY

Feathers

Feathers probably account for more sea fish catches around the coast of Britain than any other form of terminal tackle. Mackerel feathers are an absolute must for any sea angler who wants to catch fish to eat.

A string of mackerel feathers, at its most basic, is a combination of three, four or six hooks, each tied about 18 inches apart, along a length of clear monofilament fishing line. The individual hooks each have a small pluck of chicken feathers lashed to them.

Shop-bought mackerel feathers come in a variety of colours; mostly these sets are all white, or all orange, or multi-coloured with each of the hooks sporting a different hue of plumage including red, blue, white, orange and black.

I refuse to get too colour conscious about mackerel feathers. It really doesn't hurt to have a colour selection of feathers in your tackle box, to ring the changes when the fish aren't biting. But to get hung up on one mackerel feather colour or another is a sure sign of madness.

I do believe in having more than one *size* of feather though. The size of the feather relates to the size of the hook it's mounted upon. There are several types of small feathers available from tackle shops. The smaller feather sets (which may also be called micro feathers, mini feathers, Sabikis or Hokkais) are really worth having in your collection simply because they might work when bigger ones won't, or they

Mackerel feathers

might work on different species. They may lure mackerel who are being a bit shy, and they may also work on some of the smaller species like herring, sprats, horse mackerel, garfish and even large sand eels.

The size of the feather (or mini lure, as it really is) and its efficiency at attracting fish will relate to the size of the prey prevalent in the water at that time. If all the mackerel are busy feeding on ¼–½-inch-long fish fry, then a great big 3-inch-long feather isn't going to successfully imitate what the mackerel are feeding on. It might even scare them off.

The smaller-sized 'feathers' often don't involve any feather plumage at all. They are simply mini fish lures, tied with flashy and sparkly man-made materials. I would recommend having a couple of sets of smaller feathers in your box.

The little micro feather sets sometimes contain even more than six hooks to each string. I've come across sets of eight or ten mini lures on a string, which are set closer together than the big feathers, but they can be very tangly and tricky to use. However, without too much faffing, you can simply cut a long string of micro feathers in half and make two shorter, more manageable ones.

Why feathers work A string of feathers will attract fish, especially mackerel, because of the way they move and glint. Some feathers have silver flashy material tied into the feather, but also the hooks themselves, if kept clean, will gleam and reflect sunlight as they're jigged through the water. Movement is key. A stationary feather hanging limply in the water will rarely attract a bite, as it won't resemble anything a mackerel might regard as food. Movement makes it interesting. It makes capture seem more urgent.

A hungry mackerel, hunting in a competitive group, sees a movement and a flash of reflected light, and instantly nails what it assumes is a small fish, before any of his mates get a look in.

The mackerel-seducing movement that you can induce in your feathers will differ depending on whether you're afloat on a boat, perched high above the water on a pier, or else down at sea level on the beach.

Feathering from a boat This is the easiest and most effective way to use feathers, because you can simply drop them down to the seabed, weighted by a bomb-shaped lead, and then wind them back up again. Fish will take either on the way down or up; they're not fussy about direction, just movement.

Instead of simply letting the feathers fall through the water, it's more effective to lower them 10 or 15 feet at a time and stop, then jig them up and down, two or three times, at each new level. The 'jigging' should be done in rhythmic sweeps, moving your rod from waist height to head height and down again. This way you can cover the water column efficiently, jigging the feathers through every stage from the boat to the seabed. Mackerel can feed at any depth; sometimes they're only 5 feet under the boat, other times they're way down deep, practically on the seabed. When you're reeling the feathers back up, do the same jigging sequence in reverse. Keep stopping every half a dozen reel turns, to jig up and down at least two or three times.

If you do feel a 'rattling' on your line, it means a mackerel is hooked up. Mackerel will hook themselves, you don't have to 'strike' (see p.174) to drive the hooks home. Mackerel feather hooks always have a pronounced barb on them, so fish rarely escape if they're properly hooked in the mouth. Instead of winding up furiously when you first feel the telltale rattle, to bring your precious quarry up to the boat, try 'hanging' your line for 10 seconds. Hanging means suspending it without jigging or retrieving it.

More mackerel will often hook themselves on your spare feathers while the string hangs in the water with the first mackerel already hooked up. The simple explanation for this is that if one mackerel sees another mackerel obviously engaged in some hunting and eating activity, it's very likely to pile in and try to get some action for itself. So by hanging, you can make competitive feeding and unchecked mackerel greed really work in your favour.

Feathering from the beach For the very reasons that feathering from a boat is so easy (you're surrounded by water deep enough to contain fish), feathering from the beach is much more difficult. In order to get to water deep enough to contain fish, say upwards of 10 feet, you'll normally need to be able to cast your feathers at least 20 or 30 yards. Apart from anything else, this can be a hazardous business. Casting a string of stainless-steel brutally barbed hooks from a standing position out to sea is fraught with potential danger.

At the same time, feathering from the beach is one of the most satisfying ways of catching a feed of mackerel. So, I feel it's my duty to help you to catch some mackerel from the beach without maiming anyone. In order to do this, there are some things we need to rule out. The first of these is the use of a beachcaster rod.

If you walk along Chesil Beach in Dorset in the summer, you'll see lots of anglers chucking out strings of feathers with enormous rods. These are beachcaster rods (see p.117) and they're normally around 13 feet long or more.

As I mentioned earlier, I don't enjoy using these big rods at all. This is for two reasons: firstly, they're not easy to cast and definitely not by anyone new to fishing; secondly, they're uncomfortable to hold and not very pleasant to play a fish on. Beachcasters are unwieldy, uncomfortable sticks, capable of chucking a weight and bait up to 300 yards. But you will only achieve distances of 100 yards or more if you practise and have a well-tuned, expensive and tricky-to-use multiplier reel attached to it. I'm not saying you won't one day progress to using a beachcaster and casting further than I could even dream of, but for the sake of getting started, let's forget beachcasters altogether.

The next option is to use a beach rod. This is usually 11–12 feet long and is built like a very beefy spinning rod. It's designed to take a big, beefy spinning reel with heavy-duty 20lb line. It's much easier to use than a beachcaster, not much more difficult than a spinning rod or carp rod, but it is a hefty, ungainly thing that has no use other than to chuck out big baits and feathers off the beach or rocks.

A simple spinning rod (or carp rod or bass rod – all basically the same thing) has myriad uses in the sea and fresh water, but more importantly it can be used by practically any size of person – man, woman or child – with ease and comfort. To fish from the beach with a spinning rod or a carp rod with feathers, you will need at least 15lb line on your spinning reel, a shock leader (see p.131) and no more than a 3oz lead. The trick is to keep the tackle light and well balanced in terms of weight to rod ratio. I never use anything heavier than a carp rod and I can cast far enough to catch fish in comfort. I also never use more than three feathers – to reduce the chance of snags.

When you're fishing with feathers from the beach, you have to keep the feathers moving through the water, not just to attract fish, but also to avoid them sinking to the bottom and getting snagged as you wind them shorewards. Remember, even with only three feathered hooks there are still at least three opportunities to get your tackle hung up on rocks. And because of the low angle at which you have to retrieve them, it's often impossible to pull them free without breaking your line once they've snagged. This means leaving a string of dangerous tackle wrapped around a rock, uncomfortably close to the shore where people are likely to go swimming.

Your retrieve should be fast. You can intersperse each few winds of the reel with a long steady jig upwards, which, if you hold the rod high, will make the feathers 'swim up' in the water.

Tangles and knots need to be avoided, so keep your line simple and in good working condition. An unwanted knot in your reel line, which forces you to stop winding in order to untangle it, will cause your feathers to sink and might then lead you to hook up with the seabed.

Spinners and wedges

Simple spinners have been around for hundreds of years. They are clever pieces of mechanical engineering, which work on the principle that as they're retrieved through the water, the force of the water passing through the spinner blades will make them rotate like a propeller. The rotation of this blade (or blades) causes vibrations in the water (imitating a wounded fish) as well as creating flashes and glints of light from the shiny metal surfaces as they revolve. The flashing and the vibrations will both attract fish, either out of curiosity or an intention to attack.

The 'Mepps' spinner is an ancient French design, which has been copied and 'improved' upon many times by many manufacturers. But I have to confess I have a real soft spot for the original Mepps, which are very efficient at spinning and creating a vast amount of vibration and flashing, because of their simple but effective design. Original Mepps tend to be more expensive than the myriad imitations, and yet I don't mind paying the extra.

Mostly sea fishermen these days only use the smaller Mepps for mullet spinning, and the rest of the sizes often get left for freshwater pike anglers to use. Mepps is a design classic and you really should have one in your box – there's not a predator species in the world that hasn't been caught by a Mepps.

A wedge (aka Dexter) is like a heavy version of a spinner. It's usually got a much heavier body and an aerodynamic shape, which makes it easy to cast, even into a head-on wind. It can also be used from a boat, either cast out and allowed to sink and then retrieved, or just dropped down over the side, allowed to flutter down to the seabed and then retrieved up 20 turns of the reel handle and dropped back down again. So with this method you're working your wedge up and down in the bottom 20–30 feet of the sea beneath the boat. A wedge doesn't rotate like a spinner and it doesn't have mechanical blades to whirl as it's retrieved. Instead it is carefully designed to wobble and kink as it's retrieved, moving in the way a wounded fish might swim.

The wedge is aerodynamically designed to cast efficiently. The bigger the wedge, the further you should be able to cast. But the bigger the wedge the fewer fish you're likely to attract, simply because a small wedge of ¾–1oz looks like potential prey to a small mackerel, horse mackerel or pollack, but a big wedge of 1½oz could scare them away because they might think it's about to prey on them. Certainly, a big bass might attack a big wedge, but remember there are far fewer big bass around than there are small mackerel. And big bass are a lot smarter too. So if you're just looking for a fun couple of hours with the prospect of a decent nosebag at the end of it, stick to smaller wedges.

Using a spinner or wedge from the shore Casting a spinner or a wedge from the beach is a much easier alternative to casting a string of feathers. A spinner or wedge has only one hook (even though it'll probably be a treble hook with three barbs),

Spinners, including the Mepps spinner (middle left)

Dexter wedge

so it's less likely to get snagged on the seabed as you retrieve, and less likely to tangle up during repeated casting. Both a spinner and a wedge are normally used without additional weight. All of their weight is intrinsic to their body shape, and so they sink more slowly than a string of feathers, which has a weight attached to the terminal end of the string. A string of feathers with a weight at one end can be cast out further than most plugs or spinners or spoons, because it is normally heavier. However, because spoons and plugs are lighter, they sink more slowly and are less likely to snag on the bottom, which makes them more relaxing to fish with.

Feathering from the beach will also normally require tying on a shock leader (a plug or spoon won't) and fishing at a frantic rate, retrieving fast, to avoid snagging on the seabed. With spinners, spoons and wedges, the pace of retrieve can be slowed down to a much less frenetic pace. Personally, I can only stand half an hour of frantic feathering before I want to swap to a more sedate method.

With spinners and wedges and spoons (see below), which imitate one single bait fish, rather than a small string of them, as feathers do, there is also the strong possibility of attracting the attention of bigger, more selective predators in the area like sea bass or pollack. It's unlikely (though by no means impossible) that you'll hook a big bass on mackerel feathers, but there's every chance you'll hook one on a lure like a spoon or plug.

Using a spinner or wedge from a boat You can cast a spinner or a wedge from a boat and let it sink, then slowly retrieve it. This can work well when the fish (especially bass and pollack) are hunting near the surface, or else if you let your lure drop into the tide and be taken away from the boat with the current for a few minutes, before you start a long slow retrieve. I should add, though, that most mackerel boats or charter boats don't allow or don't encourage clients to cast lures from the boat, mostly for safety reasons. When a group of paying clients are dropping their feathers or baits over the side, it's possible to limit any accidents. When a bunch of punters are casting plugs with up to three huge treble hooks mounted on them every couple of minutes, wheeling back behind them to cast, lurching with every wave, the health and safety issue becomes a nightmare.

So, if you've got your own boat, or have a friend with one, or else have chartered a boat all to yourself, then you'll be able to cast plugs, spoons and anything you like, but when you're cheek by jowl with your fellow anglers in the care of an experienced skipper, you're unlikely to be allowed to cast your spinner from their boat.

Toby spoons

Tobys are more like wedges than spinners. They wobble and they rotate too, but not with the ferocity and frequency of a spinner. They also imitate a wounded fish's behaviour. Tobys can be really effective when cast and retrieved, or else trolled slowly

Toby spoon

behind a moving boat. Being generally lighter, they don't usually cast as far as a wedge, but nor do they sink so fast. So a Toby can be retrieved more slowly than a wedge, which can be handy in shallow water to avoid hooking up with the seabed.

However, like wedges, bigger Toby spoons look great and cast further. They do offer the opportunity of catching a big fish, but a ½lb mackerel (which would be delicious to eat) is going to swim in fear of his life from a big Toby spoon, rather than try to swallow it.

Plugs

There are two distinct types of plug: floating and diving. Both might be used from the shore or possibly from a boat. The depth you desire your plug to dive under the surface depends on where you think the fish may be feeding. Bass, for example, will feed on wounded fry right on the surface, practically grabbing them out of seagulls' mouths, while pollack like to hunt a few feet down from the surface at least.

A floating plug stays on the surface all the time, even when it's being reeled in, because it's very buoyant and simply wiggles its way across the surface of the water. A diving plug, on the other hand, may well float on the water when it's still, but as soon as you start to wind it towards you, the diving vane at its head forces it under the surface of the water.

Some diving plugs are deep divers, some are shallow, depending on the size and angle of the diving vane. And some are integrally weighted too, so they sink down in the water as soon as they're cast out.

Plugs

Plugs are beautiful. Irresistible, perfectly proportioned pieces of tackle that sing to anglers and wannabe anglers with a siren song that will have you parting with your cash faster than you can say John Dory. I once had a guest on my angling radio show, *Dirty Tackle*, who had a collection of plugs worth over £10,000. These weren't antique or vintage collectors' plugs. They were brand-new ones; and none of them were ever used in anger. He just hoarded them in huge multi-drawered tackle boxes and pored over them with gloating obsession. He was a man totally smitten by the lure of the lure. But be warned, there are plugs designed specifically to catch the cash-rich angler first, and fish second.

Apart from simply casting and retrieving a plug or a spinner, both can be used as a 'trolled' bait, let out behind a slow-moving boat. Trolling is a method of fishing originally developed for bluewater game fish, such as marlin and sailfish. All it means is that you tow a lure (plug, spinner, wedge or large fly) 30–100 yards behind the boat, which must be moving very slowly. The lure is positioned either on the surface, near the surface, or deep down, depending on the type of lure and the species of fish you're after.

Plugs are not essential kit. Yes, they are sexy, alluring, and fun to use. They just don't as a rule catch an awful lot of fish. If you really *must* have a plug, then buy a floating plug and a shallow-diving plug of around 3½–4 inches. Try casting them off rocks or a steep, sloping beach, so they're working in at least 10 feet of water. You might get lucky and pick up a pollack. Work hard at dawn and dusk, and you might even attract the homicidal attentions of a bass. But don't hold your breath.

Rubber fish, 'Shads' or 'Storm lures'

Just as all vacuum cleaners get called 'Hoovers' and plastic food wrap is always 'cling film', so any rubber fish lure usually ends up being called a 'Shad' or a 'Storm lure' after the most famous of the rubber fish manufacturers.

Rubber fish come in a variety of colours, sizes, shapes and designs. They are sold both with and without hooks, and some also come with an integral weight fitted inside the body. A plain rubber fish, to which you add your own hook and then attach a weight, is obviously much cheaper than the sophisticated, pre-weighted option. However, for simplicity's sake, I'd recommend buying a couple of packets of the luxury version just to get you started. You can always experiment with rigging your own when you've got a feel for what you like.

Using a rubber fish lure from the shore Pre-weighted rubber fish are enormously versatile lures, which can be used – like spinners – for casting out from the beach or rocks, as well as for drift fishing from a boat. One cunning aspect of the pre-weighted rubber fish is the fact that the bend of the hook is upturned so the point appears upwards out of the back of the rubber fish.

The design of the integral weight means the fish always stays the right way up when it's being retrieved with the hook sticking proud out of its back. This greatly reduces the possibility of the hook catching on the seabed as it's retrieved, without reducing its effectiveness for hooking into a predator's mouth.

On a beach terrain that's not too rocky, you can even 'bounce' your rubber fish along the bottom as you wind it in, by occasionally slowing or stopping the retrieve to let the lure sink and skip on the seabed. The skip kicks up sand, causing vibrations, which might just grab the attention of a hunting bass, pollack or mackerel.

Using a rubber fish lure from a boat Rubber fish are most effective fished from a drifting boat. They can work from an anchored boat too, but not as well, simply because the lure is covering less ground.

Around Portland Bill, where we are lucky to have probably the best sea bass fishery in the British Isles, the technique of using Storm lures fished under a drifting boat is the most effective bass-catching technique. (Using live sand eels as bait is a possible exception, but much more complicated to obtain and keep alive for long enough to use from a drifting boat.)

To understand how drifting with these lures works, imagine a boat drifting along with the tide over a rocky seabed. Around Portland, we're usually fishing in less than 100 feet of water. Now, imagine connecting a line between your rod and a rounded lead weight, which then bounces across the rocks, directly beneath, or slightly behind the drifting boat. With the line held tight from your rod tip, you'd be able to feel every bump of the lead on the rocks as it is dragged over them by the moving boat.

Rubber fish and a jelly worm (right)

Now, imagine attaching your sexy rubber fish, which wiggles so enticingly in moving water, suspended a couple of feet above the weight, as it bounces over those rocks, just far enough up the line to avoid getting snagged in rocks or seaweed. And just far enough above the rocks to be silhouetted against the light above, perfectly positioned in the line of sight of any hungry predatory fish holding position in the lee of a rock, where it's ducked down out of the tiring tidal current, head pointing into the flow. This is how these big predators hunt when the tide is running fast; they hunker down behind rocks and look up, waiting for potential dinner to drift overhead.

Rubber fish lures also catch fish as they're being reeled upwards, from the seabed towards the boat. Some fish – pollack, cod, coalfish, bass and mackerel – are more than happy to chase a bait fish upwards. And because rubber fish look so much like the fish these predators hunt, a Storm lure has every chance of being attacked, simply by being in the right place at the right time. When a lure looks and behaves like a bait fish, then it's perfectly likely to get eaten.

Rubber worms or 'jelly worms'

These work on the same principle as rubber fish, although you can't normally buy them with a weight and hook already fitted. Jelly worms are slightly more limited in the fish they attract too. By all means chuck a packet in your tackle box and experiment with them one day when you're on a boat and have already filled your boots. To begin with though, stick to the pre-weighted rubber fish.

Other pieces of useful kit

Here are a few extra items of kit, which might not mean the difference between success and failure (except in the case of the drop net), but are all things you should get into the habit of taking with you.

Insulation winder

It's a special sort of person who's prepared to unclip their mackerel feather set at the end of a fishing session, dry them carefully and then wind them up neatly, returning them to the packet whence they came. Sadly, I am not made of such patient and meticulous stuff. However, after years of having a rusty, tangled, dangerous mess of used mackerel feathers lurking at the bottom of my tackle box, I have discovered the joys of insulation foam pipe lagging. A mere 12 inches of this stuff will marshal rigs and feathers, keeping them in one place, virtually tangle-free, until they're required again.

Scissors

Heavy-duty kitchen scissors with plastic handles are one of the most versatile tools you can take along with you on a fishing trip. Everything from trimming knots to chopping up bait and unwanted fishing line can be achieved with these. Buy a pair with brightly coloured handles and you're less likely to leave them behind.

Knife

There are three obvious reasons for having a knife with you when you're sea fishing: to chop bait; to gut fish; and to fillet your fish. The first two jobs don't really require a very sharp knife and, in any case, cutting bait on a bait board will blunt a sharp edge in seconds. However, filleting fish can only be done effectively with a very sharp knife. In order to do all these knife jobs capably, you either have to take along an efficient knife sharpener, or else have two knives: one for bait and one for fish preparation. The choice is yours. If you do choose to invest in a sharpener, I would recommend taking one that's easy to use, like a Chantry-style pull-through type. Using a steel or a whetstone on a boat can very quickly and easily result in a messy blood-and-sticking-plaster situation.

Pliers

If you're putting together a fishing kit for the first time, it is worth buying yourself a new pair of pliers. Don't splash out – cheap ones will do – but do make sure they have a decent cutting edge. Thin-nosed pliers are probably the most useful because they're more versatile, but don't get hung up on searching too hard for the perfect pair because, if you're anything like me, they'll be lost or rusted solid within their first few months. And don't make the mistake of taking your favourite pair from your toolbox, because they'll never be the same again.

A stout pair of pliers is brilliant for pulling buried hooks out of cartilaginous jaws, or for snipping the shaft of a hook that has got buried in a rope, your thumb, jumper or boot. Pliers can be used for mending outboard motors, squeezing flat barbs on hooks, and stripping skin off dogfish. In short, you never really know what you might need a pair of pliers for, so just make sure you have some with you.

Priest or bosher
A hammer handle, a length of copper pipe filled with sand, a truncheon, a long-shafted screwdriver, a shop-bought 'priest', a short hardwood shillelagh club, a toffee hammer, an adjustable spanner, 18 inches of blue nylon water pipe… I've seen fish despatched with all of these objects. It doesn't really matter what your chosen assassination device is, so long as it's effective and handy. Don't wait to improvise on the spot and grab for a rock or a boat skipper's best torch; either of these will cause unnecessary mess. Pack something suitable for killing fish. For cracking them with a fatal blow across the head. Pack it and know where it is when you need it.

Drop net
A drop net is a circular (or occasionally square) frame which has a 'basket' of netting hanging down from its underside. The hoop of the net is suspended from a rope in such a way that it can be lowered, off a pier or harbour wall, while the mouth of the net will remain open and parallel to the water surface below. A drop net has two main uses: for lifting a fish that's hooked to your rod line up a steep harbour wall; and for catching crabs and prawns from a pier, harbour or breakwater.

If you're fishing from a pier or rock face, high above the water's surface, the job of hauling a fish and a lead weight perpendicularly upwards may well be enough to snap your rod. By lowering the net, swinging the fish and weight into it, and hauling the net up by its attached rope, you'll minimise the risk of losing the fish or busting your fishing rod. Except, it has to be said, that getting the fish to swing into your drop net is in itself no mean feat.

The other purpose of the drop net is curious exploration. If you stick a stone in the centre of your net and lower it to the seabed, it will sit there like an inviting carpet. If you also tie a lump of alluring bait, like a mackerel head and guts, to the centre of the net, who knows what might stray on to your rug trap for a nibble.

The mesh size of the net will limit what you can catch. But, even if your drop net has a wide mesh, too big for prawns or shrimps, you can always carry a smaller-meshed lining to tie inside it. That's if your fishing trip starts to evolve more into a shore crab and prawn exploration event. There is a point to crabbing like this. Shore crabs can make good bait (see p.159), wild prawns are the pink-shelled food of the

Drop net

gods, and an amazing array of other things will occasionally crop up in your drop net too. Potentially anything from lobsters to eels and from dabs to dogfish.

Apart from anything else, a drop net is a great diversion on a slow day's fishing. And any haul from the harbour floor is a fascinating snapshot of sea life. I spent a whole day with my boys fishing off Cromer pier with just a drop net. We had a plastic bucket full of sea water in which to empty and admire each haul of shore crabs, before releasing them all back to the wild. It may sound pointless, but actually it was a thoroughly enjoyable expedition.

Cool box

An insulated cool box or a cool bag with a handful of cool blocks is an essential piece of kit for anyone who is serious about keeping their fish in its finest condition. Even in the winter, fish can spoil very quickly if left exposed to light and air. Any fish you catch need to be killed, bled and preferably gutted and chilled within an hour of being caught. I am evangelical about keeping fish cool and I always take a cool box with blocks or ice. I like the solid cool boxes and I've got one that is big enough to fit my tackle box into. So I only have to carry the one box on the way out. Insulated cool bags can be folded up and carried inside your tackle bag or box, or they can be used to carry your bait and lunch. Either way, a cool box or bag guarantees your best fish comes home in the best condition.

Bait

The best bait to choose to put on your hook is the bait that

the fish you most want to catch will most want to eat. Some fish are omnivorous and will eat a whole range of baits. The dogfish is a prime example of such a survivor fish. It will adapt to any circumstances and have a go at digesting practically any sort of food, from a mouthful of decomposing shark to a single cockle. Mullet are the opposite. They're obsessive in their finickiness and won't even consider a mouthful unless it meets their anorexic criteria exactly.

In turn, some anglers are obsessive about their bait too. Really serious beach anglers who fish in competitions will spend hours on bait acquiring and bait storing. You can, if you want, dig your own lugworms and ragworms and collect your own peeler crabs. But most anglers, myself included, are handicapped by time and sloth and would rather buy bait when we need it. However, there is a limit to the range of good baits you can buy. Most ordinary seaside tackle shops will sell frozen squid, frozen mackerel (usually whole, sometimes whole but headless, and occasionally in fillets), live lugworms and live ragworms. Some may also stock frozen sand eels and possibly frozen peeler crabs.

If I'm off on a boat fishing trip, I'll normally grab a small block of frozen squid and a couple of quids' worth of ragworms. The squid is a great all-round bait and the ragworm will always work on pouting, plaice, whiting and black bream. In the summer, I wouldn't bother about buying any mackerel because I'd assume we would be able to catch some on feathers fairly easily and we could use the fresh mackerel, filleted and cut into slices, as bait. In the winter, I might buy a couple of frozen mackerel too (or better still, take a couple from my freezer – if I've been wise enough to lay some down for the lean times).

If I'm going shore fishing I would take some squid and some ragworms, possibly a frozen mackerel, but I'd also have a forage around, looking for fresh mussels and limpets when I arrived at my chosen destination, if there were suitable rocks and crevices to be searched.

Time and time again fish will gleefully prove anglers wrong by sticking up two stubby fingers (or fins) every time we think we've made a new angling rule. So, don't expect what a fish eats to be what you think it should eat; they'll trip you up as often as they can. But, as a rough rule of thumb, the adjacent chart indicates the baits that consistently work best for the species you're most likely to encounter.

Bait for sea fishing

Key: ● = Best   ○ = Might get lucky

	SQUID STRIP	WHOLE SQUID	MACKEREL STRIP	WHOLE MACKEREL	SAND EEL	LIMPET/MUSSEL	PEELER CRAB	LUGWORM/RAGWORM	BREAD
MACKEREL	●		●		●	○	○	○	
DOGFISH	●	●	●		●	○	●	●	
POUTING	●	○	●		●	○	●	●	
POLLACK	●	●	●	●	●		●	●	
COD	●	●	●	●	●	○		●	
WHITING	●		●		○	○	●	●	
GARFISH	●		●		●				
RED GURNARD	●		●		●	○	○	●	
BLACK BREAM	●		●			○	○	○	●
PLAICE	●		○		●	●	●	●	
SEA BASS	○	●	○	●	●		●	●	
DAB & FLOUNDER	○		○		○	○	●	●	
HORSE MACKEREL	●		●		●	○	○	●	
HERRING	●		●		○				
SQUID				●	●				
SLOB TROUT								●	○
GREY MULLET								●	●

Key: ● = Best   ○ = Might get lucky

ENCORNET
DE CALIFORNIE
GRADER CONGELÉ

Squid

Squid is one of the most versatile baits you can use. Nearly all of the fish mentioned in this book will wrap their gums around a mouthful of squid if given half a chance.

Squid is very convenient to use because it freezes and keeps well. You can even refreeze it (once or twice at the most) if you don't use it all on a fishing session. You can buy squid from tackle shops in frozen 5lb lumps, or in smaller bagged portions, which contain just a handful of individual squid.

Bait squid are usually about 4–8 inches long, but sometimes you can buy much smaller squid, often known as Japonica, which are only an inch or two long at the most and can be used whole.

The larger squid can be used whole too, if you're targeting large-mouthed fish, like bass. In fact, a whole squid, or even two, threaded on a large 4/0 hook or on a 4/0 pennel rig (see p.167), is a very popular bait for bass, fished off a beach, close in, just behind the surf breaking line. This approach works especially well just after stormy weather, when bass will come in close under the cover of murky water looking for food that's been scoured out by the storm waves.

A squid head and tentacles are terrific bait too; good for bream, pouting and gurnard. The head and tentacle cluster have a thick, almost cartilaginous texture, which will stay on the hook well, through several casts.

The classic way to fish squid is with the mantle (the white bell-shaped body) cut into cigarette-sized strips. These work best when they're very lightly hooked, just through one end, so they can flutter and flap in the current in an enticing and irresistible way. The fact that squid is so white means that it shows up well in the water too. Cuttlefish strips, and even whole small cuttlefish, can be used in exactly the same way as squid.

Lugworms

Lugworms are dug by bait diggers from sandy and muddy beaches when the tide is at its lowest point. You can dig your own lug if you like, but it's a back-breaking and often fruitless, frustrating business. Having said that, the few times I have successfully dug my own marine worm bait, each worm in the bait box has felt like a major achievement. And subsequently it is hook-mounted and used with great care and expectation. But for simplicity's sake, to begin with, just buy your lugworms from a tackle shop.

Normally, lug are sold either by number or by weight. A dozen lug is plenty to get you started. Lug are traditionally sold in a folded newspaper package and if you don't use them all in one session, they'll keep for a few days, wrapped in damp newspaper, stored in the fridge. They work best for cod, bass, flounder, dabs and whiting when fished on a fine-wire Aberdeen hook.

There's a knack to threading lug on to a hook. Start by inserting the hook point in the centre of the bulbous head end, then try to slide the worm all the way up the hook shank and push an inch of the worm over the knot. Don't squeeze the lug too hard with your thumb and forefinger as you thread it, or else you'll get showered with lug juice and your bait will end up looking shrivelled and anorexic.

Ragworms

Treat ragworms the same as lugworms; keep them in the fridge wrapped in wet newspaper. There are king rags (very big ones), ordinary rag, white rag (very rare and sought by serious competition anglers) and even farmed rag (some purists baulk at ragworm farmed in the hot-water outflow of power stations, but in truth, any rag is worth a try if you can get hold of it without having to re-mortgage your house).

Like lug, you should thread them on a thin wire hook, though rag have the added frisson of possessing a pair of clamp-like pincers in their mouth parts. Getting a nip from these hairy, wiggly critters as you're trying to slide a hook down their throat can really make you jump and even squeal like a schoolgirl at a Jonas Brothers gig. Which all adds to the fun of a day out fishing.

An inch or two of ragworm used on the tip of a Mepps No. 5 spinner (see pp.138–40) sometimes works a treat for harbour mullet too.

Sand eels

Live sand eels are a bass's favourite food, but they're often very difficult to find for sale in tackle shops, and are even harder to keep alive. They require a large bucket of sea water with a bubbling battery-operated aerator device to provide a constant stream of oxygen to keep them alive. And even then, with oxygen bubbles and fresh sea water, they'll still die with alarming and disturbing regularity.

Packs of frozen sand eels are the alternative. They never seem to work quite as well as live eels, but if the fish are hungry and you're in the right place at the right time, they're the next best thing.

There is more than one way to hook a live sand eel. Different anglers will swear by different methods and the bigger-sized eels (sand eels can vary from 3–10 inches in length) might require a different technique from the smaller ones. What you're trying to achieve is a position for your hook that is unobtrusive enough to allow the (live) sand eel to swim as freely and as unhindered as possible. You also want to avoid sticking your hook through a part of your sand eel which will kill it. If you've gone to all the trouble of finding and storing live sand eels then you want them to stay alive on your hook as long as possible.

The two simplest methods to hook a live sand eel are either through the tip of its beak-like mouth, from under its chin and up through the top of its nose, or alternatively sideways, from one side of the head through to the other, just in front of the sand eel's eyes.

You can hook a dead sand eel in exactly the same way, but most anglers prefer to stick the hook right through the eyes on a dead sand eel so the curve of the hook is threaded through both bony eye sockets.

With a very big sand eel, whether it's alive or dead, it's better to thread the hook down through its mouth and out through one side of its gills, then nick the point of the hook in and out through the flesh an inch below its head and pull the line taut so the hook shank lies flat and straight, up through its gill and mouth. This method holds a big eel more securely, which reduces the chance of it being accidentally pulled off. It also sets the point of the hook further down the sand eel's body, which means there's a better chance of a big attacking fish being hooked.

Limpets

If you're fishing off rocks or a rocky beach, then limpets are always likely to be close at hand. Take a blunt knife or screwdriver along with you and use it to lever them off a rock, then scoop the foot and flesh out of the shell. The foot is very rubbery, like thick squid, and it will stay on the hook for ages. It always feels good to me to be using fresh bait from the location in which I'm fishing, but sadly limpet is not every species' favourite lunch.

Mussels

Fresh mussels, teased off rocks or harbour pilings, are soft, juicy and laced with pungent attractants. Many more species will make an effort to eat fresh mussel than they would fresh limpet. The only trouble with de-shelled fresh mussel is that it's so soft and succulent, it's very difficult to keep on a hook unless it's been lashed on with a foot or two of bait elastic. It's well worth a try though, as some fish, such as plaice, will sell their souls for a mouthful of fresh mussel. It will also get nibbled off a hook by small-mouthed scavengers like crabs faster than you can blink.

Mackerel

Fresh or frozen mackerel is one of the best baits to use. For most of the fish featured in this book it works most effectively in small strips cut from a medium-sized fish fillet. A whole fillet, fished 'flapper' style (with the central spine removed so the two fillets flap in the current), works well for large flat fish and for rays, conger eel and tope. A mackerel head, cut off at an angle with some of its guts still attached, is cracking bait for a large bass.

Although mackerel is a bait much loved by many fish, it's also the bait that is all too often badly presented. Mackerel works well because it's oily, and gives off lots of exciting smells, as well as having a flash of iridescent skin to attract sight feeders. However, if you simply stick a fat, misshapen lump on your hook, it won't attract anything except a brain-dead, half-starved dogfish, or crabs.

The best bait is one that hangs delicately and enticingly from the hook and can flutter in a natural fashion in the current. Size isn't nearly as important as presentation. Ideally, your mackerel strip bait should look like the one shown below.

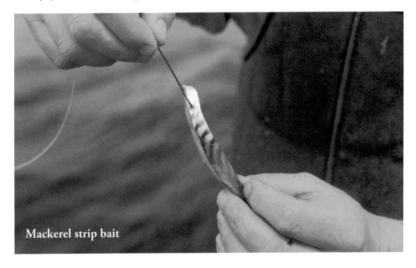

Mackerel strip bait

Peeler crab

This is the name given to a common shore crab when it's about to moult its shell, which it does once a year between early May and late June. The crabs are filled with yellow body fluid and have soft, squidgy internal organs at this point, which makes them irresistible to cod, bass, smoothhounds and dogfish, to name but a few.

You can collect your own live peeler crabs, especially at the higher reaches of the tide around muddy estuaries, though they are tricky to catch. Peelers that are just about to shed their shells are the best. To identify a peeler, look for cracking between the top shell and the leg sockets. To check, remove the tiny pointed end of one leg; if a perfectly formed leg is revealed, rather than just white sinew, you have a peeler.

Peelers will stay alive in the fridge for several days and peeler aficionados often hold them there until they're at their peak. Collecting your own bait is undoubtedly satisfying, but peeler 'farming' in your fridge might feel like a step too far.

If you do get hold of a peeler or two, remove the soft shell before you either lash it to a hook with bait elastic (see p.131) or cut it in half, remove the legs and carefully 'weave' your hook through the leg sockets.

Bread

Bread is only really used for catching grey mullet. It can either be fished under a sensitive float (see p.165), pinched on to the hook, or else squeezed on to a hook and ledgered in one lump on the harbour bed. This is usually presented amongst a 'carpet' of ripped-up tiny pieces of bread, laid out to act as ground bait, to attract a cruising mullet's attention. The worst cotton-woolly white sliced bread works best.

Fishing Skills

There are a few things you can do beforehand to prepare for the day you first go down to the sea, armed and dangerous, such as practising tying essential knots, and unpacking a rig and working out how to attach it to your line.

You can't practise killing a fish, or releasing a fish, but you can take yourself down to the local park or football field with your rod and reel to practise casting – carefully. Instead of flinging a lump of lead around your local park, try attaching a small rubber super-ball to your line, either by drilling a hole through it or taping your line to it with duck tape. Or else use a rubber fish lure with the hook snipped off, or a Toby spoon lure with the treble hook removed for safety.

Obviously you'll need to watch out for runners, dog walkers, cyclists and any other park users. When I started out, I spent hours practising like this, casting with a fly rod or even practising with a beachcaster rod and a tricky multiplier reel. At times, I may have looked like a bit of a twonk, but it made all the difference to my fishing when I eventually got to the water's edge.

Assembling a rig

A rig can be location-specific; a pier rig is a tackle set-up which works well when fished from a pier, for example. A rig can also be technique-specific; a float rig is a set-up of line, hooks, weight and float that allows you to float-fish. A rig could also be species-specific. A bream rig might vary slightly from a whiting rig in its construction or choice of hook size, even though they're both used in roughly the same location, fishing the same technique.

There are hundreds of different rigs. Proficient, experienced anglers take great pride in inventing new ones and customising existing ones. But there are only a handful that you really need to know about.

Shop-bought rigs

Before going into the individual rigs, a quick word about shop-bought ones. Serious, experienced anglers will shake their heads and make tut-tutting noises at the mention of shop-bought rigs. In their opinion, such things are expensive, badly made, and an unnecessary luxury, only indulged in by those with more money than sense. Taking this kind of stance is fine if you know how to tie knots and are confident about what you're hoping to achieve.

Personally, I believe you should never be embarrassed about buying a rig from a shop. Tackle dealers will love you, and you'll be able to get your bait wet quickly instead of fumbling around, all fingers and thumbs, for half an hour before your terminal tackle ever makes a splash. Even purist home-rig-building, experienced sea anglers would agree that you can't catch fish if your bait isn't in the water.

Paternoster rig

The paternoster rig, also known as the 'pier rig', 'bream rig' and 'boat rig', includes one, two or three hooks suspended above the weight. In other words, when the weight is on the seabed and the line above it is held tight, your baited hooks, spaced 12–18 inches apart, hang off the side of the main line on their own individual branches, known as 'snoods'. These snoods should flutter around in the current, presenting your hook baits in a visible position just above the seabed where bottom-feeding fish will easily notice them.

The paternoster rig can be fished from the shore too, as long as the ground you're fishing over isn't too snaggy with rocks. A two- or three-hook paternoster fished from the shore is good for flat fish as the shallow angle of the line will position the baits on or near the seabed.

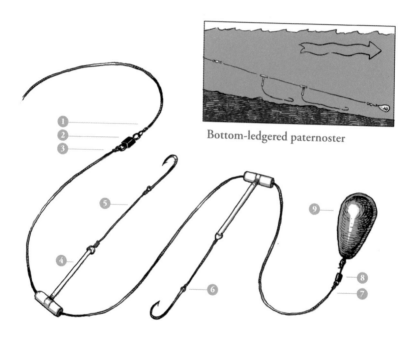

Bottom-ledgered paternoster

1. Half-blood knot
2. Swivel
3. Half-blood knot
4. Boom
5. Hook link
6. Half-blood knot
7. Half-blood knot
8. Clip swivel
9. Bomb weight

Running ledger rig

In angling speak, a ledgered bait is a bait that is located on the seabed by the use of a lead weight. And, just to make life more confusing, a 'running ledger' is often used from a drifting boat, where the bait is not resting on the seabed, but is bouncing along the seabed, or is even held, suspended a couple of feet above the seabed. So in fact it's not really a 'ledgered' rig but a moving one.

The 'running' part refers to the fact that the reel line, if pulled from the hook end, will 'run' through the weight. So, if a fish grabs the hook, it can run with it for a few feet before it feels the strain of the rod bending. The weight isn't fixed to the line, so when a fish pulls the hook it doesn't initially feel any resistance of the weight which might make it suspicious and cause it to drop the bait. Of all rigs, this is the easiest to make.

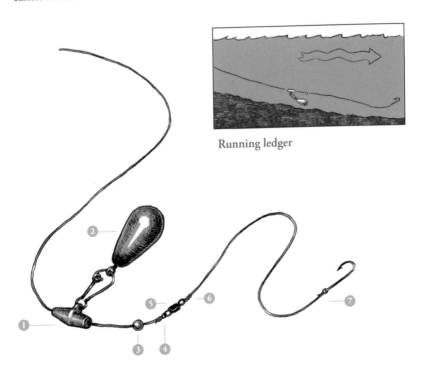

Running ledger

1. Zip slider
2. Bomb weight
3. Bead
4. Half-blood knot
5. Swivel
6. Half-blood knot
7. Half-blood knot

Float rig

Use a float rig when you want to keep your bait clear of a snaggy or weedy seabed, or if you want to present your bait near the surface of the water rather than near the seabed, because that's where the fish you're targeting are feeding. A float rig allows you to present a small bait high in the water, where certain species like garfish, mackerel and mullet prefer to feed.

If you're fishing from rocks over snaggy ground, a float rig suspends your bait out of reach of the snags, allowing it to travel naturally with the current, presenting the bait in clear water just above the rocks or weed where fish should be lurking and waiting to ambush their food.

The key to keeping your bait at exactly the right depth under the water is the stop knot (see pp.169–70), which stops your float from sliding up the line.

Float-suspended rig

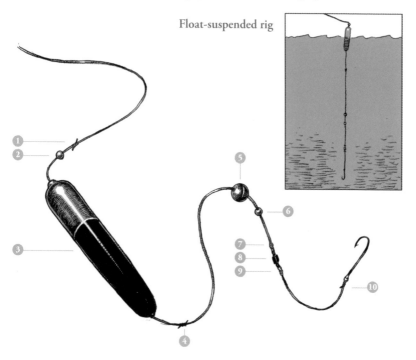

① Stop knot		⑥ Bead	
② Bead		⑦ Half-blood knot	
③ Float		⑧ Swivel	
④ Stop knot		⑨ Half-blood knot	
⑤ Drilled bullet weight		⑩ Half-blood knot	

Spinner/wedge/spoon rig

You can just tie a clip swivel to the end of your line and clip on a spinner, wedge or spoon (see pp.138–41). This will work adequately most of the time. You can add an extra swivel 2 or 3 feet above the clip swivel, to give the line greater protection from becoming twisted by the spinner's revolving action. This is most valuable if you're fishing in very strong currents, or across the mouth of an estuary with a strong outgoing or incoming tide. It also provides a little extra weight, which might help with casting, especially if you're using a very lightweight spinner, or else you're fighting against a facing wind. In extreme windy cases, or where you want your spinner to work deeper in the water, you can add a 'drilled bullet' lead weight, which you thread on to the line above the swivel (towards the reel). This provides extra overall weight which makes casting easier.

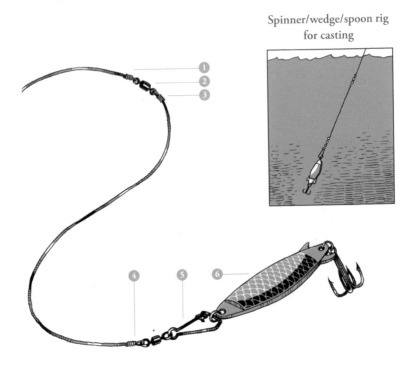

Spinner/wedge/spoon rig
for casting

1. Half-blood knot
2. Swivel
3. Half-blood knot
4. Half-blood knot
5. Clip swivel
6. Toby spoon

Pennel rig

The pennel rig performs two functions. Firstly, by putting two hooks on one line, it allows you to mount a much bigger bait than you could safely secure on a single hook. Secondly, it increases your chances of hooking into a fish, because it gives you two potential hook points on the same bait.

If you fish with a big bait that only has one hook threaded through it, at the head end, then you can easily miss a fish if it bites at the tail end. The fish gets a mouthful of your bait for free, and you, most likely, get *half* a bait back, but no fish. With a pennel rig your hooks are spread across a big bait, making both ends deadly.

To tie a pennel rig, thread the line through the eye of the upper hook, wind the line five times or more around the shank, and tie it to the eye of the second hook, so the first hook can be easily moved up or down the line. This increases or shrinks the distance between the two hooks, in order to match the size of the bait you're using.

Not only is the pennel rig useful for beach or boat fishing, presenting big baits on your line, and holding them in place whilst casting, but the rig also has its uses when squid fishing. If you use a pennel rig – either with two single hooks as shown, or even with a small treble hook at the terminal end – you're simply increasing the number of sharp, barbed hook points that stick out of your bait.

When fishing for squid, the more potentially snaggy points you have protruding from your bait fish, the better. If you're squidding with pennel-mounted small dead pouting, or poor-cod baits, the squid will explore them with his tentacles as he tries to drag the dead fish to his beaky mouth. The more hooks there are, the more chance you have of snagging him on the barbed points as you reel him up to the surface.

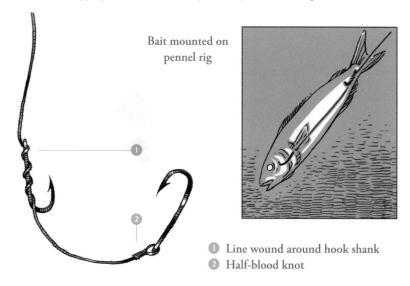

Bait mounted on
pennel rig

❶ Line wound around hook shank
❷ Half-blood knot

Tying basic knots

Knots are things of deep joy. We can so easily freewheel through life never needing to know more than a simple granny knot, but once you learn a couple of new ones, suddenly you'll find all manner of uses for them. Being able to tie knots is unexpected food for the soul. Whilst you don't need to know many knots for fishing, the half-blood knot is the essential one for attaching your hook to your line.

Whenever I'm learning a new knot, I take a spool of line, a big blunted hook and I practise while I'm watching telly. Tying and re-tying the same knot when you're only half paying attention to what you're doing is the best way to learn, because your hands get used to the movements and you learn them by heart and by touch. This way you can avoid the sad and soggy business of referring to a book when you're on a boat or the beach.

Half-blood knot

This is the most used knot in angling. It works well with monofilament but not with braid.

- Put your line through the eye of the hook, pull 3 inches through and hold it parallel to the reel line (step 1).
- Twist the short end around the reel line five or six times while holding the hook or swivel eye still (steps 2–4). After the last turn, bend the end down and poke it through the hole created in the line just above the eye (step 5).
- Pull it through slowly, while easing the knot down towards the eye. Lick the knot as you're doing this. Saliva helps lubricate the line, which stops it kinking or causing too much friction on the line as you pull the knot into place.
- Pinch the knot down with your fingernails as you give the last tug to the reel line to make it sit hard on top of the eye.
- With a pair of kitchen scissors, trim off the tag end close to the knot (step 6).

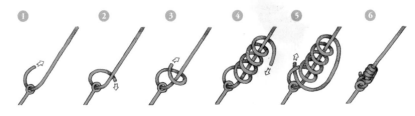

Tucked half-blood knot

This is the cautious belt-and-braces version of the half-blood knot. In an ordinary half-blood, when you pull the tag end of the line tight, you then simply trim it off. But in the tucked half-blood you make the knot even more safe by tucking the tag end through the topmost loop (steps 4–5). The extra tuck through the loop created at the top of the twists, furthest away from the eye, secures the knot better than the simple half-blood.

I'm ashamed to admit that I never tuck my half-bloods. I know I should, but I'm too impatient to do that extra bit of work and I don't like the look or feel of a tucked one, especially on monofilament line of 15lb or more. It's a bit like choosing whether to tuck your shirt into your trousers and cinch it with your belt, or let it hang loose and risk having a draught up your tummy. I'm not proud of it, but I have to confess, I don't give a tuck.

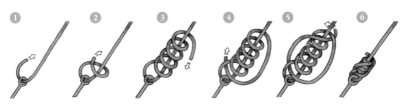

Stop knot

A stop knot is a handy knot to know because you can use it whenever you want to create a 'stop', either for a sliding boom or, most commonly, when you're float-fishing and want to create a stop to mark the furthest point the float will slide up the line, which sets the predetermined depth that your bait will be suspended beneath the float.

There are two types of stop knot that I normally use: one is a cheaty, quick one, which can be tied as a simple overhand knot with a thinnish rubber band. The elasticity helps it grip the line, just enough to hold the bead and float in position, but, at the same time, not so much that it can't be easily repositioned if you want to alter the depth.

The other stop knot can be tied with ordinary monofilament line (usually it's better to use slightly thicker line than the reel line, but it's not essential). Or there's some lovely rubbery string stuff sold in tackle shops for rig-building called Powergum, which makes a quick and efficient stop knot that can be repositioned up and down the line easily to alter the depth of your float-suspended bait. (See diagram and tying instructions overleaf.)

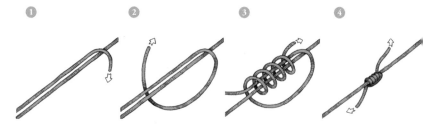

1   **2**   **3**   **4**

Monofilament line or Powergum stop knot
- Decide where you want the knot to sit on the main line.
- Cut a length of about 4 or 5 inches of monofilament or Powergum, just enough to comfortably tie an overhand knot with. Lay it alongside your main line and then curve your stop knot line into a loop (steps 1–2).
- Hold the loop against the main line and pass one end of your line through the loop four or five times (step 3).
- Now moisten the loops with spit and pull both ends of your line apart so that the loops begin to close into each other (step 4). The harder you pull the tighter the coils of the loop will grip around the main line.
- Trim off the excess monofilament or Powergum from the ends, leaving the tight knot with ½ inch at either end.
- Whenever you want to slide this knot up or down your main line, use a lick of spit to lubricate the knot and the line.

Elastic band method
- Snip through an elastic band (I love those red ones postmen leave) so that it becomes an elastic length rather than a circular band.
- Determine the position you want it to sit on your main line above the float and simply tie it around your line in an overhand granny knot.
- Pull it tight and trim off the excess rubber. It should still move up and down the line if you want to shift it. But so long as you pulled it tight enough in the first place, because of the friction of the grippy nature of the rubber, it will hold itself on the line.

Casting shock leader knot
This is a very important knot. It is used to join your reel line of 10–15lb to your shock leader of 30–40lb. Because of the job that it does – providing a small, neat join between two vastly different diameter lines undergoing the enormous strain and shock of casting several ounces of lead with great force from a standing start – it needs to be tied efficiently. This is definitely a knot to practise at home until you've really got the hang of it.

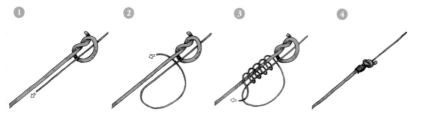

- First, tie a simple overhand knot at the end of the shock leader. Then thread the reel line through the centre of the leader knot, pull 4 or 5 inches through and lie it alongside the leader (step 1).
- Now twist the reel line loosely five or six turns around the leader (steps 2–3).
- On the last turn, fold it back towards the overhand knot and tuck it under the first twist, between the reel line and the leader.
- Pull the tag end of the reel line gently as you work the tightening twists down towards the overhand leader knot. The trick is to lubricate these turns with spit and help them to sit evenly butting up against the leader knot.
- Pull the leader knot tight with your teeth and make sure the turns are neat together and snug against the leader knot (step 4).
- Test it by pulling hard on both ends of line leader and reel.

Braid knot

There are some very complicated braid knots. Generally, it's much more difficult to tie knots in braid than monofilament because braid is very thin and shiny (see p.121). A lot of conventional monofilament knots just won't work on braid. They slip open. The easiest braid knot to tie, and to remember, is also called the Uni-Knot.

- Pass the end of the line through the eye and pull it back up the line for a few inches and then bend it back to form a loop (step 1).
- Wrap the end around the two parallel lines, passing it through the loop.
- Do this five times or more (step 2) and then pull the tag end away from the hook until the knot tightens (steps 3–4).
- Then lubricate the knot with spit and push it down the line to the eye.
- Pull the reel line firmly to seat it neatly above the eye.

Casting

The most casting you are ever going to do is when you're spinning or mackerel feathering from the beach. That's because both these techniques involve fishing a moving lure through shallow water, and in order to stop your lure or feathers from sinking and snagging on the bottom, you have to keep reeling in, which of course means you then have to keep casting out again, over and over. This may seem like I'm stating the obvious, but it's a valid point, especially if you're new to casting, or you're fishing with a child, or someone else who's new to casting. Don't attempt a technique that revolves around being able to cast passably well when you're not sure if you can.

Easier venues for first-timers or children, or those unsure of their casting ability, are piers, harbours and rock marks, where you can float-fish for mackerel, for instance. Float fishing from a pier involves occasional casting. After one cast, you could leave your bait suspended beneath your float, dangling seductively in the current, for half an hour or more before you have to reel in and cast again. On the other hand, while feathering off the beach, you'll probably have to cast every 2 minutes.

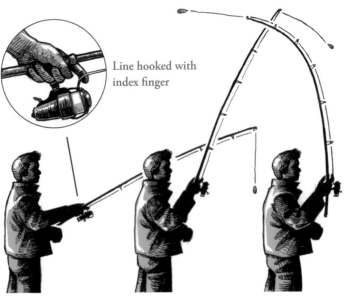

Line hooked with index finger

Start position: rod at 10 o'clock, dangle of 18 inches. Cock back bale arm

Raise rod sharply up to vertical

Stop at 12 o'clock...

How to cast a spinning rod

Hold the rod in your dominant hand, fingers either side of the reel seat stem. Your forefinger and middle finger should be on the up side, your two other fingers on the down side.

- Point the rod upwards at 10 or 11 o'clock.
- Next, reel in your casting weight until it hangs between 18 inches and 2 feet below your rod tip (this is the optimum casting 'drop').
- Wind the reel, so that the roller on the bale arm of the reel is in the nearest position to your index finger.
- Now, you should be able to extend your index finger and hook it around the line.
- Take the weight of the line in the crease of your finger beneath your fingertip, and hold it, while you cock the bale arm back using your other hand. You don't need to trap the line between your finger and the rod shaft. You just need to hold it far enough back towards the reel handle so that line doesn't fall from the spool. You're simply putting enough tension on the line to keep it on the spool.
- Now, with the rod still pointing at 10 or 11 o'clock, make like you're a crane, swivelling your waist, so the rod goes from being just in front of you to being

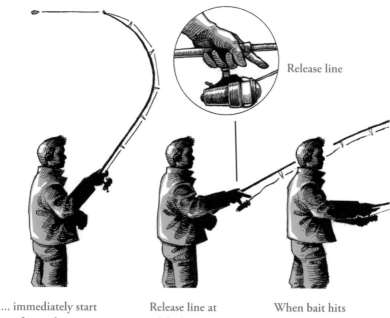

Release line

... immediately start forward cast

Release line at 10 o'clock position

When bait hits water, wind reel to release bale arm

just behind you. So you're turning your body, not your feet, half a turn. During this action, your other hand should be on the lowest point of the rod butt.

- Now, the rod is still at 10 o'clock position, only it is pointing behind you. So if you imagine you're the centre of a clock face, it's now at 2 o'clock.
- At this stage, you need to turn your wrist over, so you rotate the rod through 180°. Basically, instead of the reel and rings pointing towards the ground, you need to turn your wrist so they point to the sky.
- Now, you are locked and loaded and ready to cast.
- Keep your rod behind you, but turn your head to face forward – towards where you want to cast. Imagine the rod as a big flexible pole, which you're going to whip forward by pulling your bottom hand towards you as your reel hand punches out, thus whipping the tip of the rod forward.
- As you bring the rod over, snapping it forward, stop as you reach the 10 o'clock position. At the same moment, straighten your index finger to release the line. The rod tip shouldn't come lower down than 9 o'clock in the forward cast.

Describing it makes it sound more complicated than it really is. I'd urge you to practise. Spend time casting away from the waterside and try to 'feel' when it goes right. Casting is like hitting a tennis ball on the 'sweet spot' of a racquet, or a rounders ball with the meat of the bat. You soon *know* when you've done it right.

Striking and playing a fish

'Striking' is what you do when you feel a bite on your bait. But 'striking' is a misleading word really, because it suggests a lot of action – a big violent, powerful movement, which it actually shouldn't be. More people lose fish by striking too hard, or else by reeling in too fast and too furiously, than at any other time. (Losing a fish whilst you're reeling is known as 'bumping' a fish.)

A strike should be when you raise the rod tip quickly and firmly, but not with a heavy hand, from your normal fishing position of rod at 9 o'clock, up to 11 o'clock.

Most of the time, you don't really need to 'strike' so much as simply raise the rod tip up to the 11 o'clock position and start reeling, steadily. When the rod is starting to bend in the 11 o'clock position it's already exerting pressure on the line, pulling it taut and pulling the hook point upwards.

The only time you need to strike with any real determination is when you're bottom-fishing for black bream or possibly float-fishing for garfish. But even then, with the black bream's nibbly bites and the garfish's sometimes tentative takes, you may well find that it doesn't work, even though you strike fast and positively. In these circumstances, you'll often find that reverting to not striking, instead simply raising the rod tip and reeling steadily, solves, or at least reduces, the problem of missed fish.

Releasing your catch

Some fish, like wrasse, rockling and poor cod, are simply not worth eating. Wrasse are too bony, with flesh like soggy cotton wool, and rockling and poor cod are just too small and fiddly to process. So if you catch any of these, they need to be handled and released carefully in order to survive. Similarly, bass less than 40cm from the tip of their nose to the fork of their tail are classed as undersized, and you are required by law to release them. Also, you'll most probably catch various individual fish, which, although they belong to an edible species, are just too small for the pot, and so deserve a second chance to return to the sea to do some more growing.

Releasing fish is something you need to do carefully and quickly. The more you handle a fish, either to admire it, or possibly photograph it, the more chance there is that you'll damage it. With smooth small-scaled fish like mackerel, even the merest contact with dry hands will remove and abrade enough scales to cause it potentially terminal damage. So, if you can, always dampen your hands before you handle a fish that you intend to release. If it's too slippery to hold, you can use a damp cloth to help, but the cloth must be properly wet. A dry cloth will rasp off scales even quicker than dry hands.

If you're on a boat, or fishing from rocks or a harbour wall where you have water directly beneath you, it is possible to release small fish without even touching them, simply by taking the shaft of the hook in your thumb and forefinger, turning it upside down, so the point is aiming downwards, and then giving a firm flick with your wrist. The fish should just fall off and land back in the sea.

Some fish, the wrasse family in particular, are very sensitive to the change in pressure when they're being reeled up from any depth over 20 feet. They're normally bottom-dwelling fish, and the pressure change that occurs when they are reeled to the surface causes them to 'blow'. This means their insides, including their swim bladder, may start to protrude out from their anal vent. Their eyes will also expand and pop out (see pouting, pp.53–5), as the air pockets in them rapidly expand as they ascend.

In this 'blown' state, they're unable to swim back down to the seabed and are best killed and saved for the stock pot. But, with a little experience, you'll soon get to recognise when you've hooked a wrasse. Wrasse bites and subsequent fights are very distinctive: a sharp rattle at your rod tip, followed by a short-lived, but very aggressive head-shaking fight. So, if you think you've hooked a wrasse from a boat, or a pier, or any depth of 20 feet or more, simply reel it in very slowly. I know it's hard if you're excited and just want to see what it is that's fallen for your bait, but, if they're raised from the seabed super-slow, they often won't 'blow'. Without bug eyes and protruding swim bladders they can be released successfully, to continue their important, rudely interrupted wrasse work.

If you reel in a fish on the beach, and you instantly know that you want to release it, then don't bump it up the pebbles to your tackle box. Leave it in the shallows while you locate your pliers.

Try to keep any fish at least semi-submerged at all times. And never just 'throw' a fish back. Hold it in a few inches of water for half a minute, if you can, to give it enough time to re-orientate itself and get water flowing through its gills. This movement of water through its gills will give it a boost of oxygen, which should be enough to make it flick its tail and depart.

Killing fish

The best way to kill any of the fish you're likely to catch is with a swift, sharp crack to the head with a blunt instrument. Take something suitable with you – don't rely on finding something deadly at the scene of your catch. Scrabbling around trying to find the 'right' stone on the beach, or a heavy enough screwdriver on a boat, or a lump of driftwood at your rock perch, causes delay.

Delaying a fish's death while you hunt for a murder weapon is cruel; it prolongs the suffering of the fish out of water, and it is also detrimental to the quality of the flesh that you want to eat. A fish, lying alive on the deck of a boat or on sand, shingle, rock or the timbers of a pier, is going to flap and struggle, and beat its tail madly, trying to escape the only way it knows how: by attempting to swim. In so doing, it will thrash itself against a hard surface which will bruise its flesh, causing its naturally firm, muscular texture to deteriorate, and creating tissue damage that will potentially attract bacteria and make it go off quicker.

Allowing a fish to flap longer than necessary also depletes the energy reserves within the muscle tissue. These energy reserves would otherwise be kept within the dead muscle and would be used to maintain the cellular metabolism, which slows the onset of rigor mortis and subsequent spoiling.

In other words, if you do not have a rolling pin, priest, hammer handle, long-handled screwdriver or a shop-bought bosher at the ready, you will unduly extend the fish's death throes and deliver yourself a substandard portion of prime fish flesh for supper.

To kill a fish, the method is quite simple. You need to hold the fish down on a stable, flat surface. Keep a clean rag or tea towel handy to hold it firmly while you hit it hard on the head, at least twice. This should kill the fish instantly. Don't mush the head in some crazed axe-murderer-like frenzy – you want to be able to use the head later for fish stock. But don't be too soft either. You need to hit it hard enough and accurately enough – across the back of its head – to bring its life and its flapping to a swift and decisive end.

Killing mackerel

Instead of banging mackerel across the head, I prefer to snap their necks. Killing them by this method does two jobs at once. It kills the fish and it bleeds them in one swift movement.

The easiest and most effective way to simultaneously kill and bleed a mackerel is to put a thumb or forefinger in its mouth, and bend its head back acutely, at 90° to the body. This snaps the neck and at the same time rips the gills out from where they're attached under the throat. This kills the fish instantly and the rip in the gills starts the bleeding process all in one move.

This method is used with mackerel and not with other fish because, quite often, you'll catch a few mackerel in quick succession if you luck into a shoal. In order to continue fishing and maximise on the brief bright window of non-stop rod-bending action, you need to employ a method that kills and bleeds quickly, leaving your hands free to fish on. Mackerel are also suitable for killing this way because they tend to be small fish, and their necks are easily broken. They don't have sharp spines or razor-sharp gill covers, like bass or bream do, and they don't have thick, fat unbreakable necks like cod or pollack.

Snapping mackerel necks and tearing their gills upwards will not be everyone's cup of tea. And it may well just be too brutal for the gently acclimatising novice fisher. If so, then don't do it. Stick to a simple bosh with a blunt instrument. Just kill your fish quickly and efficiently in the manner that suits you best and feels right.

Bleeding fish

I don't promote 'bleeding out' as an alternative to boshing it on the head. Death by bleeding out, which involves cutting an artery and allowing the fish to die through loss of blood and lack of oxygen, is too cruel for me. And the fish will still flap and thrash in the process of its death throes, causing bruising to the flesh.

I do like to bleed my fish, but I advocate cracking them on the head first. A fish's heart will continue to beat for 2–3 minutes after it's been killed by a blow to the head. So a crack over the head will stop the flapping, and because the heart continues pumping, the majority of blood can still be flushed from the flesh.

The reason I advocate bleeding any fish is because when a fish is killed and it isn't bled, its blood remains within its circulatory system throughout its flesh. This blood will coagulate, creating weblike patterns and streaks through any fillets you might later cut from the bones. This blood doesn't really do any damage or affect the flavour of the fish too much, but without it, the flesh is cleaner-looking and potentially it will keep much longer because it's the blood in the flesh that will normally first attract bacteria.

Bleeding a fish

In order to bleed a fish, I crack it over the head and then, as soon as I can, I snip through one set of bright-red gills with a pair of tough kitchen scissors. A major artery runs through the fish's gills. So by snipping all the way through a gill arc, just after the fish has been dealt a firm blow, this will open up the artery to allow the thick crimson arterial blood to be evacuated from the body by the still-beating heart.

Chilling fish

The single biggest threat to your life-enhancing fish supper is heat. Most people like going fishing in good weather, yet excessive warmth will spoil your fish stunningly quickly. One of the worst things you can do with your lovely fresh-caught fish – and I've seen it often – is to stick it in a black dustbin liner bag and leave it in the sun.

It helps to take the fish's guts out before you chill it (see gutting, pp.183–6). It's not essential and it might not be possible, depending how and where you're fishing, but a fish's gut, incorporating decomposing food, will attract bacteria quickly. So, the sooner you can safely remove the fish's insides, the better. But even if you can't gut the fish soon after catching, you should still chill it whole and gut it later.

To keep your fish in peak condition, put it in an insulated cool box with some ice or a few freezer blocks. I usually carry my lunch in the same box and hopefully swap lunch for the raw materials of my fish supper during the day. It doesn't have to be a big cool box. I'll often take a 2-litre cool box with one ice block, and sometimes I'll even fillet fish as I catch them, in order to keep them compact and well chilled.

Fish Preparation Skills

I've always really enjoyed the job of preparing fish. It's a hard thing to explain. You either want to take fish apart, or you don't. From the very first mackerel I ever caught, aged five, I had an urge to take its insides out. Now, transforming a fish – fresh from the sea – into a perfect glistening portion of flesh, begging to be cooked, gives me great satisfaction. Fish cookbooks often suggest you 'ask your fishmonger' to do every task from filleting to cutlet cutting, but thankfully, as a fisherman, you don't have that luxury. Instead you have a duty to learn how to get the fresh, flapping thing you've caught into the best possible shape for cooking.

How you treat the fish you've landed and how you then transport them to where you intend to cook them is an issue of respect. Nothing depresses me more than seeing anglers leaving a charter fishing boat with a black dustbin liner bag, bulging with once beautiful wild fish, which I know will already be halfway to becoming slime-covered mush, fit only for cat food or fertiliser.

To enjoy the great fish you catch – and get the best out of them in terms of flavour and texture – you need to understand the basics of good fish prep.

Once a fish is dead, your first two concerns should be scales and guts. Only certain fish will need descaling (such as bass, black bream, pollack and grey mullet, which have very heavy scales), and it's easiest to descale them before they've been gutted, when the belly cavity is still intact. (However, don't fret if you haven't time to descale the fish before you gut them; it's still feasible, just not quite so easy.)

It is most crucial to gut your fish as soon as possible after catching it, because the longer you leave the guts inside, the more potential 'harm' they'll do, as they start to attract bacteria, which break down and spoil the fish flesh from the inside. Ideally the fish should be gutted within an hour or two of being caught, and the belly cavity filled with ice.

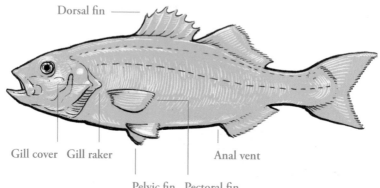

Dorsal fin

Gill cover   Gill raker

Anal vent

Pelvic fin   Pectoral fin

Scaling

Obviously, you remove scales from a fish because you don't want to eat them. But, if you are going to skin a fish, it's easier to do so with the scales intact, as the skin can become very thin and papery once the scales are removed.

I also leave the scales on my fish if I'm intending to barbecue it, as they help to protect the flesh from the intense heat of the coals, keeping the flesh more moist.

Removing scales from fish is easy. You just rub them up the wrong way, from tail to head – opposite to the way they overlap and lie. You can use the back of the blade of a short, strong knife. Some proper fishing knives sold in tackle shops come with a special crinkle-cut pattern along the back of the blade designed for descaling fish. Alternatively you can use a shop-bought descaler. These come in a variety of forms and shapes; my favourite are the plastic-handled descalers with a semi-circle loop of crinkle-edged steel mounted off the top of the handle. You can even make your own descaler by nailing upturned bottle caps on a handle-sized lump of wood.

It's best to descale a fish in running water or in a bucket of water, to stop the scales flying around. Work from tail to head and rinse the fish when you've finished.

The fish you really need to descale are black bream, bass and grey mullet, unless you're going to barbecue them.

The fish that could do with a quick rub over with a descaler but aren't heavily scaled are pollack, pouting, garfish, whiting and herring.

Flat fish, dogfish, squid and mackerel don't require any descaling.

Gutting

Gutting is the messiest prep stage, so even if you intend to take your fish home with you (rather than cook them on the beach), it's a job which is better done at sea or at the water's edge. Fish guts and scales are best returned to the sea, because they provide food for crabs and gulls and other carrion-feeding fish. Fish heads and frames are best taken home, for making stock. However, do be sensible and sensitive about where you deposit any fish guts. Don't just dump them into a harbour at slack tide or leave them on the beach in the belief that the next high tide will take them away, causing a sight and stench for other beach users to endure in the meantime.

The two main types – or rather shapes – of fish that you're most likely to catch are 'round' fish, or, if you're very lucky, 'flat' fish. These are fishmongering terms, which describe the shape of the fish's cross section. A mackerel sliced in half would be round. A plaice would be flat. Arguably, there are a few oval-shaped fish too, such as black bream, John Dory and trigger fish, but these can be treated in the same way as round fish.

Gutting a round fish

To gut a round fish, such as a mackerel, pouting, pollack or even a dogfish, the best place to start is by inserting the tip of your knife into its anal vent. This is the downstream end of the digestive tract, so if you cut upwards from here, slicing the belly wide open, you'll expose all of the fish's stomach and internal organs.

The safest way to do this is with the fish lying on its side, tail towards you. Place the flat of your hand on its upper side to hold it steady and insert your knife at about a 5 o'clock angle, with the tip pointing headwards and the cutting edge facing outwards (pic 1), in order to slice the belly from the inside out, as you work the knife upwards (pic 2).

Then stick your thumb inside the belly to hold the belly flaps open while you scoop out the contents (pic 3). Drag as much as you can out, either with your free hand or with the blade of the knife (pic 4). Some of the insides will naturally still be attached to the gullet or throat end, and if they won't come away with a pull, snip them off with kitchen scissors or carefully cut with the knife (pic 5) as close to the head as you can manage.

If you're intending to cut the fillets off your round fish, then you need to do no more; if, however, you're going to cook it 'on the bone' you might want to finish cleaning out all the internal residue. What's left in the belly cavity can be scraped out with the blade of your knife (pic 6). You'll find a line of dark goo, held beneath a thin membrane along the underside of the spine where the two ribcages meet. This looks like thick coagulated blood, and functions as the fish's kidney. It's preferable to remove this, because when cooked it can give the flesh that presses against it a slightly bitter, coppery flavour. And, for the more visually sensitive diner, it can appear somewhat off-putting.

The best way to remove the kidney blood is to puncture the membrane with the tip of your blade, slice it from one end to the other, and scrape the dark goo out with the blade, or with the back of your thumbnail, while holding it under a trickling tap or rinsing it in a bucket of water. It's not the end of the world if you don't remove this blood line. And often, if I'm cleaning and cooking a whole bunch of mackerel on a barbie, I'll leave it in and simply pack the belly cavity with a few extra bay leaves to cover the blood line and counteract any possible bitterness.

First and foremost, the importance of gutting round fish is to rid the tasty muscle flesh of possible contamination by the digestive juices, or decomposing food that is inside the fish's belly. Organs such as heart, liver, sex organs, roe or milt (sperm) can be left in and cause no detriment to the fish flavour whatsoever.

Personally, I love most fish roe and I'm quite happy to pick around any amount of liver and heart. Again, the fastidiousness of your gutting, beyond taking out the digestive essentials, is really down to personal taste.

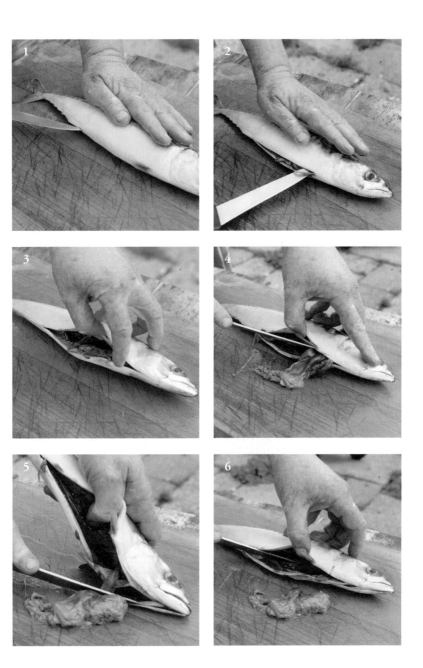

Gutting a flat fish

Unlike a round fish, the innards on a flattie are found quite close to the mouth. To locate the internal cavity, feel around the flat fish's collar. To one side of the head you'll feel firm neck muscle, on the other a soft, squidgy spot. Sometimes, especially on good-sized plaice, you'll sense what feels like a collection of stones just under the skin. These are seed mussel shells, sometimes crunched up, often whole, which the plaice has sucked up, cramming his belly pouch-style, for consumption later.

To eviscerate a flat fish, stab the point of a sharp knife into the flesh on his upper side, just below the single pectoral fin (pic 1). Once you've cut through the skin and the knife point is in the belly cavity, cut sideways for 2 inches, following the curve of the skeleton (pic 2), creating an incision just big enough to poke a finger and thumb inside (pic 3) and extract the digestive tract and contents of the stomach (pic 4). The liver and roe can be left in, and the heart too, if you like, or you can pull everything out, finishing off with a good rinse to remove any digestive goo.

Removing gills

The only time I bother to remove the gills from a fish is if I'm going to cook it whole with its head on. Gills extract oxygen from the water and transfer it to the lungs. They also work as a filtration system, trapping potentially harmful bacteria, which can accelerate the decay of a fish once it's dead. They are one of those indicators that you should look at when you're assessing how fresh a fish is, for example if it's lying on a fishmonger's slab and you're considering buying it for your tea.

Bright red gills, on which the gill strands stand apart and proud – like the teeth on a comb – is the sign of a truly fresh fish. Grey, gummy, gooey, sticky gills suggest that a fish is past its best.

It's easy to remove gills. Lift the gill plate (pic 1) and snip through either end of the gill arch with kitchen scissors (pic 2). Cut around the base of the gills where they attach to the body (pic 3) and pull them away with your fingers (pic 4).

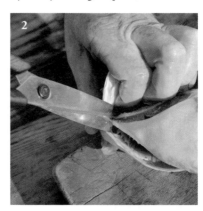

Filleting

Filleting is a wonderful skill to learn. It's not nearly as easy as it looks when someone professional is doing it. Nor is it as difficult as it first seems. It's a case of learning the basic principles and then letting yourself loose on some fish. Don't rely on the fish you catch. Buy some unfilleted fish from the fishmonger, such as mackerel, dabs or whiting. Once mastered, it's an impressive and useful skill for life.

Filleting a round fish

There are many ways to fillet a round fish and this is my preferred method. The approach is simple, repetitive and designed to remove maximum flesh. If you feel you've left more flesh on the bone than you wanted to, don't be scared to take your knife and carve any little clinging morsels off. So what if they're not attached to the rest of the fillet? They'll still taste the same. And don't forget the stock pot (see pp.218–20) is the absolver of all filleting sins and oversights.

First cut off your fish's head with an angled cut that goes from behind its head, at the top of its neck, across and under its pectoral fin, on the lower side of the fin, in a line that cuts through the top of its belly. Use a strong-bladed knife for this. If it's a big fish with a thick spine, a flexible filleting knife won't be man enough and will quickly blunt or get chipped if regularly used to chomp through the bone. Once the head is off you should have a fish body with a 45° angled slice where its head once was (pic 1). The apex of this angle is where your first fillet-cutting slice starts.

Keep your fish flat on the board at all times. Angle your knife across the sharp corner of the sliced neck and start with the heel of your blade, where the blade joins the handle (pic 2). Position the blade just above the central line of the spine, aiming to cut the uppermost side of the dorsal fin. The first cut should ideally penetrate about ½–¾ inch into the flesh, about two-thirds of the way down towards the tail.

Stop two-thirds of the way down and then, keeping the blade level and parallel to the board, work the point across the fish, over the top side of the central spine until it pokes out of the belly side of the fish. Now your knife should look like its stabbed right through the fish (pic 3). From here, work it down in one, two, or three (fewer is better) cuts towards the tail, with the cutting edge of the blade angled very slightly downwards so that it effectively 'shaves' the flesh off the central bone.

Once you've cut right down to the tail, move back up to the start of the first cut at the sharp pointed neck angle. Using the thumb on the hand that isn't holding the knife, fold open the cut to expose the spine. Your next cut wants to deepen the first cut, keeping the knife at a gentle angle, but striving to cut to where the ribcage starts to bulge upwards (pic 4).

Then, work this cut down to the point where the free-flapping tail section starts (pic 5). If your knife is sharp, these cuts shouldn't require much pressure. Don't force

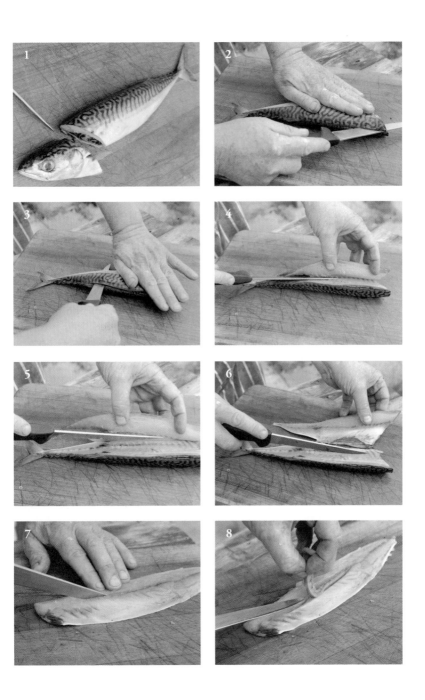

your way through the flesh. Use smooth, gliding, angled cuts and try to use all of your blade, not just the tip.

Your next cut should be your last. It should take you up over the curve of the ribcage and down across the belly cavity (pic 6, p.189).

To remove the other fillet, flip your fish over. This time start with the head towards you and commence your first cut at the tail end, working up to the head end. Then stab through to release the tail fillet. And finally, use two or three more cuts to remove the whole fillet, working across the ribcage and down across the belly as you did on the first side. Trim each fillet of excess skin.

Now you need to remove the line of small bones from the centre of each fillet. To do this, cut lengthwise down each side of the line of bones (pic 7, p.189). Angle these cuts into a V-shaped trough. Then, using the tip of the knife, carefully lift out the central line of flesh containing the bones (pic 8, p.189).

Filleting a flat fish

Filleting a flat fish is more straightforward than filleting a round fish, mainly because the anatomy and skeleton are easier to navigate. The body is squashed flat, so it's a two-dimensional puzzle, rather than a three-dimensional one. Because of this, there's no central ribcage and belly cavity to have to cut around.

Having said that, it's only really worth filleting flat fish that are at least 1½–2lb. Smaller flat fish are best cooked whole in the oven as the flesh depth is very shallow and filleting is simply too wasteful. Eating flat fish 'off the bone' is so easy anyway; a grilled or baked flat fish sits flat on your plate, you peel back the skin and eat the flesh off one side of the bone, and then flip it over and eat the other side.

But should you find yourself happily in possession of a nice plump plaice or an enormous flounder that you want to fillet, what you need to do first (after removing its guts) is lay it white side down, on your board.

Your first cuts should be a V shape of two cuts, which run down either side of the head. From the bottom of this V, the next cut, turning your V shape into a Y shape (pic 1), should run right down the centre of the fish from neck to tail, dividing the upper side into two sections. Each of these sections are known as quarter fillets, because there's two on each side, and four in total. Your downward cuts will always cut down to the wide flat skeleton – so you can't cut too deep. The bone is your end point, so just cut to the bone and stop.

The central cut will fall to one side or the other side of a small central ridge of bone, which is where the spines of the skeleton meet in the middle. For the next cut, angle the tip of the blade under one side or the other (pic 2) – I usually go for the right-hand side (because I'm right-handed) – and just ease the tip ½ inch under the flesh. Then with the tip scraping flat against the skeleton, cut all the way down the length of the fish.

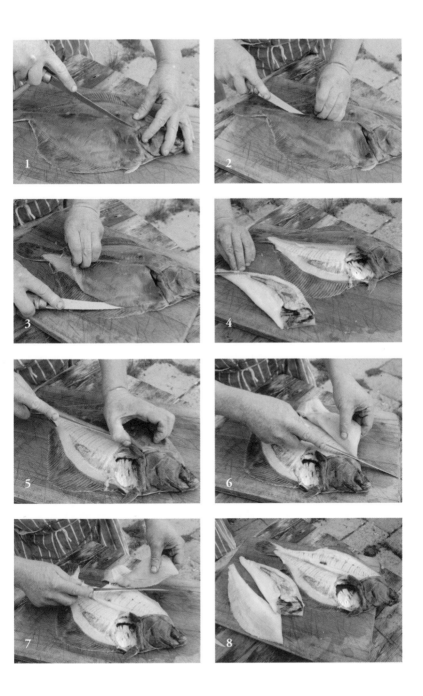

The next cut is exploratory, allowing you to slide the blade of your flexible filleting knife deeper under the flesh, with the blade always scraping against the fan of the skeleton bones. Effectively you're working from the centre of the fish outwards, scraping the fan of the bones, until you reach the outer edge and are able to cut out through the skin that meets the outer ribbon of fins (pic 3, p.191). Then remove the quarter fillet (pic 4, p.191).

Do this on both sides, left and right (pics 5, 6, 7 and 8 p.191), then flip your fish over. Now you need to repeat the process on the white side. This will give you four almost identical fillets, with the two upper ones being slightly thicker with brown skin, and the underside ones thinner but with white succulent skin. Trim the fillets with your knife or scissors to remove any fin spines or tag ends of skin.

Skinning

Skinning a fillet always looks an impressive feat, but it is much easier to achieve than you might think. One thing worth bearing in mind though, as I mentioned in the scaling section, is that it is more difficult to skin the fillet from a fish that has been rigorously descaled than one which still has its scales intact, or one that has only had a quick swipe or two to clean the worst of the moulting scales. This is because rigorous descaling can leave the skin paper thin and therefore more likely to tear under the knife.

The mechanics of skinning a fillet are easy. Lay the fillet flesh side up, skin side down on a clean flat board. Start from the tail end. If the tail's very slippy to hold with your fingertips, a pinch of salt will give you a little more grip.

Hold the tip of the tail firmly down on the board and cut down through the flesh with your blade angled slightly towards the head end. Stop when you reach the flesh side of the skin.

Now, turn your blade so that it's steeply angled towards the head, just as though you were trying to shave the flesh side of the skin. Hold the tail down and move the blade ½ inch, to start the cut. Then stop. Don't move the blade any more. Instead, wriggle the tail with your other hand and pull it towards you, away from the blade. This is where that sprinkle of salt helps with the gripping.

The trick is to move the tail, not the blade. The blade is held rigid while you wiggle and pull the tail towards you. You'll soon see how easy it comes. Keep the downward pressure on the blade constant, but not too hard. Make sure the fillet always remains flat to the board as you tug and wiggle the tail.

How to skin a dogfish

Skinning a dogfish is a skill really worth learning. Dogfish are as easy to catch as mackerel, but nowhere near as easy to cook and eat, because their delicious flesh comes wrapped in a thick, sandpaper-like skin, which appears to have been fitted with super-glue. There is, however, a surprising amount of satisfaction to be had from mastering the technique of peeling off this skin, as well as the more obvious culinary reward. Of the various techniques I've come across, I use the following two methods (both illustrated), as I've found them to be the most reliable.

Skinning with pliers

This involves removing the two fins on the fish's back, with deep horizontal slices, to cut the fin off right down to its root (pic 2), then doing the same on the underside with the tail fin.

Now slice beneath the anal fins, cutting across the fish, deep into the belly cavity, and then turn and slide the knife upwards towards the head, slicing away the whole belly and stomach walls (pic 3). This can be done in one long deep cut, which removes everything abdominal, right up to the underside muscular column of the main body.

Remove all guts and stomach flaps right up to the throat, before turning the knife from the horizontal to the vertical and cutting downwards under the throat, right through to the back of the neck, removing the head. This leaves a headless, finless, gutless dogfish, with a tail (pic 4).

Then, using just the point of the knife, while holding the fish by the tail, head end pointing away, cut a skin-deep line between the holes where the fins once were. This cut ideally penetrates just below the skin, and continues in a line from tail right up to decapitated neck, all along the back (pic 5).

Then flip it over and make the same longitudinal cut along the underside of the tail, joining up the oval-shaped hole (where the fin was) to the gaping hole that was the belly. So the skin is now divided longitudinally in two halves. The thinking is that to strip the skin from two halves, one down each side, is easier than trying to take it off in one sock-like piece.

In order to start peeling the skin, you need to cut a ring around the tail, just to the depth of the skin, and then lift up a tab-end of skin, big enough to clamp with the jaw of the pliers. Each half of the skin is then stripped off, using pliers, from tail to head (pic 6).

With practice it's possible to peel the skin off in two long pulls, one on each side (pic 7). And when that happens, believe me, it is a supremely satisfying feeling. Not only is the sensation of one long peeling action very pleasing, but to see the perfect skinned eminently edible-looking flesh appear from under what previously looked

like something you'd use to sand your kitchen floorboards is like discovering the Holy Grail over and over again. But do be prepared for it to go wrong. Often the pliers keep slipping and failing to hold on to the slimy tag and you'll find the skin coming off in tiny pieces, which makes the process slow and irritating.

A few tips:

- Dogfish skin is phenomenally tough stuff and will dull the edge of a sharp knife in seconds, so avoid using one of your best knives. My favourite dogfish knife is a cheap nylon-handled meat boning knife, which will stand a lot of abuse, yet can still be re-sharpened easily.
- Use square-nosed rather than thin-nosed pliers.
- Use a tea towel or rag to hold the pliers and even a thick rubber glove to hold the tail. The skin is very abrasive and unless you've got hands like a pot hauler, you'll easily rasp some skin off. It's very painful and takes ages to heal!
- When you manage to get a good grip, pull like you mean it. Try to get a whole side off in one rip – restarting on a half-stripped side is never easy.
- When I was first shown this technique I was told that it could be done without pliers, using just your teeth instead. Which of course I had to try. And yes, it can be done, but I grazed the tip of my nose and my top lip in the process, and really wouldn't recommend it, unless you're desert-island desperate.

Skinning by hand

This method doesn't require pliers, but a glove or a rag, to protect your skin and give you some grip, won't go amiss.

As for the previous technique, cut off the back fins right down to the root, so that it leaves two oval-shaped holes in the back, exposing white flesh.

Flip the fish over, slice off the fins under the tail and the anal fins too, but don't slice off the belly. Instead, cut the belly open all the way up from the anal vent to the throat, like you would to gut any round fish (pic 1). But continue the cut right up through the chin, effectively splitting the underside of the head wide open in two. Then remove all the guts (pic 2).

With the fish on its back and the flaps of the belly opened out, make two cuts at 45° between the head and the pectoral fins at either side of the head (pic 3), almost through to the spine. This creates two flaps, incorporating the fins, which can now be used as 'handles' (pic 4).

With one foot planted firmly on the dogfish's head, and what's left of its chin facing downwards, it's now possible to peel each flap around towards the spinal column, ripping the skin at the neck. Then, holding the head and body down with your foot while pulling the two flaps together (pic 5), it's possible to remove the entire skin in one long pull (pic 6). Finally, cut off the head (pic 7).

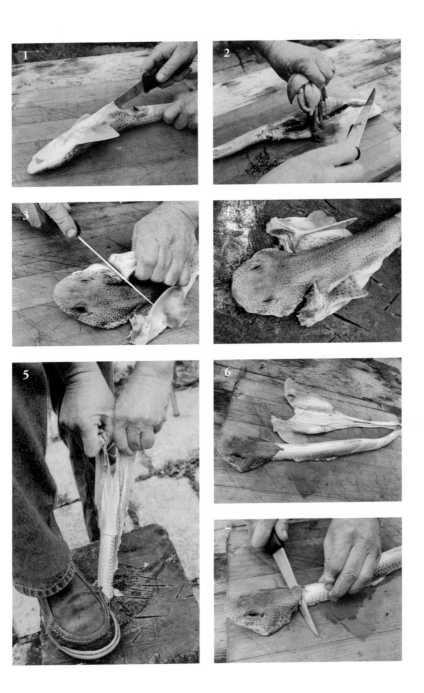

How to prepare squid

Freshly caught squid are very satisfying to prepare. They're just so weirdly beautiful, and when you've successfully deconstructed one, they're so simple to cook. All the flesh is more or less the same thickness; there are no bones or cartilage or skin to bother fussy fish diners and the bulk of the flesh is easy to cut into any shape or size you desire, from butterflied curls, to rings, chunks or cubes. And then there's those delicious tentacles, which in my house we all fight over.

Squid is best cleaned under a slowly running tap. First rinse it to remove any ink, which might have leaked out of the ink sac (pic 1).

Then pull the head (hopefully still attached to the guts) out of the mantle (body). To do this, hold the mantle in one hand, take the head and tentacles in the other and pull. Be careful though, if the head feels like it might part company with the guts, leaving them inside, then you need to slide your fingers into the head end of the mantle and tease the guts out (pic 2), by detaching them from their fixings on the inside. This might take a couple of attempts. Just keep gently tugging at the head until you can feel the insides come free. Then draw the whole lot out.

Lay the head and tentacles and guts on your board and cut through the head just on the tentacle side of the eyes (pic 3). This should leave you with a bunch of tentacles just joined together at their base, which you keep, and a set of eyes attached to a set of guts, which you throw away.

Now rinse out the mantle; put your fingers in and give it a slosh around. Then turn it tail end up and grab both fins in one hand (pic 4). Depending on how big your squid is and how thick its covering membrane of stretchy translucent skin is, this will either simply peel off in your fingers, or else need to be poked and prised off by puncturing the membrane skin with your fingernail (pic 5). Having watched Korean and Chinese women clean squid, I realise a tough fingernail is a most useful tool for removing the membrane from fins, mantle and tentacles. Sadly, I bite mine.

Once you've teased as much membrane off as you can, or can be bothered to, you're good to go – and start cooking. However, if you're going to cook squid rings, one last thing you can do is invert the mantle. Turn it inside out by pushing the tail up through the neck, just like you're turning a sock inside out. Use a wooden spoon handle to push the thin end in and up.

The reason for doing this is twofold: first it allows you to clean out all the residue of the guts which might cling to the interior of the mantle, without having to cut it open. And secondly, because it reverses the stresses of the cylindrical wall of the mantle, it means you'll always cook perfectly round squid rings, rather than floppy figure-of-eight ones, which you get if you don't flip the mantle inside out. It's not compulsory, but it's a neat little trick that never fails to impress! The mantle and fins are now ready to cut as required and cook with the tentacles (pic 6).

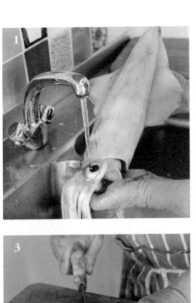

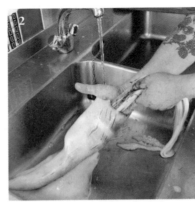

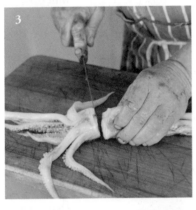

Cooking Fish

I rarely do anything fancy or faffy with the fish I catch,

mainly because I usually cook it and eat it while it's still blisteringly fresh. Good fresh fish requires very little cooking and very little in the way of extra flavouring. If it's straight from the sea, then it has the freshness and sea flavour that I most want to taste. I rarely use specific recipes – and I never use complicated ones. Instead, I just choose the cooking method that I think will best suit the particular bit of fish I've caught, and the people I'll be serving it to. Added ingredients, seasonings, accompaniments and quantities are all very flexible.

So, in this section, I am simply giving you my general fish cooking techniques. You will find some recipes here, but they're intended as guides, rather than prescriptions. I'm hoping that you'll customise them to your heart's content. The way to become a happy fish cook is to feel your way along, turning the basic principles of good fish cookery into your own recipes. If you still feel like getting stuck into some slightly more structured fish cookery, Hugh and I have included a whole range of tried and trusted recipes in *The River Cottage Fish Book*.

There are really no absolute 'wrongs' in my approach to fish cookery, other than overcooking, which is the most common mistake. But this is easily avoided. Just remember that fish flesh is very different from animal flesh. This is largely to do with the creatures' different lifestyles.

Fundamentally, fish don't have to deal with gravity. They don't have to bear their own weight all day long whilst trying to keep themselves propped up on two or four legs. Instead they have the luxury of water to take their body weight and so their muscles don't need to be encased in membranes and lashed into place by sinews and ligaments. Fish muscle is much softer, held together in precisely stacked flakes and bound only by layers of collagen, a substance which dissipates at very low cooking temperatures. In short, fish flesh is much more delicate than meat or fowl, and it's a lot quicker to cook.

The adjacent table matches different species with different cooking techniques, simply as a quick reference guide. As always, these are suggestions, not rules. Just because flounder sashimi hasn't lit my fire, it doesn't mean it won't work for you.

Sea fish cooking techniques

	SASHIMI	SUSHI	CEVICHE	STOCK	BARBECUE	PAN-FRY	DEEP-FRY	WHOLE FRY	GRILL	BAKE	FOIL PARCEL	STEAM
MACKEREL	✓	✓			✓	✓			✓	✓		
DOGFISH				✓		✓	✓		✓	✓	✓	
POUTING	✓	✓	✓	✓		✓	✓		✓	✓	✓	
POLLACK	✓	✓	✓	✓		✓	✓		✓	✓	✓	
COD				✓		✓	✓		✓	✓		
WHITING	✓	✓		✓		✓	✓			✓	✓	✓
GARFISH						✓	✓	✓	✓	✓		
RED GURNARD	✓	✓	✓	✓	✓	✓	✓	✓	✓	✓	✓	✓
BLACK BREAM	✓	✓	✓	✓	✓	✓	✓		✓	✓	✓	✓
PLAICE				✓		✓			✓	✓	✓	
SEA BASS	✓	✓	✓	✓	✓	✓			✓	✓	✓	✓
DAB & FLOUNDER				✓		✓	✓		✓	✓		
HORSE MACKEREL	✓	✓			✓	✓			✓	✓		
HERRING					✓	✓	✓		✓	✓		
SQUID					✓	✓	✓	✓	✓	✓		
SLOB TROUT	✓	✓	✓	✓	✓	✓			✓	✓	✓	✓
GREY MULLET				✓		✓	✓		✓	✓	✓	✓

✓ = recommended cooking technique

Herbs, seasonings and accompaniments

I tend to ignore the kind of rules about seasoning and saucing fish that have been handed down over the years from various messiahs of fish cookery. The selection of herbs and seasonings that I would deem essential to fish cooking is pretty small, mostly interchangeable, and can be used with all the species I cover, although some flavourings do work better with certain styles of cooking.

One notion I am inclined to agree with is that oily fish are best served with a piquant, citric accompaniment such as salsa verde, while white fish works better with a creamy sauce, like tartare. Citrus flavours cut the richness of oily fish flesh perfectly, of course, but then a fried mackerel fillet smeared with a dollop of creamy horseradish sauce is equally gorgeous, which totally contradicts the theory. So, rather than offer you rules about cooking and serving fish, I'm simply going to list my most-used herbs and seasonings and favourite fishy accompaniments:

My essential seasonings are:

- Sea salt
- Black pepper
- Garlic
- Chilli
- Wasabi
- Horseradish
- Chives
- Thyme
- Bay leaves
- Parsley
- Lemons
- Limes
- Capers
- Crabapple juice (verjuice)
- Vinegar

My top accompaniments for fish are:

Homemade mayonnaise

Put 2 egg yolks in a bowl with a scrap of crushed garlic, some salt and pepper, a pinch of caster sugar, 1 tsp Dijon mustard and 1 tbsp cider vinegar or lemon juice. Whisk lightly together. In a jug, combine 150ml rapeseed or light olive oil with 150ml sunflower oil. Whisk the oils very gradually into the yolk mixture: start with just a few drops, then slowly increase to a thin stream. Keep whisking all the time so the oil is emulsified into the yolks. (You can also do this in a blender.) When you've added all the oil, adjust the seasoning with more salt, pepper, sugar and lemon juice if necessary. Cover and chill until needed. Keep in the fridge for up to 3 days.

Garlic mayonnaise

Follow the mayonnaise method above, but start off with more garlic – 2 fat cloves, crushed to a paste with a little salt, should be about right.

Tartare sauce

Combine 2 heaped tbsp good mayonnaise with a roughly chopped hard-boiled egg, 1 tbsp chopped parsley, 1–2 tsp chopped dill or chives (optional), 2 tsp chopped capers and 2–3 chopped gherkins or cornichons. Add a squeeze of lemon juice to taste and season with pepper, and salt if necessary.

Salsa verde

Roughly chop the leaves from a large bunch of flat-leaf parsley, along with a few basil and/or mint leaves if you have any. Add 1 finely chopped garlic clove, a few capers and a couple of anchovy fillets if you like. Chop it all together until quite fine. Scrape into a bowl and mix in 1 tsp hot mustard, a good squeeze of lemon juice and enough olive oil to make a thick paste. Season with salt, pepper and more lemon juice if needed. Use within a day or two.

Dill hollandaise

Put 1 egg yolk in a bowl. Melt 150g unsalted butter (or salted if that's all you have), cool until tepid, then trickle it gently on to the egg yolk, whisking all the time, until it's all incorporated. Add 2 tbsp finely chopped dill, a squeeze of lemon juice, and some salt and pepper. Serve straight away.

Sweet chilli dipping sauce

In a small saucepan, combine 3 tbsp redcurrant (or other fruit) jelly or jam with 1 tbsp cider or white wine vinegar, a dash of soy sauce, 1 finely chopped hot chilli and 1 finely chopped garlic clove. Heat gently, stirring, until the jelly melts, then simmer gently for a couple of minutes. Season with pepper. Leave to cool. Before serving, whisk in a little warm water and/or more soy sauce to give a runny dipping consistency. Once cooled, this will keep in the fridge for at least a week.

Soy and garlic dipping sauce

Combine 3 tbsp soy sauce with a good dash of Worcestershire sauce, 3 tbsp mirin or rice wine (or cider or apple juice), 3 tbsp water, 1 finely chopped red chilli, 1 finely chopped garlic clove, 1–2 tsp grated fresh root ginger and a good pinch of sugar. Bring to a simmer and cook gently for 2–3 minutes. Let cool slightly. Serve warm as a dipping sauce for deep-fried battered fish or tempura, or dribble over mackerel fillets or any sort of hot fish. Once cooled, it'll keep in the fridge for a week or so.

Horseradish sauce

Combine about 100g grated fresh horseradish root with 2 tsp cider or white wine vinegar, 1 tsp hot mustard and a pinch of sugar. Leave for 10 minutes, then stir in 125g crème fraîche or soured cream. Season with salt and pepper. Use within 24 hours.

Raw fish: sashimi and sushi

Sashimi

Sashimi is simply bite-sized pieces of raw fish fillet served with a splash of soy sauce and a smidgen of wasabi (or strong English mustard). In some respects, it's the most basic way to prepare fish because it doesn't involve any cooking. But that doesn't mean it's the easiest. Sashimi involves a certain knowledge of fish anatomy and skill with a filleting knife. It's arguably a lot easier to throw a whole head-on guts-out mackerel on a barbecue than to render it into elegant, boneless, uncooked bite-sized pieces.

I'd seriously encourage you to try sashimi-making. There's something undeniably exciting about eating fresh raw fish – especially fish you've caught yourself. There's no more natural way to enjoy freshly caught fish. A little goes a long way though – you don't necessarily need a whole plateful of it. Every summer, when the black bream fishing starts, I like to ceremonially carve a few slices of a just-caught new-season bream on my boat. It's a joyous nature-taster of things to come.

'On board' sashimi should be a quite rough and ready affair, where you simply slice off some nice boneless strips of just-caught fish flesh and dunk them in soy and wasabi. But an accidental mouthful of bone or gristle can be off-putting, so it's worth developing a bit of a technique of your own, a little sashimi routine that'll help you to deliver a clean, boneless, scale-free result. In my experience that means at least keeping a spare cutting board just for sashimi, and pack some kitchen roll or a clean tea towel too.

You could argue that cramming the finer points of sashimi preparation into a few paragraphs is impossible. Sushi and sashimi chefs train for up to 10 years to perfect the deep and complex art of raw fish preparation and presentation. So, this is a cheat's guide, but it's all you'll need – as long as you're working with top-notch super-fresh fish, and you don't mind fairly free-form presentation…

There are a few bits of essential equipment:
- A sharp filleting knife (and a sharpener)
- A clean tea towel and/or some kitchen roll
- Two chopping boards. Whether you're making sashimi on board a boat, on the shore, or in your kitchen, your gutting and filleting board must be different from your sashimi cutting board. Cross-contamination from one to the other can ruin the end result. Doesn't hurt to have a separate knife too.
- A bowl of clean tap water or sea water: this helps to freshen a piece of fish while you prepare it, and is essential for dipping your knife into between cuts. The dipping of the blade stops the steel 'dragging' in the flesh. If you use a sticky knife, it can create furry, broken edges in even the firmest fish flesh, rather than clean, crisp-cut lines.

Things to remember:

- Keep cutting surfaces clean.
- Keep your cutting knife very sharp and very clean. Dip it frequently in clean water as you work.
- Accept that there will be some waste when you fillet. Sashimi-cutting requires you to jettison anything that might have bones or membranes (use these bits for stock). And don't use anything that has got too warm or looks unappetising.
- Try and handle the fish as little as possible. Warm hands will make the flesh soft and slimy.

My all-time favourite sashimi fish are:

- Sea bass
- Red gurnard
- Pollack
- Pouting
- Mackerel

My basic technique:

Don't descale your fish. You'll need to remove the skin and it's easier to do this with the scales on. (Descaling makes the skin thin and more likely to tear.) However, be careful not to let any scales transfer from the skin side of the fish to the flesh side.

- Working on your filleting board, gut your fish (see pp.183–5). Rinse it really well to get rid of any traces of blood, innards or scales.
- Fillet the fish as carefully as you can (see pp.188–90), then remove the skin from each fillet (see p.192).
- Pat the fillets dry with a clean cloth or kitchen paper and transfer to the clean cutting board. Trim and tidy each fillet, discarding any remaining bones and any membranes or unappetising bits. You should now have a couple of very neat and clean-looking naked fillets.
- Cut the fillets into bite-sized pieces, remembering to keep dipping your knife into clean water. It's best to work at a 45° angle to the grain of the flesh, cutting it first into thick strips, then slicing these into smaller 'bites' if necessary.
- Arrange your sashimi on a clean plate. Top each piece with a mere smear of wasabi or hot mustard, sprinkle on a few drops of good light Japanese soy sauce (such as Kikkoman), and serve immediately.

Sushi

If you can cut sashimi, the next step is to have a go at sushi. At its most basic, sushi is nothing more than a mouth-sized oval of perfect rice with a smear of wasabi and a sliver of thinly sliced good fresh fish (i.e. sashimi) draped on top (shown on p.207). Cooking, seasoning and storing the rice correctly is 95 per cent of the art of good home sushi-making. It's not difficult, nor does it require a lot of special equipment. Once cooked, the rice can be shaped by simply pressing it into balls, then flattening slightly. But, if you fancy a cheap, clever gadget, buy yourself a sushi portion press.

My favourite sushi fish are:
- Sea bass
- Red gurnard
- Pollack
- Pouting
- Black bream
- Pickled mackerel (see p.210)

Sushi rice

A failsafe recipe for cooking rice to make nigiri sushi – simple finger-shaped sushi.

Serves 6

200g sushi rice	1 tbsp caster sugar
100ml rice wine vinegar	¼ tsp fine sea salt

Rinse the rice in a sieve under cold running water until the water runs clear, then rinse it again. Drain and tip into a large saucepan. Cover with plenty of cold water. Leave to stand for half an hour, then drain, return to the pan and add fresh water to cover by an inch or two. Bring to a fast boil. Cook for 5 minutes, then turn the heat down and simmer gently for a further 15–20 minutes, until nearly all the water has been absorbed. Take off the heat, cover the pan and leave to stand for 10 minutes.

Meanwhile, put the wine vinegar, sugar and salt in a small pan and heat gently until the sugar has completely dissolved. Leave to cool. Add the mixture to the warm cooked rice, combining it well. Tip the seasoned rice on to a large tray and spread it out to help it cool. Perfectionists will also fan it at this stage. Don't refrigerate it.

To make nigiri sushi, have a small bowl of clean water to hand. Dip your fingers into it frequently as you work, to stop the rice sticking to them. Take a roughly bite-sized portion of rice (it can be still slightly warm, or completely cooled – warm is best). Roll it between your palms to form a ball. Squash it slightly and smooth and mould it with your fingers to form an even oval shape. Repeat with the rest of the rice.

Once the rice ovals are all formed and cooled, top each with a smear of wasabi or hot mustard, then a piece of sashimi (see p.207). Serve with soy sauce for dipping.

Lightly pickled mackerel

Mackerel makes great sashimi, eaten with no more than a smudge of green wasabi and a dribble of soy sauce. However, when mackerel is used to make sushi portions, it's traditionally lightly pickled first: quickly salted, then marinated in vinegar. This is because, being an oily fish, it deteriorates very quickly, and in its raw state it can be prone to parasitic worms. Hugh and I eat yards of raw mackerel every year without any problems, but then our mackerel is always fresh and straight from the sea. If yours is more than 24 hours old, or you're not quite sure how super-fresh it is, or if you just fancy a new flavour, try this quick mackerel-pickling recipe.

Makes enough for 40 sushi pieces
100g fine sea salt
4 large mackerel fillets

For the marinade
500ml rice vinegar
50ml mirin, apple juice or sweet cider
(or water with 1 tsp sugar added)
10g sea salt

Sprinkle about one-third of the fine salt over a non-metallic dish. Lay the mackerel fillets skin side down on top, without overlapping them, then sprinkle over the rest of the salt in an even layer. Leave for just 5 minutes, then turn each fillet in the salt and transfer to a bamboo basket or a plastic colander. Leave for another 10 minutes, so the salt continues to draw out the juices. Then quickly but *thoroughly* rinse each fillet in cold water and pat dry with a cloth or kitchen paper.

Mix all the marinade ingredients together and put into a non-metallic container, such as a ceramic dish, or a plastic box. Add the mackerel fillets and leave in the fridge for 1–1½ hours by which time the flesh will have turned creamy white.

Remove the fillets, shaking off the marinade, and pat them dry. Discard the marinade. Carefully peel off the papery, thin outer skin of the mackerel, from the head to the tail, leaving the iridescent pattern underneath on the fillets (but don't worry if a little of it comes away with the skin).

Lay the fillets skin side down again. Use tweezers to remove the pin bones from the lateral line along the middle of the fillet. Or you can cut each side of the line of bones and lift them out with a filleting knife (see p.190; pic 8, p189).

Your pickled mackerel is now ready to cut for sushi. Slice across each fillet at ½ inch intervals at a 45° angle, to get roughly diamond-shaped pieces. Place each one on a shaped oval of sushi rice (see pp.207 and 209) on to which you've first smeared wasabi or mustard.

Marinated fish

Marinating is an incredibly simple way to add flavour to fish. You can do it with raw fish, using a cold marinade – a technique that generally works best with white fish. Alternatively, you can bathe cooked fish in a hot marinade to get a quite different result – usually best with oily fish. There are a couple of classic dishes, both South American in origin, which make the most of these techniques and I frequently turn out a version of one or both of them at home. They share two particularly attractive characteristics: first, they can be excellent make-ahead dishes, which don't rely on split-second timing. Secondly, they're just begging to be tweaked and tinkered with, depending on the ingredients you have to hand.

Cold marinating: ceviche

Cold marinating can be as simple as tossing chopped or sliced super-fresh raw fish with a few aromatic flavourings and herbs – maybe olive oil, Tabasco, parsley, chopped red onion – and serving it up as a kind of fish 'tartare'. However, I nearly always include some citrus juice in a cold marinade and, as soon as I do that, I am entering the exciting realms of 'ceviche'.

Ceviche is a way of 'cooking' fish, but without heat. It relies, instead, on the chemical properties of citric acids. When fish is cooked in the conventional way the protein fibres, which resemble coiled springs running through the flesh, begin to unwind and straighten out. This starts to occur at about 55°C and, within a short time, the fibres will have straightened out and begun to merge and coagulate. At this point, fish is deemed to be cooked. The exact same reaction can be created by immersing fish flesh in citric acid, which in the case of ceviche means a delicious marinade of lemon, lime and orange juices. When you immerse fish flesh in these juices, there's an almost immediate visible chemical reaction. As the acid is absorbed, the translucent flesh becomes opaque and milky (just as it does when you heat it).

Ceviche celebrates the natural textures and flavours of good fresh fish, without being quite as hardcore an experience as eating sashimi or sushi. If you find totally raw Japanese-style fish preparation just too alien, but like the idea of eating fish in its natural state, ceviche is definitely worth a try. Firm white-fleshed fish, such as black bream, bass, pouting, whiting and pollack, work best. I'd certainly consider using salmon or trout too. But really oily fish like mackerel, while they can make an interesting addition, don't tend to work as a main ingredient. Ceviche is often made with a mixture of fish species but it's equally good with just one type.

You can vary the amount of time you allow the fish to marinate before you eat it. When I first started making ceviche, I would leave it for an hour at least. Over the years, my marinade time has got shorter and shorter, and quite often now I'll just prepare it and eat it straight away – especially if I've made it with some eye-wateringly fresh bass or black bream, because I can't keep my hands off it. It's actually perfectly safe to keep your marinated fish in the fridge and eat it the next day, when you'll find the texture much softer and less 'raw'. But my own preference is for a just-marinated fresh, zingy, crunchy experience.

Hot marinating: escabeche

When I find myself looking for something a little different to do with oily fish, such as mackerel, herring or garfish, and I have a little bit of time on my hands, I'll plump for the hot marinade option. While this involves cooking the fish, the final dish itself is served at room temperature. It's a great recipe for using up a glut of oily fish, and it's perfect for a large group of fish diners. Or as a tapas-style dish, served alongside other delicious fish treats.

All I do is fillet the fish then fry the fillets quickly over a fairly high heat to give them some colour on the flesh side and just a little crispy edge. I might dip the fillets in flour first too so they'll have an extra crispy coating – this crispness works well with the marinade as it soaks up the flavours a little more than the flesh alone might do. Over these cooked fillets I'll then pour a hot and fragrant marinade: a mix of, say, vinegar and apple juice, spiked with garlic, shallots, grated ginger, lemon zest and chilli. The fish will then be left to cool in its aromatic bath, and I'll serve it later with some good crusty bread to soak up the juices. A dish like this is great to make in advance because it actually improves with being chilled for a day, although I always serve it at room temperature, never cold.

What I'm describing in my ad hoc way is actually a Latin American classic called escabeche. Like ceviche, it exists in many forms, so you should feel totally at liberty to create your own version. For my money, it's a great way to use up an excess of oily fish. I'll often use it on a few skinny, sad mackerel that I've got left after a barbecue, or with the results of filleting accidents. I'll even do it with bony fish like sprats or small herring or garfish, where the bones are too tiny to remove without a full surgical team as back-up. In this case, I'll fry the fish hard, cranking the oil up a few degrees and crisping them good and proper. This way, the bones, fins and skin become crunchy, and the marinade soaks into them deliciously. The result is both soft and crisp, spicy and sour, turning something that could have been wasted fish into a sweet, tangy, crunchy delight.

My ceviche

A ceviche marinade must contain strong citric juices – lime, lemon and orange are all essential, in my view – but everything else is optional and variable. What you're after is a marinade that is bitter and acidic, but which also has sweet tones. I always add a little sugar and salt to take the edge off the acid taste. The rest is up to you. Try soft brown sugar instead of caster, try Tabasco instead of fresh chilli, add smoked paprika or a few glugs of peppery olive oil. I also love to mix in some raw salad vegetables to bulk out the mixture and give it some crunch – thinly sliced celery and onion are my favourites, but use whatever you like. I've made very good ceviche with sliced carrots. Even tomatoes can work, though I'm not a huge fan unless they're partly green and very tart and firm.

Serves 5–6

500g fish fillets (black bream, sea bass, red gurnard, pouting and pollack are ideal)
Juice of 3 limes
Juice of 2 lemons
Juice of 1 orange

1 red chilli, deseeded and chopped
1 clove garlic, peeled and crushed
1 tsp caster sugar
1 red onion, peeled and sliced
2 inner stems of celery, sliced
Salt and freshly ground black pepper

Trim your fish fillets carefully, as for sashimi (p.208). You need completely 'clean' fillets, without bones, skin, scales or membranes. Slice the fillets into pieces, about 2 inches long and at least ½ inch thick. If the pieces are too thin, they'll 'overcook' and turn mushy. Pour the lime juice over the fish and toss lightly. Limes have more acid than other citrus fruits, so adding this first kick-starts the 'cooking' process. Refrigerate or keep in a cool box while you prepare the rest of the marinade.

In a bowl, mix the lemon and orange juices with the chilli, garlic, sugar, a good pinch of salt and lots of pepper. Taste the marinade and tweak the flavours to your liking: it should be citrus-sharp, but also fragrant and with a hint of sweetness. Once you're happy, pour the marinade over the fish chunks. Add the onion and celery and mix it all together. Leave in the fridge for a minimum of 15 minutes to 'cook'. I personally wouldn't leave it longer than an hour, but you can leave it overnight if you choose.

Serve in little bowls, making sure that each has a generous portion of the marinade along with the fish and vegetables. Toasted crusty bread is a great accompaniment. When you've eaten all the fish and crunchy salad, the leftover marinade is a joy to drink. It's sour and fruity-fishy – in a good way – and truly wakes up your tongue. In Ecuador, they call these few gulps of marinade *leche de tigre* or 'tiger milk'. Mixed with a generous shot of vodka, it's a customary hangover remedy!

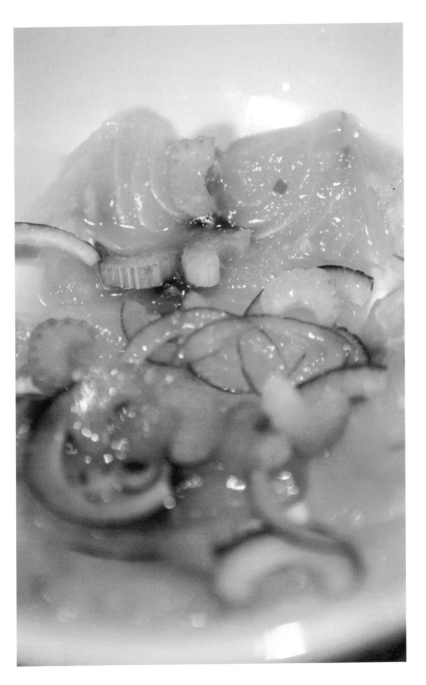

My escabeche

Try adding your own blend of flavourings to the marinade. Spices such as cumin, coriander or allspice, and aromatic herbs like thyme or marjoram all work well. Orange zest could replace the lemon. Thinly sliced onion, carrot, celery or pepper can be added too: sauté them until soft in the fish frying pan before you add the marinade liquid. It's sometimes nice to finish the dish, just before serving, with a sprinkling of a fresh herb, such as parsley or even mint. I'll also add some thinly sliced raw onion and hot chilli – and maybe even very thinly cut carrot – right at the very end. The crunch and bite of the onion and chilli set against the sweet, crunchy-coated softness of the fish fillets is enough to make you start writing sonnets.

Serves 6

Olive or rapeseed oil, for frying
12 fillets of mackerel or scad mackerel,
　garfish or herring

For the marinade
100ml cider or balsamic vinegar
200ml apple juice
1 hot red chilli, finely chopped
2 shallots or garlic cloves, peeled
　and chopped
A couple of bay leaves
Grated zest of 1 lemon
Salt and freshly ground black pepper

Heat a thin layer of oil in a non-stick frying pan over a medium-high heat. Fry the fish fillets, in batches, for a couple of minutes each side, until lightly coloured and just cooked. Transfer to a large dish in which they will fit snugly in one layer.

Combine the vinegar and apple juice and add to the frying pan with the chilli, shallots, bay leaves and lemon zest. Heat until simmering, then cook for a couple of minutes, scraping up any crispy bits from the pan as you do so. Season well with salt and pepper. Pour this hot marinade over the warm fish fillets in their dish, to cover them completely.

Leave to cool, then chill for a few hours – or up to 24 hours – before bringing back to room temperature. Serve with lots of bread for mopping up the marinade.

Fish stock

Stock is a precious thing, a commodity that opens the door to all manner of fast and flavoursome meals. It freezes well, but I'll often keep a bowl of jellied stock in the fridge for a week, where frankly it seems to improve with age. It's incredibly useful for quick fish dishes. If, for instance, I'm frying a couple of fillets, I often add half a ladleful of stock to the pan after the first few minutes of cooking. The liquid semi-poaches the fish and reduces to form a rich and tasty little 'gravy' in the pan.

I make my own fish stock because it's easy – and far better and far cheaper than any stock I could buy. I have some on the go most days, primarily so I know there'll always be plenty of tasty base for soups and risottos. Stock-making also enables me to render raw offcuts of fish edible to my dog, chickens and pigs. However, the stockpot has another purpose: it is a salve for a guilty conscience. If I've made a hash of filleting a fish, or have only used the very best bits – for sushi or sashimi – leaving lots of odd morsels of flesh clinging to the bone, then I feel absolved of guilt knowing that nothing is going to waste: all these odds and ends will contribute to a perfect stock. I view the stockpot as a filleter's confessional, into which all the sins of the flesh (left sticking to the bone) can be washed away and made good.

The only special equipment you need for stock is a good large pot. I have two actually: one has a 9-litre (about 2-gallon) capacity; the other's about 13 litres (nearer 3 gallons). Both are heavy-based so they conduct heat evenly, and have well-fitting lids to stop excess evaporation. Big, easy-to-grab lug-like handles help too.

What do I put in? Skin, heads, bones, fins, livers and roe (eggs or milt) all go into my stockpot. In fact, with the exception of the guts, I'll put in any part of any white or semi-white fish (pollack, cod, pouting, whiting, bream, bass, gurnard or dogfish). Flat fish are great for stock too – the frames, heads and skins of plaice, dabs and flounders make some superlative stock.

I don't normally use oily fish, like mackerel or herring. I find they make the stock too greasy and too fishy in flavour. On occasion, I'll chuck in the odd mackerel frame, but rarely the heads. (Incidentally, even these still get used – generally on my next fishing trip. I'll freeze mackerel heads and use them singly as bait, or put several together in a tangerine sack and use for baiting crab pots. I might also mince up the heads to make chum – rubby dubby – for a special black bream trip.)

It's impossible to be precise about quantities when you're using up trimmings, bones and oddments. But, as a rough guide, I don't think it's worthwhile making stock with less than 500g of fish trimmings – 1.5kg would be better. If you don't eat as much fish as I do, try saving up a stash of fish trimmings in the freezer, adding to it whenever you can. (See recipe overleaf.)

My three favourite recipes using fish stock are fish risotto (see p.221), fish soup (see pp.222–3) and fish stew.

Simple fish stock

I never really use the same combination of flavouring veg and seasonings twice, though I regard celery, carrots, onions and bay leaves as essential. The rest largely depends on what I find in the bottom of the fridge or in the garden.

Makes 2–3 litres

500g–1.5kg fish trimmings (see p.218)
2–3 stems celery, roughly chopped
    or whole
2–3 carrots, chopped or whole
2–3 onions, peeled and halved
6 bay leaves
Salt

Plus any of the following:
A few green peppercorns
A couple of dried chillies
A head of garlic, sliced in half
A couple of slices of fennel bulb, plus
    a handful of feathery tops
    and a few seeds if available
Leek tops
Parsley stalks
Thyme sprigs

Simply chuck all your fish heads, bones, skins and filleting sins into a large pot, then add the all-important seasonings and vegetables. Now cover the lot with water and add some salt – I use 2 tsp to every 5 litres water. But don't go overboard, the saltiness will increase as the stock reduces; you can always add more salt later.

Bring to the boil, reduce the heat, cover and let it simmer gently for a minimum of 20 minutes; ideally no more than 30 minutes. And it'll probably be fine if you forget about it and leave it on for a bit longer, as long as it's not boiling hard.

Taste the stock to make sure you're happy with it. I normally make mine quite watery. (You can always reduce it later by boiling it hard once the bones and veg have been strained out.)

While the stock is still hot, or at least warm, attack the contents with a potato masher, pulping up the veg, knocking all the flesh off the bones, and mushing up any heads. Then pour through a colander into a bowl. I use a wide-holed colander rather than a sieve because I like bits in my stock. You can strain it through a fine sieve, or even through muslin, if you're anally retentive and prefer a clear, translucent result.

When the fishy contents are in the colander, give them another bashing with the spud masher or the end of a rolling pin to extract every last drop of juice. Then leave the stock to cool, before putting it in the fridge, or possibly bagging and freezing it. My fish and bone mush goes to the chickens or the pigs, after I've hived off a few of the better-looking bits for my dog Spike.

A simple fish risotto

The fresh fish you add to your risotto at the end of cooking can be almost anything: oily fish, white fish, shellfish, squid or cuttlefish. Just make sure it's all carefully skinned, deboned and cut into large bite-sized pieces (except prawns or shrimp, which can be put in whole). To be honest, though, if I've got a really stonking fish stock, I sometimes don't add any fresh fish at all – a plain, soupy fish stock risotto is simply one of the most flavoursome and soothing dishes.

Serves 4

A large knob of butter
2 tbsp olive or rapeseed oil
1 onion, peeled and chopped
1 garlic clove, peeled and chopped
About 700ml fish stock
350g risotto rice (arborio or carnaroli)
1 glass dry white wine or cider
(optional)

About 300g fresh fish and/or shellfish
(chunks of white or oily fish fillet,
whole scallops, squid rings, whole
shell-on prawns or shrimp)
½ lemon
A little chopped parsley or chives
(optional)
Salt and freshly ground black pepper

Heat half the butter with 1 tbsp oil in a large saucepan. Add the onion and garlic and sauté gently for 5–10 minutes. Meanwhile, bring the stock to a low simmer in another saucepan.

Add the rice to the onion, stir and cook for a couple of minutes. If you're adding wine, do so now, and let it simmer until all the liquid has evaporated. Now start adding the stock, one ladleful at a time. Stir well after each addition and add the next ladleful as the previous one is absorbed. Keep the risotto simmering gently, and stir frequently. It should take about 18 minutes to add all the stock, and for the rice to be just cooked. When it's done, season with salt and pepper.

When the rice is nearly done, cook the fish and/or shellfish. You can steam it, but I usually fry it. Heat the remaining butter and 1 tbsp oil in a large frying pan over a medium heat. Add the fish and shellfish and fry gently for about 2 minutes until just cooked, or even a little undercooked. Finish with a generous squeeze of lemon juice.

Add the fish and shellfish to the rice for just the last minute or so of cooking, folding them in very gently so they don't get broken up. Remove the risotto from the heat and serve right away, sprinkled, if you like, with some parsley or chives.

Variation
If you've got a good rich stock, simply bring to the boil and pour it over couscous. Add a knob of butter, cover and leave to stand until it has soaked up all the stock.

My fish soup

I've never made this exactly the same way twice, but it's always very quick, simple and deeply satisfying. All I do is create a tangy, salty thin soup base – really just a poaching medium for the fish – add a few noodles and thinly sliced vegetables then, at the last minute, some chunks of fresh fish.

Everything about this soup should be fresh and very lightly cooked. I can make it in 4 minutes once I've got the stock up to temperature. It's very easy and adaptable, so do play with it – try it without noodles, add some broccoli sprigs or kombu seaweed, or make it really spicy, or squeeze in a lime at the end to make it sour. The soup should change through the seasons, reflecting the vegetables and fish that are at their best. You can even make it with just stock and white fish and nothing else.

If I've got a good batch of stock ready, I'll use that alone for the soup base. But, if I only have a small amount, or it's a bit watery, I'll augment it with miso (Japanese fermented soya bean paste) or dashi-no-moto (a Japanese soup base made from dried bonito fish flakes). There are lots of different kinds of miso; it doesn't matter much which you use, but a paste is preferable to granules.

The most important issue with this soup is timing. You must avoid overcooking the vegetables and fish. If in doubt, err on the side of undercooking and you'll probably hit it right. If I've made you feel nervous about timing, you can always cook the fish separately by steaming or frying it, then add it to the hot soup just before serving. Small quarter-fillets of dab and flounder work well fried first and then placed on top of a bowl of soup, or risotto for that matter.

Serves 4

500ml–1 litre fish stock
1–2 tbsp miso paste or ½–1 sachet of
    dashi-no-moto
About 150g medium dried egg noodles
1 large leek, trimmed and sliced
1 fennel bulb, trimmed and sliced
1 garlic clove, peeled and sliced
1 red chilli, sliced

300–400g mixed white fish and
    shellfish, such as 4–5cm pieces of
    skinless, boneless pollack, pouting
    or gurnard, squid rings, whole or
    halved scallops, shell-on prawns
Toasted sesame oil or chopped parsley
    or coriander, to serve
Salt and freshly ground black pepper

Put the fish stock into a large saucepan; you need roughly a mugful for each person. If you're using miso paste or dashi, first mix this with some boiling water to a sloppy paste. Once in the pan, bring up to a simmer, stirring to make sure the miso or dashi is all dissolved.

Now add your noodles: break flat bundles in half first; let nests open out in the water, helping them along with a big-pronged fork. Simmer for 3 minutes, stirring occasionally, until the noodles are pliable but not fully cooked.

Now add the leek and fennel (or other veg) and start your mental clock. Once the veg is in, you're about 3 minutes from pouring this into bowls. You want the veg to be still crisp when it's served, so don't dither. Taste the broth and add salt and pepper if you think it needs it. Turn the heat right down, then add the garlic and chilli and, finally, the fish. Thicker, denser items like scallops or squid should go in first: they'll need a couple of minutes to cook through. White fish pieces will only take a minute, so add these right at the end (they'll go on cooking even once you've served up).

When the fish is just cooked, take off the heat and ladle the soup immediately into warm bowls. Finish with a trickle of sesame oil, or chopped parsley or coriander.

Gurnard with tomato and fennel

This is a gloriously rich, warming braise. You can make it using only tinned tomatoes as the liquid element, but I think it's immeasurably enhanced by the addition of some lovely homemade fish stock. If you can't get hold of gurnard, try thick cutlets of grey mullet or dogfish goujons or cutlets (both of these need only 10–15 minutes in the oven). To make this more substantial I've included a can of chickpeas, but you can leave these out if you prefer it more soupy.

Serves 4

2 tbsp olive or rapeseed oil
100g chorizo or smoked streaky bacon, cut into small chunks or lardons (optional)
2 onions, peeled and chopped
4 celery sticks, sliced
2 fennel bulbs, trimmed and roughly chopped
4 garlic cloves, peeled and chopped
1 fat red chilli, deseeded for less heat if preferred, and sliced
400g tin chopped tomatoes

2 tbsp tomato purée
About 400ml fish stock (or use another 400g tin of tomatoes)
400g can chickpeas, butterbeans or other pulses, drained and rinsed (optional)
2 tsp smoked paprika
2 bay leaves
A pinch of sugar
4 red gurnard or mullet cutlets (about 400g each), descaled and gutted
Salt and freshly ground black pepper

Heat the oil in a large casserole or saucepan over a medium heat. Add the chorizo or bacon if using and fry for a couple of minutes, until the fat starts to run. Add the onions, celery, fennel, garlic and chilli. As soon as they all start to sizzle, reduce the heat, cover the pan and let the vegetables sweat and soften, stirring them from time to time, for about 15 minutes.

Add the tomatoes, tomato purée, stock, chickpeas if using, paprika and bay leaves. Bring to a simmer and then cook, uncovered, for about 40 minutes, until you have a thick, rich sauce. Season to taste with sugar, salt and pepper. Meanwhile, preheat the oven to 180°C/Gas mark 4.

If you're using a large casserole dish, you may be able to fit the gurnard in it – nestle them snugly into the hot sauce. Otherwise, transfer the sauce to an ovenproof dish and add the fish, pushing the portions down gently into the sauce. Bake in the oven, uncovered, for 15–20 minutes, or until the fish is cooked through.

Serve each portion of fish with plenty of the chunky tomatoey sauce, and mashed potato or crusty bread to mop it all up.

Barbecued fish

When I think of barbecues, I think of the beach – that's where I tend to do a lot of open-air cooking. Lit by the setting sun, accompanied by friends, family and a cool box brimming with freshly caught fish, there is just nothing better. But of course you can enjoy the wonder of a fresh fish barbecue, with all its smoky, fire-cooked, lip-smacking, finger-licking flavours, in your garden, on a roof terrace, or wherever.

One thing I really would encourage you to do is barbecue in the autumn and winter. I love an outdoor fire when the weather is cold and cooking is a cosy joy, rather than a sweating chore. In my opinion, the best time for beach barbecues is late October. This time of year can produce some stunning clear but mild days. What's more, the mackerel are plentiful and at their best, absolutely chock-full of omega oils – they've spent all summer feeding on high-grade protein and slowly converting it to oil to keep them fuelled through the winter months.

Whenever you choose to do it, there are just a few simple things to be aware of in order to make your barbie the thing of joy it should be. And, believe me, I've done my research over the years: my advice on how to run a successful barbie is inspired by my multiple failures as well as my modest successes.

The right kit

When it comes to equipment, I suggest you buy a bucket barbecue. I think they are the safest and easiest to use, particularly on the beach. Here in Dorset, where beaches are mostly made up of pea shingle, a bucket barbie works best because it keeps the main concentration of heat well up off the shingle, which has a habit of splitting when it gets too hot and pinging around like ricocheting bullets. Bucket barbies are also great for beach cooking because they're easy to carry (they come with a handle) and you can stash your charcoal and firelighters or kindling inside the bucket.

I abhor disposable barbies. The coals inside them are made of reconstituted coke-mush and they come ready-impregnated with evil ignition chemicals that make your fish taste like diesel fuel. Most of all, I hate them because too many people think 'disposable' means 'just leave on the beach when you're finished'.

For fuel, I always use local hardwood charcoal made from coppiced wood – it's increasingly easy to buy these days. I never ever use charcoal briquettes – the fuel of Satan – ungodly things that shouldn't be used to cook good fish. I don't like the chemicals put into them and I find they always get too hot, too late – they don't give the good hour of steady heat that a well-laid hardwood charcoal fire will provide.

Personally, I can't see any point in cooking on the beach if you've got to lug tons of gear along with you. So, when we barbecue as a family, we don't take knives and forks. We eat our mackerel like a fleshy corn-on-the-cob, using fingers and teeth to tease off the flakes of flesh. All the kit I ever take is one big sharp knife – and a pair of tongs when I remember. If we bother to take plates, which doesn't happen often, we'll pack plastic ones that can be washed in the sea or recycled paper ones that can be burned. However, most of the time I just serve grilled fish on flat beach stones. Hunting for their own stone plate is a great game for the children too.

One other bit of kit I often take with me when I'm barbecuing on the beach is a pair of thick leather gardening gloves. They are a godsend when things are suddenly getting too hot and you need to move searing hot metal around in a hurry.

Lighting your fire

Despite my dim view of disposables and briquettes, I'm not a fanatical purist: I do often use firelighters to get a barbecue going (my justification is that these are all burnt away and obliterated by the time any food gets near the fire). Thin, dry twigs or scraps of cardboard make good kindling too. If you're using these, they should go into the bed of the barbecue first.

Lay your charcoal out in a thick layer in the barbecue – one golden rule is to always use more charcoal than you think is needed. If using firelighters, distribute a few bits of them between the coals. Now light your kindling, cardboard or firelighters, pile more charcoal on top, stand back and let things start to catch. As soon as the charcoal starts to burn in places, start piling up the coals over these hotspots, fuelling the flames. Don't be afraid to redistribute and rearrange the coals several times during this firing-up period, so that all the coals get a chance to start burning. Tending the fire is as much of a creative role as cooking the food. Once all the coals are burning well, knock them down again into an even layer. Now you've got to wait, wait, wait before you put your fish anywhere near the fire. Do not cook anything until all flame and smoke has died away and the coals are glowing and covered in grey ash.

Cooking your fish

The best fish to barbecue are oily ones because they're self-basting and won't dry out over the intense heat, as white fish can. My absolute favourite for the barbie is mackerel (see p.230), but I've also had wonderful feasts of barbecued garfish, herring and scad mackerel. I don't particularly like to barbecue white fish like pouting or pollack because the intense heat of charcoal doesn't do white fish flesh any favours; it just scorches it and makes it too dry.

If I've got pouting or pollack to cook on the beach, I'll take an old heavy-bottomed frying pan along and shallow-fry fillets or small, whole gutted fish. Alternatively, I'll parcel them up in foil or wet newspaper so they can steam-cook on the barbecue grill. Little dabs and flounders, with their relatively thick skin can work surprisingly well on a barbie, especially one that's cooling down, and where the fierce heat has gone from the coals. A slow-cooked whole dab or flounder, turned regularly and then picked apart with a sharp knife and eaten straight from the blade, feels like fresh fish at its freshest. And one of my favourite ways to cook fish on a barbecue is in a pot or bucket of fresh sea water (see below).

A barbecue can descend into disaster when great fish get ruined by being burned or stuck to the grill. It's nothing short of a tragedy when you've carefully landed, killed and chilled a fabulous fish to see it cremated on the spars of your barbie, inedible to man or beast. So, a crucial investment in my view is a good-quality 'sandwich'-style grill basket – one you can fit a few fat mackerel in and still be able to close properly. It needs to have an inch or two of depth on each side, and the bars need to be made of good-quality steel (preferably stainless) and be strong. The puny wire ones will rust, buckle, break and slice through your dearly beloved fish.

The best grill baskets I've found came from Susmans, a South African import company I found online. South Africans seem to know a lot about eating outdoors and make seriously heavy-duty kit. I'd spend more on a decent grill basket (that will last for years) than I would on the barbecue itself, which really is just a receptacle for hot coals.

You don't have to buy a grill basket: you can just cook on the flat grill that fits on top of your barbecue, of course. However, I find I can never get a fire-threatened fish off quickly enough, without major risk to life, limb and mackerel. If you're going to cook whole fish directly on the barbecue grill, leave the heads on. And, when you gut the fish, try not to make the slice in the belly too long. A head-on fish with a mostly complete belly will hold together better on the flat grill, while the head gives you something to grab hold of when you turn them over.

Barbecuing using a bucket of sea water

One of the most delicious and natural ways to cook mackerel on the beach is to poach them in a bucket of sea water. Of course, you don't have to use a bucket; a pan or a stockpot will do perfectly well. And it doesn't hurt to use a vessel with a lid – it'll help the water heat up faster. If you don't have a lid, lay a chopping board or a sheet of tin over the top of the bucket as you bring it up to boiling point.

The way I normally cook mackerel by this method is to heat a gallon of sea water in a pot on top of my barbecue, making sure there's enough water in the pot to completely cover the fish. When it's about to start boiling, I take the pot off the heat, submerge the head-on, guts-out mackerel in the water and cover the pot to keep the heat in. You can throw bay leaves or fennel tops into the water before you submerge your fish, but I'm happy to just enjoy the simple, natural seasoning of the sea.

It will take only 10 minutes to poach a one-portion-sized mackerel, weighing ½ –¾lb, in the residual heat.

The texture of mackerel poached in sea water is firm and deliciously moist. I like to peel the skin off and then gnaw at the flesh, eating it flake by flake, chunk by chunk, straight off the bone.

Barbecued mackerel with bay

Barbecued mackerel with bay or fennel

The smoky flavour of a freshly grilled mackerel, cut with the aromatic punch of bay or fennel, is unbeatable. I would definitely advise using a grill basket, so that as soon as you think the fire is too hot, or the dripping juices are making it too smoky and everything is about to go pear-shaped, all you need do is lift the basket off entirely and set the fish aside while the fire dies down.

Serves 6
A little olive or rapeseed oil
6 whole mackerel, gutted but heads left on
Lots of bay leaves or fennel tops and/or lightly crushed fennel stalks
Salt and freshly ground black pepper
A couple of lemons (optional)

Prepare your barbecue (see pp.226–7).

Massage the fish all over with a little oil, then season them generously with salt and pepper inside and out. Scatter a layer of bay leaves or fennel in the base of your grill basket. Lay the mackerel on top. Tuck some more bay or fennel inside the fish cavities. Put some more bay or fennel over the top of them. Close the grill basket.

When the fire has died down and the coals are glowing and covered with a good layer of white-grey ash, put the basket of fish on the barbecue, low down and very close to the hot coals. This technique is very dramatic: you'll often get clouds of thick scented smoke and even crackling flames roaring up if the oil in the bay leaves ignites. But the fish doesn't come to any harm – in fact, quite the opposite. The herbs actually protect the fish from the intense heat of the grill and they create a scented steam – fresh fennel tops in particular – which penetrates and cooks the fish while keeping it moist. When you come to eat, you'll probably find bits of charred bay leaf or fennel stalk clinging to your mackerel flesh like lumps of shrapnel, but these only enhance the flavour and crunchy skin texture of the cooked fish.

Cook the mackerel for 4–5 minutes each side. Open the grill basket and check one fish to see if it is done, then serve straight away, with a squeeze of lemon juice if you happen to have some, and some good bread. A salad of some sort – maybe peppery green leaves, or sliced ripe tomatoes – is a great accompaniment.

If you don't have a grill basket, make sure the barbecue grill itself is good and hot, then lay the bay or fennel directly on to it when the coals are ready. Stuff more bay or fennel inside the fish, and lay them directly on top of the smoking herbs on the grill. Turn the fish after about 5 minutes and cook the other side. Remove the mackerel as soon as it's cooked to the bone and serve.

Baked fish

The foil parcel method

Nothing could be easier than cooking fish in a foil package. It's a wonderfully simple and very forgiving technique, yet the result is really quite elegant. All you're doing is sealing your fish – which could be a whole gutted specimen, or a couple of fillets, or even thick cutlets, cut from the fish at right angles to the spine – inside a little chamber with a bunch of aromatic flavourings. These create a fragrant steam in which the fish will cook. The parcel goes into the oven or on the fire, and in just 15–20 minutes you'll have beautifully cooked moist fish in a little pool of aromatic juices.

When cooking fish in this way, my favourite additions are lemon juice and lemon zest (loads of it), fresh garlic, bay leaves, fennel tops, sliced ginger, chives, black pepper, butter, lime juice and, most important of all, salt. I can never resist a hit of hot too, so I'll add some sliced fresh chilli, seeds and all, which never fails to deliver a little extra frisson.

The liquid might be a splash of cider, beer, wine, verjuice or apple juice. The more you add, the more of a poaching technique you'll achieve. Conversely, if you don't use any liquid – only add butter or oil – the cooking that takes place will be like a combination of frying and poaching, which is also very good. Don't be shy about experimenting with flavourings when you're doing your own foil-baked fish.

If you're cooking your parcels in the oven, one sheet of foil should be enough. Put it, shiny side down, on a sturdy baking sheet, give it a lick of butter, add the fish, then draw up the foil to fashion a 'pot' around it. Pasty-shaped packages work well. Into your foil-fashioned pot, put your herbs or spices, oils and liquids, then scrunch the foil closed at the top. The parcel should be well sealed but baggy: there should be room inside for hot air and steam to circulate. Put it in an oven preheated to 190°C/Gas mark 5. Keep an eye on it, checking it every 5 minutes or so. A small fillet will be cooked in about 10 minutes, whereas a whole 1.5kg fish could take 35 minutes. Just keep opening the parcel and prodding until you see the flesh flake invitingly and peel away easily from the bone (if there is any).

If you want to cook a foil parcel of fish over, or in, a wood fire or a pile of glowing coals, you'll need a couple of layers of foil at least, but the technique and the timings are similar to oven-cooking.

Sometimes, if I'm doing parcels with small fillets, I'll stick some veg in too. Calabrese and purple-sprouting broccoli, celery and green beans all cook at the same rate as a white fish fillet and chucking them all in the same parcel saves on pans.

When it's time to serve, bring the foil parcel – or parcels – to the table and open them up so everyone can enjoy the cloud of delicious scent that's released. Share out the fish and don't forget to pour some of the sauce from the bottom of the foil parcel over each portion.

Baking without foil

This is what I think of as 'naked baking', without a foil parcel to protect the flesh and hold in juices. The fish I most like to bake naked are large whole plaice, whole headless mackerel, whole bass, whole pollack and slob trout.

I choose this technique for these fish because I want their flesh to be cooked in a harsher way – a way that forces out moisture more quickly from the flesh, crisps the skin and turns the ends of the fins crunchy and even singed. It's a more violent and dynamic way of attacking your fish with heat, which produces different textures and flavours from steaming, poaching or parcel-style 'wet' methods.

You can cook whole fish more or less naked, with perhaps just a splash of oil or butter, or maybe a rasher or two of streaky bacon to provide a little extra oil to lubricate the skin. However, baking also works well with cutlets or fat fillets, which can be smeared with oil and herbs to create a 'crust' as the exterior dries out in the intense heat.

To prepare a whole fish for baking, I'll leave the skin on but take the scales off – either when I'm still at sea or in the sink as soon as I arrive home with my catch. I dry the fish with a tea towel and then, using my hands, massage oil or butter all over its skin, fins and head. Fish heads and fins love to stick to baking trays. They will do their level best to stick, whether you oil them or not, but the more time you devote to putting oil on them, the easier it will be to part them from the pan when you finally take them from the oven. I then fill the bellies of my fish with bay leaves and a generous knob of butter.

The skin of the fish acts almost like a porous, natural foil parcel to hold the heat and the moisture inside. However, the skin can also be slashed open two or three times, which makes the skin retreat from the cut and the flesh start to gape underneath. This can look very dramatic and it provides a great opportunity to add a little extra seasoning of salt, pepper or lemon juice directly on to the grain of the flesh – which can then penetrate deep into the fish.

Slashing works especially well on flat fish like large plaice, but be a little careful when you put slashes in the sides of a round fish – don't cut too deep or do too many slashes. I've gone overboard in the past with Jack-the-Ripper-style slashes only to watch my beautiful whole fish fall apart in the oven as the skin retreats and shrivels, leaving the flesh to tumble out.

The prepared fish go on to a baking tray and into the oven, which I've preheated to around 200°C/Gas mark 6. The time taken depends a great deal on the size of the fish, and the position in the oven (see right), but, as a rough guide, a few fish cutlets can take as little as 12 minutes, while a big plaice might need to be in there for upwards of half an hour.

Positioning your fish in the oven

How aggressively a fish is baked is partly a result of where in the oven you choose to place it. Baking at the top of the oven, in the hottest zone, isn't really that much different from grilling. In my oven, if I bake a mackerel or a slob trout on a flat baking tray, with nothing more than a smear of butter and a sprinkle of salt and pepper, I'm able to cook it all the way through in 15 minutes, and just begin to crisp up the top layer of skin. It won't be quite as crisp as it would be if it was cooked under a grill, but it's enough to give the skin a roasted look and a sharp tangy flavour.

The middle and bottom rungs of the oven are where I'll put fish that's fairly thick and needs a longer, slower cooking time in order for the heat to penetrate the flesh right to the bone.

Sometimes when I'm baking a big fish, I'll move it around the oven – up or down, depending on whether I want to put more heat on to the surface of the fish or into the centre. With a big plaice, for example, I'll start it low in the oven for 10 minutes before moving it up to the top rung for a further intense skin-crinkling, flesh-roasting 10 minutes to finish it off.

I also do a bit of moving around with one of my favourite mackerel dishes, where the fish is baked on a bed of par-boiled chunky potatoes with onions, olive oil, whole garlic cloves and huge chunks of peel-on lemons. This I'll start in the bottom of the oven and progress upwards every 10 minutes, before giving it a final skin-crisping blast at the top. I often cook garfish in the same way.

If I think a fish is cooked in the middle but I want it to be crisper on the top then I'll migrate it upwards to where the heat is greatest. And the opposite is true if the topmost skin of the fish looks ready, but, from a quick prod with a fork, I can feel the flesh in the centre, near the spine, is still firm and clinging to the bone. If it's underdone in the centre it needs to be left for a few minutes in the bottom of the oven where the lower heat can penetrate deeply without overcooking the surface.

Baked cod or pollack with green beans and pesto

This simple little dish is a real winner. It's very easy to just knock it up for one person, and no more work to make it for two or more. Instead of beans, you could use tender stems of purple-sprouting broccoli or, in early summer, some slender spears of asparagus.

Serves 2

About 200g trimmed French beans
About 150ml hot fish stock
2 thick fillets of cod or pollack (about 250g each), skinned and boned

3 heaped tbsp pesto (homemade or good-quality bought)
Salt and freshly ground black pepper

Preheat the oven to 200°C/Gas mark 6. Scatter the green beans in an ovenproof casserole dish and pour the stock over them. Lay the fish fillets on top, then sprinkle on a little seasoning (remember that the pesto will be quite salty). Spread the pesto in a thick layer over the fish. Bake in the oven for 10–15 minutes, until the fish and beans are cooked, and the pesto has formed a delicious crust. Serve straight away, with new potatoes.

Steaming

Any kind of fish – white, oily, flat or cartilaginous (dogfish) – can be steamed quickly and easily. Any cut or portion will work too, from whole fish to cutlets to individual fillets. The joy of steaming is that it's gentle. Lightly steamed fish will retain its shape and size; it doesn't wrinkle, crisp, buckle, shrink or harden. It stays moist, flaky and, once steamed, it is extremely easy to deconstruct. Bones will just fall out of steamed fish and skin will peel off with minimum effort. Steaming is also very fast – it can take just a few minutes – and so easy to control. All you need to do, to check how your fish is doing, is lift the lid and give the fish a gentle prod with a fork – if the flesh is cooked it will easily break into flakes.

Steaming seems to me a very pure and honest way to cook fish, but also if I'm honest, a bit boring. Mostly I steam fish when I'm planning to do something else with it *after* it's been steamed – to make fish cakes perhaps, or add to a risotto just before serving. Or I might let it cool and serve it with salad, or possibly mix it with mayonnaise and make sandwiches.

I might occasionally steam a whole fish or a large fillet if I want to eat it cold. Slob trout is fabulous steamed then flaked off the bone, allowed to cool and served with lemon or garlic mayonnaise and steamed vegetables, or with salad and rice.

So steaming is a useful tool in the fish cook's armoury. Granted, simply steamed fish can be a bit bland, but I do love the texture, and a plain piece of steamed fish is a great backdrop to other ingredients. Sometimes I serve up plain steamed fish and vegetables drizzled with something punchy – a splash of warmed sesame oil, warmed olive oil, or a spicy chilli and rice vinegar sauce – to put a little edge to the flavour.

The two best fish-steaming tools are a fish kettle and a collapsible stainless-steel steaming basket (also called a 'petal' basket) which fits inside one of your saucepans or your wok. Put a little water into the base of the kettle or the pan and bring to the boil. Then put your fish on the fish kettle tray or into the steaming basket, add to the pan and cover tightly. Single fillets can be cooked in a matter of minutes. A large whole fish in a fish kettle might take 20 minutes.

Always make sure that the water you add to create your steam isn't deeper than the tray at the bottom of the fish kettle, or deeper than the feet on your petal steamer. You don't want the boiling water to actually touch the fish, only the steam that it delivers. It takes a remarkably small amount of water, in a pan with a good tight-fitting lid, to sufficiently steam even the firmest of fresh fish.

I rarely bother to flavour the water that I use to create the steam. Sometimes I might add a handful of fennel tops or a couple of bay leaves to make the steam aromatic, but I'll never do more than that because the fish is in the steam for such a short time so it's not worth going to too much trouble. Any additional seasoning is going to happen after the fish is taken out of the steam.

Steamed white fish and broccoli with soy, chilli and garlic

This is a very puritanical recipe that makes me feel very righteous. It's the type of meal I like to make best of all at lunchtime, just for my wife Helen, and myself, when all the children are at school. Personally I'm an addict of hot chilli and will always liven up what is quite an Amish-type meal with a Mexican-style kick.

Serves 2

2 fat fillets of white fish, such as pollack or pouting (about 250g each)

A good handful of purple-sprouting broccoli, tough ends trimmed

3 tbsp soy sauce

3 tbsp mirin or rice wine

1 clove garlic, peeled and chopped

1 red chilli, chopped

1 tsp grated fresh root ginger

A good pinch of sugar

Toasted sesame oil, to finish

You'll need a collapsible steel steaming basket, or 'petal' basket, for this. Put a little water in the base of a large saucepan, deep frying pan or wok, into which the basket will fit snugly. Bring the water to the boil.

Put the fish fillets, skin side down, in the basket, trimming them to fit if necessary. Tuck the broccoli stems around the fish. Transfer the basket to the pan (making sure the water doesn't touch the fish). Cover tightly and steam for 5–7 minutes, until the fish is done.

Meanwhile, combine the soy sauce, mirin, garlic, chilli, ginger and sugar in a small pan with 3 tbsp water. Bring to a simmer and cook gently for 1 minute, then remove from the heat.

Serve the fish and broccoli on warmed plates and trickle some of the warm soy mixture over them. (You probably won't need it all, but it will keep well in the fridge for at least a week.) Finish with a splash of toasted sesame oil and serve with rice.

Deep-fried fish

I passionately enjoy deep-fried fish. I love to cook it. I love to eat it. And I love to see all my children's hungry, greasy-chinned mouths devouring my deep-fried fish.

The things I deep-fry most are:
- Fish fillets in 'chip shop' batter or tempura batter
- Fish fillets in homemade breadcrumbs
- Fish fillets in Japanese panko breadcrumbs
- Squid rings dusted in spicy flour
- Fish fillets dusted in spicy flour
- Whole small fish (head on, guts out) dusted in powdered spices

Some people are put off deep-frying because they think it requires special equipment and gallons of oil. But, to me, it's not a specialist technique: it's just a way of blitzing fish in a couple of inches of really hot oil – either sunflower or groundnut. I don't use more than 2 inches of oil – if the piece of fish isn't submerged, I can always turn it over halfway through cooking. And, because I don't use a great depth of oil, I can deep-fry in a flat-bottomed wok, or even a 12-inch thick-bottomed frying pan.

The key to success is heat. I always use my biggest, hottest gas ring and I never start cooking until my oil is searing hot. To be honest, I deep-fry at temperatures higher than are generally advised. Most sources will tell you that around 180°C – or when a cube of bread browns in 50–60 seconds – is ideal. I'm not going to argue with that as I'm well aware that overheated oil can spontaneously ignite. And if I'm cooking a large item, such as a chunky fillet encased in thick batter, I'll stick to around 180°C or a little lower. If the oil is too hot, the fish will burn on the outside before the heat has had a chance to penetrate to the centre. But if I'm fast-frying tiny little whole fish, or scraps of squid, or thin fillets, I cannot resist taking the oil over 180°C to ensure that irresistible, super-crispy effect. But please be safe: if your oil registers over 200°C on a cook's thermometer, or if it is smoking, turn off the heat.

Choosing a coating
My choice of coating is fairly random and to some extent based on what's in the cupboard), but there is a size factor. My homemade 'chip shop' batter is a substantial eggy affair, which works best on large fillets. Incidentally, the hot oil should crisp and seal the batter crust very quickly, so the fish inside isn't in contact with hot oil and never becomes greasy.

Tempura batter is much less substantial and I use it with any sized fillet of fish. All I do is mix half-and-half plain flour and cornflour with enough ice-cold sparkling water to make a thin, lumpy batter (the lumps are important – don't overmix it).

Breadcrumbs can go two ways. If you dip your fish in flour, then egg, then breadcrumbs, you can end up with a really hefty, but delicious coating to your fish. Or you can leave out the egg-dipping part of the process, as I do with Japanese panko-style breadcrumbs. Pressing the breadcrumbs straight on to the fish flesh gives a light, crispy, crunchy sheen of breadcrumbs, rather than a thick coating.

And then there's the simple light-dusting-of-well-seasoned-flour approach, which I often use with squid and small fish fillets. Sometimes I'll use cornflour to coat small fillets, or small whole fish like sprats or little whiting, really just to stop them sticking together in the pan. But this also gives them an irresistible crunchy golden sheen. Small fillets of dab or flounder will cook in the blink of an eye in a hot oil with no more than a dusting of seasoned flour to keep them decent. And then they can be slipped between the crusty embrace of a nice white bap with some salad leaves and eaten straight away.

I will occasionally deep-fry a whole head-on, guts-out fish such as a gurnard, whiting or small pollack – anything up to about 250g. I'll dust it first in spiced flour or even just in a blend of ground spices. Normally I'll opt for cumin, curry powder, chilli powder and fenugreek, but I have used only paprika (which looks wonderful) or cayenne pepper. A spicy deep-fried whole fish is tremendous fun to cook and also to eat. The idea is to get the outside as crisp as possible – even the fins and tail should be crisp and spicy and edible – while the flesh inside remains moist and tender. This requires a couple of inches of oil so hot that it practically crisps flesh on contact.

Timings

If your oil is hot and the fish is small, it will cook in next to no time. Little fishfinger-sized morsels will only need 1–2 minutes. A battered fat fillet will need 3–4 minutes, while a whole fish normally takes about 5 minutes to cook through.

My golden rules for successful deep-frying are:
- Let the oil get really hot before you start.
- Use tongs to put your fish pieces or fillets in the oil, and do it very carefully.
- Cook in small batches. Don't overload the pan or the fish bits will start to stick together and the temperature of the oil will drop.
- If you're using batter, always let the excess drip off a fillet before slipping it into the hot oil. Excess batter will break off and dirty your oil more quickly.
- Don't prod fish or turn it over too early. Leave until it's at least honey-coloured, preferably tea-coloured, then turn it. The second side will cook in half the time.
- When you remove fish from the hot oil, put each piece straight on to a couple of layers of kitchen paper. Don't stack the pieces of fish on top of one another, as this will make your batter soggy, which is a sin.
- Never use your frying oil more than twice. Just once is better.

Battered pollack

When I say 'pollack' here, I mean any decent-sized white fish fillet, so that could include gurnard, coley, mullet, cod, whiting and pouting. They'll all work. In fact, *any* fillet of fish will be delicious if you fry it in this batter. Arguably, you could dip your welly socks in this batter, deep-fry them and serve them with homemade tartare sauce and no one would complain!

Serves 4

200g plain flour
1 egg yolk
About 250ml whole milk
Sunflower or groundnut oil, for frying
4 fillets of pollack, skinned
Salt and freshly ground black pepper

To serve
Lemon wedges
Tartare sauce (see p.205)

Sift the flour into a deep bowl and season it well with salt and pepper. Whisk the egg yolk with about 100ml milk. Make a well in the centre of the flour and start adding in the egg and milk mixture, whisking well and gradually incorporating the dry flour from the sides. Once all the eggy liquid is in, start adding more milk – you'll probably need around an additional 150ml. Keep going, whisking all the time, until you have a smooth batter with a consistency a little thicker than double cream. Leave this to rest for 10 minutes.

Heat a couple of inches of oil in a deep-sided, heavy-bottomed saucepan (or use a deep-fat fryer) until it reaches 175–180°C (when a cube of bread dropped into the oil turns brown in less than a minute.

Pat the fish fillets with a tea towel or kitchen paper so they're nice and dry. Give the batter another quick whisk. Dip one fillet into the batter, hold it up and let it drip for a minute, then dip it a second time and let it drip again. Transfer to the hot oil. If your pan is big enough, repeat with a second fillet.

Cook for about 3 minutes, then turn the pieces of fish over in the hot oil, using tongs. Cook for another 1–2 minutes, or until the batter is a rich golden brown all over. Lift out and drain on kitchen paper. Repeat with the remaining fillets, then serve at once, with lemon wedges and tartare sauce.

Pan-fried fish

I know 'pan-frying' is one of those terribly cheffy phrases that gets some people's backs up. 'What *else* would you fry it in – if not a pan?' retorts Gill at River Cottage. Fair enough, but I find the term useful. For me, it neatly describes the simple frying I like to do, day in day out, with all kinds of fish.

I could call it 'shallow-frying' but that would be a bit of a misnomer as it suggests the use of a fair amount of oil. What I'm talking about here is cooking fish in a frying pan with a mere lick of grease – a smear of lubrication between pan and fish to stop the flesh or skin sticking. A tablespoon of oil or butter will do it, or a bit of melted bacon fat, or the lovely salty fat from a couple of slices of chorizo sausage.

Fry-poaching

Pan-frying, at its most basic, is a very quick and simple way to produce a beautifully browned and slightly crisped fillet. But over the years I've modified the technique a little. For starters, I don't whack the heat up too high. I do not like to 'sear' fish, because in my opinion all fish flesh is too delicate to be seared. Searing, to me, means intense heat or, in the context of fish, 'spoiling by overcooking'. The only time I'll really crank up the heat when I'm pan-frying is when the fish is not at its best. Searing and crispy-crispy pan-frying is a good way to disguise fish that has slightly outstayed its welcome.

If the fish I'm frying is really fresh and in tip-top condition, then I'll treat it as gently as possible. In fact I'm more than happy to start my fish cooking in a warm rather than a hot pan, letting the temperature increase as I go. And just to cosset my fish even more, what I usually do is to fry my fish a little bit, then finish the cooking by poaching it. A whiting fillet, gently 'fry-poached' in a touch of good olive oil with fresh garlic and an obscenely generous squash of lemon, is far preferable to anything that's been 'seared' against super-hot metal.

This is how fry-poaching works: I'll start the cooking process with just a little oil in the pan to sizzle the surface of the fish, but as soon as it's sealed and partially cooked, I'll flip the fillets over and spoon a little liquid into the pan. That could be fish stock, lemon juice, verjuice or even cider or apple juice. The liquid simmers and steams, semi-poaching the fish and, at the same time, reducing down to a soupy gravy. The result is less crisp than straight frying, but more tender – and the intense little 'jus' that forms in the pan is a real bonus.

This fry-poaching technique works best with fillets – for me, usually fillets of mackerel, whiting, bream, small bass or small pollack. And, unless you cover the pan with a tight-fitting lid while you're doing the poaching bit, it only really works on fillets less than 1½ inches thick. Fry-poaching doesn't have the penetrating power needed to cook really thick fillets or whole unfilleted fish.

You can fry-poach fillets with their skin on or off. If I'm cooking fillets at the larger end of the scale, I'll usually skin them – it helps the steam from the poaching liquid to penetrate. I'll cook small fillets, like those from small mackerel, skin on. Mackerel skin is thin and fiddly to remove, plus it can also be delicious when cooked. I normally fry fillets flesh side down first, because I find that frying the skin first makes the flesh side bulge and curl as the skin shrinks. This can make the fillets slightly more delicate to turn. I'll cook them until they just begin to brown, then flip them over on to their skin sides and add my poaching liquid a few moments later. In another couple of minutes, they should be done.

If I've put the fish in skin side down by mistake (which I often do), I wait until the skin is browning nicely, then douse the flesh with lemon juice or stock before very gently rolling the fillets over and letting them bubble for a minute or two.

With this fry-poaching technique, I'm never in a hurry to take the cooked fish out of the pan. I use a heavy-bottomed frying pan and I like to let the contents settle and finish cooking very slowly in the residual heat. To be honest, if I'm just cooking a quick fish fillet lunch for myself, what I like to do most of all is to actually eat it straight out of the pan. That little pool of fish gravy never tastes better than when it's wiped out of the bottom of the pan with a chunk of good crusty bread!

Fry-poached fillets of bream, with garlic, lemon and herbs

This is one of the ways of cooking bream that I'll never tire of. I love the filleting, the cooking – with all the lemony herb smell – and the eating. All moist and sour and sweet and hot, with a little olive oily thing going on, this is my kind of heaven. In fact I'd die happy if fry-poached bream fillets were my last supper.

Serves 2

3 tbsp olive oil
Small knob of butter
1 large black bream, descaled,
    filleted and pin-boned
1 garlic clove, peeled and
    chopped

Juice of 1 small or ½ large lemon
1 tbsp mixed chopped 'soft' herbs,
    such as parsley, chervil, chives,
    basil and/or mint
Salt and freshly ground black pepper

Heat 1 tbsp oil and the butter in a pan over a medium heat. When the butter is sizzling gently, season the bream fillets well and add them to the pan, flesh side down. Cook for about 2 minutes until starting to brown underneath. Scatter the garlic over and around the fish, then carefully flip the fillets over. Add the lemon juice and the remaining 2 tbsp oil. Increase the heat a little and cook for about 2 minutes more, until the fish is cooked through and the juices have reduced a little. Remove from the heat. Transfer the fillets to warmed plates. Scatter the chopped herbs in the pan and stir them into the juices, then spoon the herby juices over the fish and serve.

Grilled fish

Grilling is like upside-down barbecuing. You can achieve a similar crisp-skinned result, but in the comfort of your own kitchen and with the sort of temperature control that barbecuers can only dream of. You simply have to raise your grill pan a notch or two nearer the flame to increase the burn, or move it down to give your fish more gentle heat. And the easy-access nature of an overhead grill makes it easy to tweak your fish as it cooks – brush on a little extra olive oil, baste with a bubbling sauce, add an anchovy or two, or drench it with lemon juice.

For some fish, grilling is the best cooking method. Sprats, sardines and fish cutlets (cuts taken across the body of the fish at right angles) are particularly delicious grilled. It's also probably the best way to cook small flat fish like dabs and flounder, which need little more than a smear of butter or a lick of olive oil and a generous shake of salt and pepper to make them sing.

You can, of course, simply cook your fish directly on the wire grill rack, bare flesh against bare metal, if you're happy for moisture and oil to drip out of your fish. If you grill a cutlet or a whole sardine on a rack, flipping it over when the top side has browned, then cooking the underside the same way, you'll end up with a crispy, dry-cooked fish with a relatively dense flesh texture. If it's a very oily fish, like a sardine, sprat, herring or mackerel, the hot oil bubbles and burns on the surface as it escapes, making the skin crisp, sweet and chewy.

Alternatively, you could put the same piece of fish in an open parcel of foil, either on the rack or in your grill pan, or simply lay it directly in the grill pan without any foil. Cooked in this way, cupped or sealed from below, it'll be much more moist and more 'steamed' in texture.

For another kind of dish, try grilling some fillets of white fish directly in the pan, or in a foil 'bucket', with a creamy mustard or dill sauce spooned over them. The sauce will ploop-ploop around the fish, steaming and poaching the underside of the fillet. Meanwhile, any sauce on top of the fish will begin to brown and crisp, providing a contrasting crunchy top layer.

I like to add flavouring ingredients to fish when I'm grilling, like streaky bacon or chorizo. Whenever I can, I'll grill something like a fillet of whiting or pollack sprinkled with little lardons of chopped streaky bacon (smoked if possible). The bacon exudes its delicious salty fat, which bastes the white fish flesh and stops it from getting too dry. Its saltiness helps season the fish too, and the crispy bacon crunch is a fabulous complement to the moist fish flakes underneath.

If you have an overhead grill, do make the most of it, because grilling fish – from small whole pollack and trout to segments of garfish mixed with chorizo – is a great way to cook it. And don't miss out on flame-roasting fat sardines, herrings or sprats until their silver paper-like skin bubbles, crisps and browns – a real treat.

Grilled flounder (or dab or plaice) with lemon

Never underestimate the pleasure of eating a freshly grilled, freshly caught flattie. Normally I butter the fish thoroughly and whack it straight on to the tray for the fish-to-metal contact. This gives an almost caramelised crispy finish to the white-skinned underside. But, you can, if you fancy, put some thick wedges of lemon under the fish; this helps stop it sticking and adds a tang of lemon steam to assist the cooking. It also gives you hot wedges to squeeze over the fish as you eat it.

Sometimes, I'll remove the head and stomach cavity with one 45° angled cut across the neck before I start cooking. This reveals a perfect cross-section of the flattie, making it easy to tell when it's perfectly cooked through to the bone.

Serves 1
1 dab, flounder or smallish plaice
A big knob of salted butter, slightly
    softened
1 lemon, cut into wedges
Salt and freshly ground black pepper

Preheat the grill as high as it will go. Meanwhile, massage your whole fish with the butter, using your hands. Really work the butter into every inch of skin, like you were putting sun screen on a toddler. Work that butter right up to the tips of the fins – you don't want them sticking to your grill pan. Season the fish generously with salt and pepper.

Now lay your fish, dark side up, white side down, on the floor of the grill pan or a flat grill tray and grill for no more than 5 minutes, without turning. The thinner underside will 'fry' sufficiently from its contact with the grill tray. Let that salt-and-peppery top skin boil and bubble, erupting into little geyser puffs of steam. The crispy, chewy skin is a perfect contrast to the soft moist flesh within, which when it's all doused in a squirt of searing lemon juice will take your tastebuds to a sacred heavenly place.

Serve each whole fish still spitting and sizzling from the grill. Pour over any butter and fish juices from the grill pan and accompany the fish with grilled or fresh lemon wedges, new potatoes, rice or couscous and steamed lemony greens.

Directory

World Sea Fishing
www.worldseafishing.com
An amazing one-stop site run by good friend and consummate sea angler Mike Thrussell. Everything from a beginners' guide to area-by-area, up-to-the-minute catch reports, angling features, online tackle shop, tips, knots, rigs, boat recommendations and more.

Get Hooked
www.gethooked.co.uk
West Country-biased guide to fishing spots and accommodation.

General weather forecasts:
Inshore Met Office
www.metoffice.gov.uk/weather/marine/inshore_forecast.html

BBC Weather
www.news.bbc.co.uk/weather/forecast

XC Weather
www.xcweather.co.uk

Met Office Shipping Forecast
www.metoffice.gov.uk/weather/marine/shipping_forecast.html

Wind forecasts:
Windfinder.com
www.windfinder.com/forecasts/wind_british_isles_akt.htm

Windguru
www.windguru.cz/int/best.php
Designed for windsurfers, excellent.

Tidal forecasts:
Admiralty Easy Tide
easytide.ukho.gov.uk/EasyTide/EasyTide/SelectPort.aspx

BBC
www.bbc.co.uk/weather/coast/tides

Proudman Oceanographic Laboratory
www.pol.ac.uk/ntslf/tidalp.html

Angling bodies:
Angling Trust
www.anglingtrust.net
Represents all game, coarse and sea anglers and angling in England. Campaigns on environmental and angling issues, including pollution and commercial overfishing at sea.

Angling boats:
The Deep Sea Directory
www.deepsea.co.uk
UK directory for angling and diving boats, run by top skipper and friend Chris Caines. Forums, catch updates, accommodation and recommended charter boats all around the country.

West Bay Fishing Trips
www.westbayfishingtrips.co.uk
Local site for me. My favourite local skipper is Matt Toms 07967 944781.

Guides:
Guided Fishing
www.guidedfishing.co.uk
A directory of fishing guides; details of affordable fishing guides for both sea and freshwater angling around the UK.

Fly-casting instruction:
AAPGAI
www.aapgai.co.uk
Association of Advanced Professional
Game Angling Instructors.

Knots:
Animated Knots by Grog
www.animatedknots.com
Great guide to tying knots. Watch
different knots being tied and stop and
start at will. Practically knot porn!

Fisheries conservation bodies:
Marine Stewardship Council
www.msc.org
An independent charity promoting the
certification of sustainable species
around the world. Its blue fish tick
labels appear on fish products from
areas the MSC has certified as well
managed and sustainably fished.

Fishonline
www.fishonline.org
Clear up-to-date information about the
sustainability of fish and shellfish, run
by the Marine Conservation Society.

Marine Conservation Society
www.mcsuk.org
A UK charity dedicated to the
conservation of our seas and seashores.

The Association of Sea Fisheries
Committees
www.asfc.org.uk
Covers all sea fisheries committees
by area and also quotes local minimum
fish landing sizes, etc.

Useful Reference Books

The River Cottage Fish Book
by Hugh Fearnley-Whittingstall
and Nick Fisher
(Bloomsbury 2007)

*The River Cottage Edible Seashore
Handbook*
by John Wright
(Bloomsbury 2009)

The New Encyclopedia of Fishing
by John Bailey
(Dorling Kindersley 2002)

North Atlantic Seafood
by Alan Davidson
(Macmillan 1979)

The End of the Line
by Charles Clover
(Ebury Press 2004)

The Guinness Guide to Saltwater Angling
by Brian Harris
(Guinness World Records Ltd 1977)

The Sea Angler Afloat and Ashore
by Desmond Brennan
(A&C Black Publishers Ltd 1985)

*The Field Guide to the Marine Fishes of
Wales and Adjacent Waters*
by Paul Kay and Dr Frances Dipper
(Marine Wildlife 2009)

Fish
by Michael Pritchard
(Collins Gem 2004)

Acknowledgements

The construction of a book about fish catching and fish cooking requires an unholy combination of skills and kindness from a bizarre collection of people.

On the fishing front: Mike Thrussell and his son Mike Thrussell Jnr. have been endlessly generous with their time, extensive knowledge, patience, contacts and photographs. Without Mike senior's help, I would have torn my hair out in clumps. Chris Caines, Matt Toms, Richard English and Pat Carlin are all excellent Dorset charter skippers who have helped me time and time again, over the years, with their superlative fishing skills. They've also let me raid their tackle boxes and photo albums mercilessly for this book too.

On the photography stuff: Good friend and talented angler Paul Quagliana has accompanied me on countless fishing trips. He takes great action angling pictures and yet still manages to catch more fish than me, or anyone else. Gavin Kingcome's cookery photographs make me feel hungry, and I'm in debt to anglers such as Dr Richard Roberts who have kindly let me use their own hard-won fish portraits. Thanks to Toby Atkins for his top-drawer illustrations too. Also to Xa Shaw-Stewart who did great sleuth tracking down photos of odd fish.

On the cookery end of things: I can't thank Gill Meller and his crew (Emma and Richard) at River Cottage HQ enough, for letting me run amok in their kitchen. And respect is due to Jess Upton who arranged for fish, photographer and me to all be in the same place at the same time. While Nikki Duffy deserves a big shout for turning my cooking style into something resembling a recipe.

On the book production business: Natalie Hunt should be canonised for her saintly patience and unerring professionalism in collating and editing the many complicated elements of this book. Meanwhile her boss, Richard Atkinson, kept a firm hand on the tiller, while Janet Illsley got down and dirty with the editing. Will Webb then skilfully made it all look pretty once it was hung out to dry. Old friend and work colleague Helen Stiles inspired me to get on with writing the book, while my wife, Helen, provided, as always, unflinching enthusiasm, much needed encouragement, multi-fingered typing skills and endless delicious food to bolster the process. Thanks, also, to my book agent Antony Topping.

And eternal gratitude to my children Rory, Rex, Patrick and Kitty for eating all my fish meals and putting up with my various fish obsessions. And lastly, I must thank Hugh for making the whole thing possible and still being the most enthusiastic and generous angler I know.

Index

Page numbers in *italic* refer to the illustrations